THE SOUL OF CENTRAL NEW YORK

THE SOUL OF CENTRAL NEW YORK

⊢ SYRACUSE STORIES BY ⊣

SEAN KIRST

With a Foreword by Eric Carle

Syracuse University Press

The columns and the majority of the photos contained in this book were originally published by the
Syracuse *Post-Standard* between 1991 and 2015, and are used by permission of the *Post-Standard*. Some of
these columns and headlines have been lightly edited for reasons of space, grammar, context, or clarity.

First Edition 2016

17 18 19 20 21 22   8 7 6 5 4 3

∞ The paper used in this publication meets the minimum requirements
of the American National Standard for Information Sciences—Permanence of Paper
for Printed Library Materials, ANSI Z39.48-1992.

For a listing of books published and distributed by Syracuse University Press,
visit www.SyracuseUniversityPress.syr.edu.

ISBN: 978-0-8156-3483-6 (hardcover)
978-0-8156-1083-0 (paperback)
978-0-8156-5380-6 (e-book)

Library of Congress Cataloging-in-Publication Data
Names: Kirst, Sean Peter, author.
Title: The soul of Central New York : Syracuse stories / by Sean Kirst ;
with a foreword by Eric Carle.
Other titles: Syracuse stories | Post-standard (Syracuse, N.Y. : Daily)
Description: First edition. | Syracuse, NY : Syracuse University Press, [2017] | Includes index.
Identifiers: LCCN 2016043174 (print) | LCCN 2016044598 (ebook) | ISBN 9780815634836
(hardcover : alk. paper) | ISBN 9780815610830 (pbk. : alk. paper) | ISBN 9780815653806 (e-book)
Subjects: LCSH: Syracuse (N.Y.)—History, Local. | Syracuse (N.Y.)—Biography. |
Syracuse (N.Y.)—Social life and customs—Anecdotes. | City and town life—
New York (State)—Syracuse—Anecdotes.
Classification: LCC F129.S8 K57 2017 (print) | LCC F129.S8 (ebook) | DDC 974.7/66—dc23
LC record available at https://lccn.loc.gov/2016043174

Manufactured in the United States of America

For Nora, with love and gratitude for a journey made together

Contents

Illustrations

Foreword

Remembering Syracuse

I've always had a sense of loyalty to places and people. As a young child I felt alone, not having a sister or brother, and was jealous of my playmates who had. My sister Christa was finally born when I was 21; I loved her immediately and dedicated *The Very Hungry Caterpillar* to her. I have the same feeling for Syracuse, even though I moved away when I was only six years old.

As an adult looking at the photographs in my parents' photo album, I was especially intrigued by one photo of me at age three, hugging a three-year-old girl in a white dress. Little did I know that a stunning act of reporting by Syracuse columnist Sean Kirst would eventually bring the two of us back together after eight decades.

Every time I looked at this photo, it left me wondering what happened to my friend. I was too young to remember the time when the photo was taken, but the picture in my parents' photo album radiated a deep sense of comfort between these two young children, which fascinated me so much that I made a book about it called *FRIENDS*, when I was 84.

As it turned out, neither I nor that girl remembered our photo being taken. If it weren't for Sean, journalist and inspired amateur detective—who, after reading *FRIENDS*, put together the complicated pieces that 82 years later reunited the girl in the white dress with the boy in shorts—it would have never occurred to these two people, once friends of the dim past and now adults, to look for each other.

What a masterful piece of journalism that touched two people and their families deeply. By now Sean has become family of choice, and I am

1. Eric Carle and Florence Trovato embrace as young children, 1932, John Street, Syracuse. (Image courtesy of Angela Trovato)

delighted to offer here, as preface to this collection of Sean's beloved columns, my own remembrances of the city I once called home, which later became his chosen home—the setting for the inspiring stories contained herein—stories of hope, courage, and resilience.

When I was six, my parents and I returned to Germany. Whenever I had to fill out a form in Germany that required my birthplace, I thought with regret, love, and pride of Syracuse, that faraway place, as well as the

2. Eric Carle and Florence Trovato reunite, February 2015, Florida. (Sean Kirst/ *Post-Standard*)

memories of Miss Frickey, my beloved first grade teacher in Syracuse, who recognized my talent in making pictures and reminded my parents to nurture that talent.

In Syracuse I remember walking to school whistling, looking forward to that wonderful teacher's class in a sun-filled room. I remember walking on a pond during the cold season and falling through the ice into knee-deep cold water. In my parents' album, there is a photo of my beautiful mother and I standing on a rock in Schiller Park; I have at times tried to decipher the sense of happiness, security, and love looking at that picture. I remember the warmth of our Italian immigrant neighbors on the North Side, who spent the hot summer days in their cool basement. I enjoyed spending time with these kind people who treated me like family. On our last day in Syracuse they gave me the gift of a loaf of Italian bread, still warm from the oven, for my trip to Germany. I remember weekends with my parents and other members of a German club on the shore of one of

Central New York's many lakes. I remember being with my mother in a downtown Syracuse department store, where constant "ding dings" filled the air, and tubes containing bills and cash raced toward hidden accountants upstairs.

I remember my father reading the Sunday "funny papers," the comics, to me: Mickey Mouse, Flash Gordon, Superman, Blondie, Tarzan, and Dick Tracy. Heavenly memories. Oh, and the movies that my father took me to see: Charlie Chaplin, Shirley Temple, animal movies, and more animal movies.

After we arrived in Germany, my father told stories about "Syracuse and America." These stories became more and more colorful over time. And my parents made me step-dance like Shirley Temple and sing "On the Good Ship Lollipop" for my relatives. Ursula, a girl who lived next door, was my age and looked like Shirley Temple and I fell in love with her. Her curly locks were a piece of Syracuse to me, or as a psychiatrist would say, a "transfer object."

My childhood memories of Syracuse resonate with the stories Sean tells in this book—stories of neighbors and coaches, of displays of strength and resilience, and of random acts of kindness. Throughout his decades as a columnist for the *Post-Standard*, Sean offered readers an intimate view into the lives of those around them—ordinary and famous, wealthy and impoverished, young and old. Some of the best of these columns are collected here, and so Sean's words and the words of so many members of this community will once again be heard.

Perhaps for some who have moved away and still yearn for the comforts of their home in Central New York, this book will act as a kind of transfer object, as Ursula's locks did for me; for others, this collection is an entry point of sorts, an introduction to an extraordinary city made up of countless individuals with stories to tell—dozens of which are told here, in Sean's compelling prose.

Eric Carle

Acknowledgments

This book is built around column writing, the center of my life since childhood. I put off writing this note of appreciation until the last minute, because I owe so much to so many people for a career that has given me more joy than I can ever express.

As I write this, I am getting ready to attend the wake of a Syracuse woman named Marian Crinnin. I never met her, but for decades—in unique and distinctive longhand—she corresponded with me about my columns. I still have many of her letters. She was thoughtful, insightful, and she saw the larger world; over the years, I routinely heard from countless readers in Central New York who were much like her.

Marian died in July 2016, at 91. She is emblematic of everything I loved about my job, of the people who deserve my ultimate appreciation:

Readers.

◈

As for personal thanks, I often think of this: neither of my parents went to college. My father did not earn a high school degree. Yet my mother and father loved books and were voracious readers. As a child, in the days when we still walked home from school for lunch, I would eat a tuna sandwich at the kitchen table while my mother read me the classics—*Black Beauty, Treasure Island*. She was also my first editor—passionate and knowledgeable about language—when I wrote my earliest stories, little articles about junior high basketball for the *Dunkirk Evening Observer*.

My mother had a vibrant appreciation for the simplest wonders of life. Once I started writing columns, I discovered that sensibility was shared by many readers. I am deeply grateful to my older siblings: Sharon Jean,

Dennis, Michael, John, and Pam. Sharon died before I was born, but her presence—the way my parents loved her—was always in the house. My brother Dennis, my elder by 13 years, was an extraordinary storyteller. Out of nowhere, he died of a heart attack at 55. He lived with such intensity—and told stories with such ferocity—that I sense him around me, every day.

I was the youngest: Dennis, Mike, John, and Pam always looked out for me. I am thankful for the way they saw the world, for the people they married and the children they raised, for the way they understood how climbing a rusty fence or walking through the woods can lead to magic.

I lived in a little factory town where no one seemed to have much money, but I had many fine teachers who loved literature—too many to name here—and countless friends who inspired my love of reading. Jerry Reilly, a fine writer, was the guy who helped me get my first job as a 14-year-old with the *Evening Observer*; my first editor was Bill Hammond, a great and gentle mentor who taught me about journalistic rules and language.

My awakening as a writer came at the State University of New York at Fredonia, where I worked for the *Leader*, the student newspaper, and learned from a passionate faculty. I moved on to Rochester's *City Newspaper*, an alternative weekly, and Mary Anna Towler, the paper's executive editor. She was the toughest editor I ever experienced. If you slipped in any way, she'd crumple up your piece and make you do it again. But she heard the music of an individual's voice and encouraged real style; what I learned from her about writing, about the meaning and wonder of a story, I carry with me to this day.

Then to the dailies: The *Niagara Gazette*, where opinion-page editor Jerry Brydges broke newsroom rules by allowing me, as a reporter, to occasionally write columns—my first was about my parents and family wounds from World War II. Jerry admired Jimmy Breslin and was a fine craftsman. In 1988, I left for bureau work in Oswego for the Syracuse Newspapers, before the *Post-Standard* "brought me downtown" to the main newsroom. I covered suburban towns and cops and then became a general assignment reporter. In 1991, I shifted back to writing columns, first in sports and later on "cityside."

That is the work at the heart of this book.

Those were incredible years, full of wonder. I was surrounded by great editors, writers, photographers, and artists. When I first wrote this note of thanks, I tried to mention them all, and every list seemed to demand one more name, until I was mentioning dozens upon dozens of journalists, all extraordinary, all inspiring, all part of who I am. Even then, I realized I was leaving people out.

Instead of names, let me say collectively of my colleagues at the *Post-Standard* and Syracuse.com: You changed my life.

An example: in late 1993, my wife, Nora, became pregnant with twins, then lost one child to a miscarriage. Saving our other baby, the doctors said, would mean that Nora would have to spend a few months on intense bed rest. Everyone in the building bent over backwards, in response. Colleagues helped watch my older children, who were preschoolers at the time, allowing me a chance to write. The message was clear: take care of your family, and we'll be here for you.

My son Liam, born healthy and with eyes wide open, is now 22.

All I could provide in return was complete loyalty, and my best work.

I offer an enormous thank you to the quiet heroes of the newsroom, the copy editors who put together the paper late at night—editors patient with my endless tinkering at deadline. Again, I started to try and list the names, and I quickly realized the danger of skipping over great people. Better to say: thank you, all. Sometimes I'd drive downtown at midnight to look over their shoulders under crazy deadlines. They allowed it, took part in it, for one reason:

They wanted, above all else, a great newspaper in the morning.

I was lucky, so lucky, I came to Syracuse.

This book is the best tribute I can offer to this community. It is dedicated to my wife, Nora—my friend, my partner, my voice of conscience. If I struggled about the higher meaning of a column, her gut feeling—countless times—was right on the money.

A few individual expressions of thanks, for this project: To the Syracuse Media Group, for allowing me to use these columns and images. To Kellie Caimano of SMG for all her work—a lot of work—in assembling the photos. To all the photographers whose celestial images are included here. To David Lassman, for that magnificent cover shot of Syracuse. To Deanna McCay, my first editor on this project with Syracuse University Press. To Rich Sullivan, for his courage, friendship, and inspiration. To Mike Streissguth, a friend and a terrific writer whose casual remark over coffee suddenly made sense of all this, thematically. To Alison Maura Shay, the editor who brought it all together.

Finally: For my children, Sarah, Seamus, and Liam. They are at the center of everything, my greatest inspiration, a daily source of joy. From the time they toddled, they've known me as their dad and they've been patient with me, as a columnist.

To close, I return to the extraordinary human beings whose triumphs and struggles make up this collection, to the people so willing to trust me with their stories. I offer that same loyalty and appreciation to countless others I wrote about over the years; I wish this book could hold thousands of columns, because I treasure all of them. I remember each one, and I remember the readers who responded with such insight and loyalty, through e-mails or letters written in soulful detail.

It seems fitting, as I conclude this note, that I'm about to leave for the calling hours for Marian Crinnin. I never met her but I loved her, just as I love all of you.

Preface

This book hardly began as a collection. It began as a column, which became another column, which suddenly became a career, and a career grew into a mountain of tales told. I spent almost a quarter-century as a columnist with the *Syracuse Post-Standard,* and everything you'll find here was written within that time.

Still, I would say the core purpose for this book began coming together at some point during my childhood. I remember sitting at the kitchen table while my mother set up the ironing board in a cramped space, by the refrigerator. For years, we had no dryer, and my mother always hung the clothes to dry, either in the yard or by putting them on a line in the basement in the winter months. Once they were dry, still wrinkled from the line, she would gather them and carry baskets of clothes into the kitchen. Amid smoke from her cigarettes and the rich aroma of brewing coffee, she'd iron or fold every shirt or pair of pants and then place them in crisp stacks, ready to be brought upstairs.

As she ironed, she would offer long reflections on life. My father often worked nights at the steam station, where his job was moving around mountains of coal that Niagara Mohawk burned to make electricity. Many times, my sister would also be at the table, the two of us the youngest of six children, and my mother would deliver her homilies on life. We rented a house in Dunkirk, a little steel town in western New York that was going through hard economic times. My parents had been raised in Buffalo, about 45 minutes away, and my mother's reflections often centered on change and civic disintegration.

She'd lived in Buffalo until 1950, when the population peaked at 580,000, when it was among the handful of largest cities in the nation.

She'd watched, since that point, as big Upstate industries shut down or moved away, as many of her friends left for faraway states and warmer climates. She'd seen neighborhoods she remembered as fraternal and tight-knit collapse into struggle and disarray. She'd witnessed the rise of "no deposit containers" and fast-food garbage, watched litter and trash pile up in parks and along sidewalks she remembered as pristine, and at the core of these tales she always found her way to the same question:

What was it about Dunkirk, about Buffalo, about Upstate New York, that seemed destined, locked in, to this long decline? Yes, it snowed, but it also snowed in Quebec City and Chicago; indeed, many cities turned their snow into a romantic benefit. Looking back on it now, as an adult, I understand the harsh answers: The automobile changed the neighborhood dynamic of Northeastern cities. Industries fled to other regions or nations where they could find cheaper labor. Worse, few northern cities were welcoming to the wave of migrating African American families who'd left behind the cruel Jim Crow laws of the South—and that hostility caused flight, abandonment, estrangement.

All my mother knew is what she saw around her, house to house and street to street. For all intents and purposes, she had spent most of her life in three factory towns: Buffalo; Youngstown, Ohio; and Dunkirk. She was a person who could find beauty almost anywhere, and she remembered city neighborhoods as places of communal warmth: she lived as a small child in a family enclave of Scottish immigrants in Buffalo, and she would sometimes wake up in the middle of the night to walk to the home of an aunt she loved a few houses away, always feeling absolutely safe in that journey. It pained her to see this security, this human fabric, being lost.

I remember, as a preschooler, sitting on the ground in a vineyard while she picked grapes to earn a few extra dollars, how she'd soften what could have been long and tedious hours by spinning tales, by evoking wonder about grapes on the vine. I remember how she'd scatter bread in the backyard and then go to the window as dozens of sparrows and starlings gathered to eat the crumbs. In each bird, she'd see a separate personality, and she always loved robins most of all: she saw them as singular, courageous, and idiosyncratic . . .

A little like herself.

I think I knew, even then, what I wanted to do. Over the years, I have gone into countless classrooms and lecture halls to speak to young people about writing, and they often ask me a simple question: What does it mean to write a column? That can be difficult to answer, because columnists come in so many different flavors: Some use language as a powerful flamethrower, a means of fierce opinion. Some write thoughtful, layered discourse on the great social or political topics of the day. Others—and I often fall into this school—use descriptive narrative or personal essays to build a case.

What joins true columnists, I tell the students, is a simple quality:

Whatever their style, in every case, they make a point. They have something to say.

I knew what I needed to say from the time I was very small, even if the idea would not be clearly shaped for another 20 or 25 years. I knew, as a child, that I loved the Upstate sky, the way the fast-changing and tumultuous weather turned clouds and sun and moon into a kind of theater. I knew I loved the morning in spring when the maple leaves all seemed to burst out at once in a luminous green that was precious, fleeting, almost mystical—an instant made more special by the months of grinding winter before it. I knew the awe I felt on the shoreline of Lake Erie, so vast you could not see the other side, one moment at peace and in the next raised to fury by the wind. I knew I loved the taste of the first apple off a tree in September, and the scent of cut grass and moist soil in April that was the signal it was time to find your baseball glove, and the moment in November or December when the first snow fell from the sky, and entire classrooms of boys and girls—sensing great change—would hurry to the window.

Our teachers would allow us to do it, caught up themselves by the familiar wonder of that moment.

I knew I loved Upstate. I knew the harsh words and skepticism I heard so often about the region were primarily a message of warning about the dangers of such affection—implications of despair typically framed as grim Upstate humor. In the end, it came down to accepting inevitable loss, even sorrow: so many of my friends assumed they'd never find a way of staying near the places they were born, and a powerful part of my upbringing—on some deep level—was always preparation for goodbye.

I knew if I could find a way to put all of it into words, if I could bring all that love and passage and hope into narrative form, that a legion of readers would almost certainly be waiting—because they were feeling the same thing.

In other words: a column could be a means of Upstate affirmation, of communion.

The place, for me, where that truly happened:

Syracuse.

My wife and I were transient when we arrived in this city. In the first seven years of our marriage, we had lived in four different Upstate communities. In our hearts, we expected it would be the same with Syracuse— that we would stay here for a few years and then move on. Even before we arrived, we prepared ourselves to leave.

What changed everything was an apartment we rented on South Geddes Street, when our two oldest children were toddlers. It was across the street from the Woodland Reservoir, a green expanse that climbed toward a basin of sweet, clean water and then rose even higher to a lofty spot, a roundtop, with a view of the entire region. I remember the first time I went there, on a long walk with our dog, and how I looked out—stunned—at the city skyline, at modern skyscrapers side by side with art deco towers, at the valley that wrapped Syracuse in a green embrace.

It was absolutely beautiful. We had found a city neighborhood that still felt stable and vibrant, and every day it offered scenes that could always lift your spirit. Very quickly, something shifted.

We realized we were home.

I officially began writing a column for the *Post-Standard* in October 1991, although I'd gotten some practice at the craft at the *Observer* in Dunkirk, *City Newspaper* in Rochester, the *Gazette* in Niagara Falls, and at the *Leader*, my college paper at SUNY Fredonia. In Syracuse, I had just turned 32, and I was working as a general assignment reporter on a late-night shift. My executive editor sat down next to me in the newsroom and asked if I wanted to be a sports columnist. The offer was a jolt. I had not expected it.

For a few days, I hesitated—I was a news guy, and I didn't know if I was the right choice to write about sports—but I remember calling my brother John and pouring out my uncertainty. He listened, then said to me, "sometimes you get on the train, or it leaves you behind." I went for a walk that night with the dog, and I remember the stars were out in a black sky, and I realized my brother was right. This train might not stop again.

So I got on. What a gift. What a journey.

I was allowed to take a different path in sports, to write both about the celebrated heroes at Syracuse University and about the character of, say, a teen who shows up day after day for high school football practice, a teen whose sheer presence helps his team, even if he rarely gets to play in a game . . .

Even if few people ever heard his name.

The sports job would eventually lead me back to news, to the desk we called "cityside," where my editors gave me the chance to write what I wanted to write most of all: narratives about people, about men, women, and children going through everyday triumph or loss or struggle, tales that involved fundamental elements of humanity.

In those elements, somehow, was the soul of a hometown.

What I quickly learned of Syracuse was the extraordinary nature of its roots, an unbroken if sometimes overlooked heritage. The origin story of the Six Nations, the great native confederacy, happened on the shoreline of Onondaga Lake, within what are now the borders of the city; that is where a faith system began for the people of the longhouse. As I'd discovered at the reservoir, Syracuse is a city of views, a city built on hills and on both sides of a valley; the autumns are almost unbearably beautiful, and Central New York receives more snow on average in the winter than any large metropolitan area in the United States. Think of that: we'd moved to the snowiest large city in the nation. On quiet nights, when my children were small, my wife and I would take them moonlight sledding at the peak of the Woodland Reservoir.

Those memories—stars in the sky, the hushed velocity of the sleds in the snow, our joyous dog chasing the kids—are with me, sharp and immediate, when I close my eyes.

They are a blessing of choosing to stay in Syracuse.

It is a city of vibrant heritage, a city whose people have a keen and gritty sense of humor. Syracuse was a crucible of the abolitionist and

women's rights movements in the nineteenth century. Many great architects worked here, and it attracted a torrent of immigrants and newcomers,
both from abroad and from other parts of the United States. Innovations
great and small—the two-speed bicycle gear, Smith Corona typewriters,
the Brannock foot-measuring device, basketball's game-changing 24-sec-
ond clock, Carrier air conditioners, even the vision for early education that
would become Head Start—came out of Syracuse.

The city also inherited the grief familiar to so many Upstate cities
in the late twentieth century, particularly the loss of population and the
flight of industrial jobs: There was a moment more than a half-century
ago when General Electric alone, now long gone from the area, employed
19,000 people in Onondaga County. Those changes fueled the rise of
poverty and street violence, and it was as if all these waves of beauty and
heritage and pain and departure collided like a crosswind along streets
and blocks not so far from my house. My wife became a schoolteacher in
the city, and my children grew up attending the Syracuse schools, and I
was soon facing an everyday reality:

The challenge was never finding enough columns to write. My challenge was finding enough time to write them all, and I remain haunted—
even today—by the tales I did not tell. The gift of the job was the chance,
day after day, to spend time with people who had gracefully confronted
potentially crushing obstacles in life, yet who had somehow embraced the
simplest and most daunting of all strategies:

They kept going.

In every case, they had stories that were crying to be told.

Today, Syracuse is a city at a crossroads, a city of beauty, a city with a
downtown enjoying its greatest revival in more than 40 years—but a city
very much in pain. The 2010 census offered a quiet measure of stability:
for the first time since 1960, the population of Syracuse essentially held
steady, one small victory after a half-century of hard times. Yet Central
New York has been rocked in recent months by a harsh barrage of news:
Research indicates that Syracuse is home to some of the most extreme
quadrants of African American and Latino poverty in the nation, children caught in a generational cascade of suffering. Another study placed
the region's economic growth as almost dead last among the largest

metropolitan areas in the nation. It is a troubling moment, statistics giving tangible form to my mother's question about Upstate decline, and it would seem to me there is one clear answer. I hope it is epitomized by the actions and decisions of so many of the people in this book.

Some are famous, like Vice President Joseph Biden or Jim Boeheim, coach of the Syracuse University men's basketball team. Most are not. In presenting these stories, I also need to make this early apology: Between 1991 and 2015, I wrote thousands of columns. They often involved men and women going through heartbreaking struggle, men and women who trusted me with precious and often painful details of their lives, an act of faith that led to lasting friendships. Every one of those tales deserves a place in this book. In the end, we hope the 87 columns spread over these 10 chapters are emblematic, symbolic, of the point I've tried to make throughout my writing career, which is really an answer to all those questions I heard at the kitchen table:

The cities of Upstate New York have one best chance. Certainly, they can benefit from all the political or economic help they can get. But their greatest resource in the early twenty-first century is the same one that lifted them to prosperity more than 100 years ago: These are regions filled with vibrant, indomitable, and creative human beings. Bring them all together, assemble that brilliance as a whole, set aside pointless divisions and rivalries, and maybe it becomes a beacon powerful enough to overcome all the forces that too often have pushed us toward a sense of civic twilight.

What I believe you will find, in so many of these columns, is the love, courage and resilience of your neighbor.

In each neighbor, in every Upstate city, is our hope.

PART ONE

Inspiration

A Perfect Fit That's Timeless

Tuesday, December 15, 1992

Is this you, Gus?

It was. It always was. Sunday afternoon, at 3 p.m. sharp, the phone would ring at the home of Gus Charles. It would be Charlie Brannock calling, and every single time he would ask Gus that question.

The calls started years ago, a means of discussing the business of Brannock's unique invention.

At the end, they were a connection, an affirmation, between two ailing friends.

"I think he found that a little reassuring," says Charles, 70, an accountant fighting his way back from a stroke.

He has been missing the call for the past few Sundays, the first to pass since Brannock died November 22, at the age of 89.

Charles carries on the work. He still gets over to the tiny East Fayette Street factory, the one equipped with black dial phones and green metal cabinets, beneath a rack of neatly tagged devices.

Brannock Devices, named for their creator.

Nothing invented in this city has so perfectly filled a void.

"It showed incredible ingenuity, and no one has ever been able to beat it," says Tibor Kalman, a Manhattan graphic and industrial designer. "I doubt if anyone ever will, even if we ever get to the stars, or find out everything there is to find out about black holes."

Last summer, Kalman was asked to come up with ideas for a New York City design show built around functional elegance. He was struggling when he accompanied his children to the shoe store and a clerk pulled out the device.

3

There it was, exact and symmetrical, unchanged since the days when Kalman used it as a boy.

"Perfect," he says.

Charlie Brannock invented it. He wanted to find the best way to measure the foot, and he played around with the idea for a couple of years. He built the prototype from an Erector set. Sixty-six years later, 970,000 of the devices have been built in Syracuse and shipped across the world.

They remain essentially unchanged.

The device comes in green, purple, red, or the traditional black. There are models for men, women, athletic shoes, and ski boots, and for children, always with two knobs for adjusting the fit, cups at both ends for the curve of the heel, a sliding bar with strict orders to adjust "firmly for thin foot, lightly for wide foot."

If you have been in a shoe store, you know what they are, even if you never knew what they are called.

"People ask about the place where I work," says Josephine Shaw, who runs a corner of the small brick factory set aside for shipping. "When I tell them we make the metal thing that measures your foot, they say, 'Oh, yeah.'"

Syracuse is the place, the only place, where those things have been made. Charles Brannock was born here, invented the device here, died here last month. Not too many people knew about him. He hated publicity, shunned reporters.

Barely anything was ever written about him.

But his invention became an appendage for people everywhere who kneel on carpeted floors and then measure feet.

That is, literally, everywhere.

"I've been in the shoe business my whole working life, and you think of the Brannock Device as the way you make your living," says Sid Burger, shoe buyer for McB's Shoes, a women's shoe store on Market Street in San Francisco.

When Burger remembers shoes, he remembers the device. It is what they use at McB's. There are a couple of competitors, but McB's ignores them. The Brannock device seems foolproof. And it never wears out.

"They last forever," Burger says, "unless you run one over with a truck."

That is a strange kind of problem, says Gus Charles, a slender, dapper man in a wide silk tie. That is why the Brannock factory stays small. Charles Brannock believed in all the things that are supposedly dead in industry. He loved small business. He loved working downtown. And he built his product to last.

Most shoe stores don't get rid of their Brannock Devices for 10 or 15 years, until the numbers finally wear away from so much use. While Charles is guarded about production—he says the company makes "tens of thousands" each year—that total could easily be more. It would require switching to plastic, which would guarantee that each device would quickly crumble into ruin.

Charlie Brannock could not do that, no more than you can make a square box roll down a steep hill. His character prevented it, like a law of physics.

"He was very, very proud of this device," Charles says. "It meant more to him than just the money. He had no family. This was it. When he got up in the morning, this is what he looked forward to."

Kalman says it is to Brannock's honor that the device was central to his whole career. "A perfect life," Kalman says, "a perfect singularity of purpose."

Brannock never married, although friends say he had opportunities. And he had plenty of close friends, even though he dodged the wave of pop adulation that almost certainly could have swept him up. Brannock was the kind of guy built for *People* magazine, an American original, but the media never got that chance with him.

"A gentleman," says Joe Riordan, manager at the East Fayette Street plant, where 14 employees polish the incoming precast metal, attach the handles, and then prepare the devices for shipping. Riordan says Brannock treated all his employees, in suit coats or work suits, with the same quiet courtesy.

Brannock was born into the shoe business. His father, Otis Brannock, joined with Ernest Parks in 1906 to found the old downtown Park-Brannock Shoe Co. on South Salina Street. In its heyday, the store had individual floors for specific types of shoes, and offered merry-go-rounds to entertain the children.

As a young man—no one seems exactly sure when—Charles Brannock became obsessed with inventing a device that would properly measure feet, which was a science of pinching the leather and squeezing the toe.

Before the Brannock device, recalls Donnie Carbone, 64, manager of the Karaz Shoe Store at Shoppingtown Mall, the available option was a primitive block of measured wood.

"It's like night and day," Carbone says. "There's no other device on the market right now that's even used. The Park-Brannock device (is) 95 percent, 96 percent right about the size of a shoe."

During his undergraduate days at Syracuse University, while rooming with future lacrosse coach Roy Simmons Sr., Brannock would climb out of bed in the middle of the night to scribble figures and drawings.

It was the fledgling stage of the device. Simmons, 92, remembers it vividly, because he often complained that Brannock's work disrupted his sleep. Brannock would tell him to roll over. Like Edison, he feared that any idea left alone at night would vanish by morning.

"I don't know what inspired him," says Simmons, who remained close to Brannock. "Whatever it was, he was afraid that he'd lose it. Now I've seen that device all over the world, in Paris, in Japan, and I always think of him."

In 1926 and 1927, Brannock patented the device and created a company to build it. Still, Carbone says, the initial value of the invention was in the boom it caused for the downtown shoe store. No one else in Syracuse, Carbone says, could fit a shoe so perfectly. If someone had an unusual size, and the device picked it up, Brannock made sure he had a match in stock.

Faced with a surging demand, Brannock in the 1940s moved the device company out of the shoe store and into the small East Fayette Street machine shop. Each day, Charles says, Brannock would walk between the store and the factory, overseeing both the sale of shoes and orders for the device.

During World War II, the army hired him to ensure that boots and shoes fit enlisted men. Sometimes, but rarely in public, Brannock would speak to acquaintances with pride and disbelief of the way his device had swept over the globe.

The dual aspects of the business went out of Brannock's life in 1981, when his shoe store was engulfed by the expansion of the Hotel Syracuse. Brannock didn't have much choice except for selling the building, Charles says. So the two men took a tour of Upstate cities—Binghamton, Rochester, and Buffalo—to do an informal study on the health of downtown shopping.

They learned, quickly, that what happened in Syracuse was true all over. Downtowns were dying. People wanted convenience, easy parking, more than old-fashioned quality. Brannock, already 78, decided to let his store stay closed.

"I think he was shocked by that," Charles says.

At about the same time, Brannock finally let go of downhill skiing, another lifetime passion. But he remained a big fan of Syracuse University sports; thanks to his friendship with Simmons, he donated $1,000 a year to a lacrosse scholarship fund.

And he still had the factory, which kept turning out the devices used all over the world, each one bearing the name of Syracuse, New York.

Throughout the 1980s, Brannock showed up in the office every working day to take care of business—until six months ago, when his health, for the first time, began to wear down.

Now he is gone—too quietly, it seems, for a man who came up with such a striking invention.

"It's such a useful thing," Charles says.

That is the only reason Charles even agreed to talk about Brannock. He feels his boss deserves his due.

Charles is executor of the estate, and he says it has been "pretty much" left up to him to decide on the fate of the company. "The employees will continue to run it, as in the past," he says, and they will discuss as a group any of the purchase offers that Charles says have already started.

One thing is certain: just to get in the door, any would-be buyer must guarantee the device will not be cheapened or changed.

That point is not negotiable. As far as Brannock's friends are concerned, the obituaries were wrong in claiming he has no survivors. He has thousands of them, and they last until the numbers wear off.

Almost 25 years after the death of Charles Brannock, in a digital age in which almost every technology has been transformed, the most effective way of measuring shoe size remains that basic metal plate with a knob—a device that's still manufactured in greater Syracuse, although the little factory is now in Salina.

Coach Learned Early to Appreciate Life

Thursday, November 16, 1995

A year ago, right about this time, Jim Boeheim was driving along Interstate 81 with his 9-year-old daughter, Elizabeth, and her friend of the same age. They were behind a truck, and just like that—in an instant—a cinderblock broke loose off the flatbed and came flying at their car.

Boeheim had no time to react. The cinderblock took out part of the front end, then ricocheted underneath and blew away a tire. The car lurched, and Boeheim managed to veer onto the shoulder of the expressway. He knew immediately how lucky he was.

What if the cinderblock had come right through the windshield? What if he had been knocked unconscious at the wheel? What if a tractor-trailer had been right behind them? Boeheim was shaken, but it would be too much to say it caused philosophical shock. As a child, as the son of a mortician, he accepted early the idea of how quickly the lights can go out.

He grew up in a funeral home. Death, as he puts it, was always right there, and he pointed a finger at the wall on the far side of his office, as if it were a parlor in his childhood: Old people. Young people. Sickness. Accidents.

"You get used to it," Boeheim said. "You see it every day of your life." He will be 51 on Friday. His childhood sharpened his appreciation for living a long life, which was one of the reasons he jumped at the chance to help with "Coaches vs. Cancer."

Boeheim is among several Upstate coaches participating in the drive. It was started by the National Association of Basketball Coaches to honor Jimmy Valvano, the former coach and ESPN sportscaster who died after a long struggle with cancer. Jim Satalin, the former St. Bonaventure coach, is directing the effort in the Northeast. He assumed Boeheim would help out, but Satalin said Boeheim has done much more than that.

"He's been incredible," Satalin said.

There is some history to that. Boeheim knew Valvano for many years, and the SU coach speaks of one night, a few seasons ago, when they were both part of a group that went out for dinner after a game at the Carrier Dome.

Valvano was set to fly to Europe for ESPN, and he good-naturedly started to complain about the trip.

Boeheim remembers, specifically, how Valvano rolled his eyes and griped about this nagging pain in his back. "That was the start of it," Boeheim said.

The idea of the program, which holds its kickoff breakfast Friday morning, is simple. SU as a team will block a certain number of shots this season—probably in the area of 160—and donors will be asked to pledge an amount for each block. The money will go to cancer research.

To get it started, Boeheim will personally pledge $10 toward each block. He has actively been seeking corporate sponsors. On Wednesday, after doing some direct lobbying, he learned Mutual of New York life insurance will be a major backer.

He also wants the fans to get involved in the program. Boeheim has tentative plans for at least one sign-up night for the crowd in the dome. In an interview this week, he even expressed interest in taking the drive into the schools. "Maybe (schoolchildren) could pledge a penny a block," he said.

Charity work is not new to Boeheim, whose team has long been involved with the National Kidney Foundation. The Orangemen usually make at least one visit to a hospital every year. Still, Boeheim admits this cause is very personal.

"There aren't many people who haven't lost someone to cancer," he said. That includes him. Cancer killed both of Boeheim's parents before they reached old age. His mother died shortly into his 19-year tenure as SU's head coach. He lost his dad in the late 1980s, when Syracuse was cementing a national reputation.

If Boeheim someday wins a national title with the Orangemen, his folks will not be around to see it happen.

The worst part is the way his daughter often asks him what her grand-parents were like.

Boeheim does his best to answer those questions, which force him to confront all that cancer took away. His father, in certain ways, gave him a storybook childhood. There was a hoop in the backyard with a light to use at night. There were always rides to practice. Boeheim was allowed to put his basketball above routine household chores.

His father also stoked the personality we see on SU's bench. Boeheim's dad was a ferocious competitor, a guy who couldn't stand to lose, and his little boy never got a break in any game. The first time Boeheim remembers competing with his father was in table tennis, at the age of five or six. His old man pitilessly destroyed him.

It took Boeheim eight years to become good enough to defeat his father. On the day it happened, his dad put his racket on the table, turned his back, and walked out. He refused to ever play his son again.

They were the same way at golf, where their battles became almost legendary. Dick Blackwell, Boeheim's high school basketball coach, had a standing bet that father and son couldn't survive a course together. They were always, always in each other's face, two snarling competitors who couldn't even agree on the weather.

But there is another Boeheim, soft-spoken and thoughtful away from the court. That Boeheim walked away quietly last year after the Arkansas defeat, which he says now was the toughest loss he ever endured. "Worse than Indiana," he said, speaking of the 1987 NCAA championship game, because Indiana made a play to win by a point. It was SU that made the play to beat Arkansas. One technical foul changed it all around.

Boeheim lingered by himself after that one, spoke warm words in a shaking voice about his team and Lawrence Moten, the senior star who had mistakenly called for a timeout. Maybe, in that moment, we got a glimpse of Boeheim's mother, a contention the coach himself would not dispute.

"She kind of tempered me," Boeheim said. She was the best loser he ever saw, a good golfer who tried to win but was always happy for those who beat her. "She meant it," Boeheim said, sounding almost surprised.

He and his father argued constantly—as Boeheim puts it, if he said the sun was up, his dad would say it wasn't—and Boeheim remembers how his mother would step in to act as buffer, defusing the arguments before they went too far.

In that combination, that train crash of emotions, he identifies the forces that got him to this point. But his parents were definitely alike in one way: they spent a lot of energy bringing up their kids.

His mother and father played tournament-level bridge and taught the game to Boeheim, who still likes it when he gets a chance to play. They did everything they could to help his basketball career. For as long as they lived, they showed up at every one of his games.

"They made me what I am," Boeheim says now.

They have both been gone for what seems too long a time. Boeheim has this little girl who can't recall her own grandparents, who tries hard to imagine what they might have been like. He also knows a million other kids must be in that same boat, which is why he'll be looking for your pledge up in the dome.

In 2003, Jim Boeheim's Orangemen broke through and won the national title with a brilliant freshman, Carmelo Anthony. As of this writing in June 2016, Boeheim had just led SU to yet another NCAA Final Four that no one expected the Orangemen to reach—and the Hall of Fame coach was third in all-time wins for NCAA Division I men's basketball.

Tadodaho Returns

One Eye on the Present, One on the Past
Sunday, July 7, 1996

The Onondaga clan mothers felt they had no choice. Leon Shenandoah, *Tadodaho*—or spiritual leader—of the Iroquois Confederacy, was gravely ill. Eight months ago, for his own good, the clan mothers released him from the position he held for almost 30 years.

His seat by the council fire remained empty. The decision on when to return would be his. It was an attempt at helping Shenandoah to recover, an attempt at easing the burden of looking out for all Six Nations. "We believed it would help," said Evelyn Elm, a Beaver clan mother. "He is a strong man."

Throughout the winter, as Shenandoah was in and out of the hospital, many Onondagas feared they would lose him. Tadodaho himself had none of those doubts. "I figured I'd be back," he said.

After all, he wanted to welcome home the wampum.

"He's like the belts," said Oren Lyons, an Onondaga faithkeeper. "We need to have him."

On Saturday, the National Museum of the American Indian in New York City returned 74 pieces of the fragile belts and beadwork. It was only the second time such precious artifacts from museums have come home to the Iroquois.

Shenandoah, 81, is very thin. He walks with the help of a cane. But he was there, resting in a folding chair, and his presence brought joy to hundreds of his people.

"It took a lot for him to come," said Ruchatneet Printup, a Tuscarora. "It helped to strengthen him, and it helped to strengthen us."

3. Tadodaho Leon Shenandoah of the Six Nations at
the Onondaga Nation. (Peter Chen/*Post-Standard*)

Shenandoah wore ceremonial clothes and a headdress of eagle feath-
ers. Chief Irving Powless approached him, dropped a delicate red collar
around Shenandoah's neck. It was made in 1908. It is worn by Onondaga's
keepers of the wampum, belts and strings used for covenant or prayer.

For centuries, as farmland and cities encroached on old Iroquois vil-
lages or burial grounds, wampum became booty for archaeological collec-
tors. Now some things finally are coming back.

The wampum Saturday was covered and placed in a van in New York City. With an Iroquois escort, it was carried to the Onondaga Nation. "It is a special feeling," said Marylou Printup, a Tuscarora clan mother. "It is joyous, like a child coming home."

Politically, the effort to regain wampum from museums began in 1966. Powless recalled how he drove to the first of those meetings with his father, one of his teachers, and George Thomas, who was then Tadodaho. All three of his companions died during the long quest to get the wampum back. The Iroquois endured three decades of negotiations, legal roadblocks, and cultural condescension.

"What was needed through the whole thing," said Mohawk Chief Jake Swamp, "was to count on everyone having a good mind."

He spoke of calm and reasoned thinking, which is really the point of what Shenandoah does. As Tadodaho, he is stripped of his clan and his personal ties. It is his job to keep a clear spiritual view, even in times of dissension or anger.

"I would always speak to him when we were having our own problems," said Tuscarora Chief Leo Henry, recalling days of violence at his Western New York territory in the mid-1980s. "Leon would remind me that these things were prophesied, that they had to happen, and that they would pass."

Shenandoah sees a promise kept in the wampum coming home. Almost 10 years ago, Onondaga Chief Vincent Johnson quietly traveled to Kentucky with Tadodaho. A farmer had discovered a massive burial ground and, for a fee, fortune hunters took turns digging it up. Johnson said more than 1,000 graves, many of them Iroquois, were opened or disturbed.

For weeks, the two men labored to rebury their dead. They burned tobacco and tried to put the souls at peace. It was a difficult and depressing job. When it was over, Shenandoah crouched in the field and burned tobacco one more time. Johnson said the spirits of their ancestors returned to pay their debt. They asked what they could do in return for finding rest.

"What we would like," Shenandoah told them, "is our wampum back."

Johnson is convinced that moment was the turning point. Shenandoah, he said, has the gift of keeping one eye in the present and one eye in the past. Tadodaho was there Saturday to greet the wampum at the longhouse, which he described as only a first step in the return of artifacts.

He admitted his illness has taken its toll. "My stomach, my kidneys, they needed doctoring," Shenandoah said. He seemed thin, and tired, although he managed to crack a few jokes.

"It was good just to hear his voice," said clan mother Betty Jacobs, who began to weep in the longhouse when the wampum was unveiled.

As a three-year-old, Shenandoah was burned almost to death. "They did medicine over me," Shenandoah said, referring to ancient Iroquois healing rites. When it was over, when the child surprised them all and survived, an elder stood and predicted, "This boy someday will hold a high position."

On Saturday, amid much joy, Tadodaho reclaimed his job. His "horns," or his position, were restored in full. Then he sat on a folding chair in a soft breeze, while the chiefs around him spoke about the wampum. A great gift, they all agreed, always comes back for a reason.

The Onondaga Nation, ancient capital of the Haudenosaunee—or Six Nations—is only a few minutes away from the northern boundaries of Syracuse. That territory has never left the hands of the Onondaga; while the area was diminished, and the Onondaga contend much of their land was taken illegally, they are among the few Native people in this country who walk each day on land never claimed as a possession by the United States or any nation but their own.

Leon Shenandoah, longtime leader of the Six Nations, died less than three weeks after these wampum belts came home, to his people.

Call Tells Teacher He Made a Difference

Monday, April 10, 2000

The phone rings dozens of times each day for David Desimone, a guidance counselor at Henninger High School in Syracuse. So Desimone didn't think twice when it rang again last week, while two of his students hovered near his desk. Desimone, distracted, put the phone to his ear.

"This is Dan Reicher," said a voice. "Do you remember me?"

Reicher is assistant secretary for the U.S. Department of Energy, where he oversees efforts to find clean and practical fuel sources. He is also a speaker today at the SUNY College of Environmental Science and Forestry for a conference on new uses for wood and cellulose.

After 30 years, as he thought about Desimone, Reicher decided the time was right for saying thanks.

"I think we all understand the importance teachers have in our youth," said Reicher, 43, who grew up in Syracuse. "At that time, there was still a lot of idealism about the environment. People came to realize there was another way, and that's what Mr. Desimone encouraged."

Appointed by President Clinton, Reicher coordinates federal efforts to develop wind turbines and fast-growing, hot-burning willow trees as alternative energy sources. Since his undergraduate days at Dartmouth, he has moved through many public and private agencies, becoming intimate with such disasters as Love Canal and Three Mile Island.

Reicher also serves on Clinton's planning committee for the 30th anniversary of Earth Day, which falls on April 22. As that celebration approaches, Reicher was pleased to hear how his hometown is getting serious about cleaning up its garbage-laden streets.

All of that, he said, makes him think of Desimone.

"Earth Day, 1970, was one of the momentous days of my life," Reicher said.

Reicher attended junior high at the H. W. Smith School, where Desimone was a science teacher. Their meeting fueled Reicher's childhood passion. He can remember being upset, as a little boy, when he learned how raw sewage often spilled into Onondaga Lake. He can remember how his father, Norbert, a retired Syracuse physician, assisted him with simple tests of water quality.

And Reicher remembers how his mother, Phyllis, helped in crafting a protest letter about a company that used endangered wolverines to provide fur lining on its parkas. Six weeks later, a company executive wrote back, promising to spare the wolverines.

Reicher, a third-grader, had found himself a cause.

At H. W. Smith, under Desimone, it turned into a calling.

"We started what we called a 'Conservation Club,' although now it might be called an 'Environmental Club,'" Reicher said. "Mr. Desimone was one of those teachers who combined science with something relevant to society. For the first Earth Day, I remember we planted trees and picked up litter."

Desimone, an educator for 31 years, immediately recalled Reicher as a brilliant student. Desimone would search for tough questions to stick on science tests, trying to prevent Reicher from getting them all right. "He took to the environment and ecology like a duck takes to water," Desimone said.

Over the years, the two of them fell out of touch, although Reicher's call last week brought Desimone back up to date. "I knew he was doing something good," Desimone said, "but not this good."

They talked for a long time before Desimone left school for the day. Driving home, it started to hit him: a high-ranking environmental official, a grown man with the power to really help clean up the Earth, was giving his old teacher credit for that one big push.

"It didn't sink in until then," Desimone said. "What Dan learned from me was that sometimes it's all right to crawl around and get dirty. Whether it's picking up trash or planting trees, you had to respect the environment, and sometimes that means you do some things yourself. But that he'd become assistant secretary of energy? And that he'd say he went into the business because of me?"

Desimone, overwhelmed, tried to tell his wife. Every time he started, he could not finish the story. He kept getting too choked up to explain, and that was because of every teacher's simple truth: you can spend a lifetime waiting for one phone call like that.

Dan Reicher is considered an international authority on climate change and clean energy. David Desimone, now retired, says Reicher was "destined" to do great things; the good teachers, it seems, have a way of knowing.

In Fulton, Quik's Inventor Made Magic

Monday, October 21, 2002

Kim Siebers Cornetet grew up in Fulton, across the Oswego River from the Nestlé chocolate plant. Her dad, Bart Siebers, was a legend in that place, which gave Kim and her sister Lynn a kind of magical childhood.

At Christmas, every year, Nestlé executives would treat the families of employees to gift boxes of chocolate. The company would also spring for a free movie.

Kim, 43, who now lives in Florida, swears that she could tell when it was about to rain by a change in the chocolate aroma from the factory.

Beyond all else, Kim feels honored to have grown up as the daughter of a man who turned a glass of cold milk into a treat, a man who was sometimes known as "Mr. Quik."

Before Bart Siebers retired in the early 1980s, he helped to develop and improve many Nestlé chocolate products, including the company's renowned chocolate chips. During the creation of Nestlé's "Triple Decker" candy bar, for instance, Bart brought home a precious handful of those treats for testing by Kim and her neighborhood friends.

None of that matches Bart's greatest chocolate triumph. He led the research team that invented Nestlé Quik, the chocolate milk concoction that continues to delight millions around the world, the powder now known by the watered-down title of "Nesquik."

"Bart was very heavy on the formulation of Quik," said Joseph Allerton, 83, a Fulton retiree who made his own mark by helping to create the "$100,000 Bar" as Nestlé's manager of technical services.

"The basic problem was that if you took sugar and cocoa and tried to mix them together with cold milk, they'd just sit there," Allerton said. "You had to make it so they'd dissolve quickly, and economically."

Bart and his team pulled it off, in a 102-year-old Fulton factory now destined to close its doors.

Thursday, Nestlé USA posted a "closing agreement" inside the Fulton plant, a document that described a severance package for 389 union employees. The long-feared shutdown would wipe out an operation that Allerton describes as "extremely involved" in the history of chocolate in America.

For Joyse Siebers, Bart's widow, the news felt more like a personal loss.

"I'm flabbergasted, and my husband would be crushed," said Joyse, 79, from her home in South Carolina. "It was a great plant, and Fulton brought us nothing but pleasure."

Bart, a student of chemical engineering, was hired after World War II by Lamont, Corliss and Co., a New York City company involved in chocolate research. Lamont, Corliss was soon purchased by Nestlé, and Bart relocated to the Nestlé lab in Fulton.

He was introduced to Joyse in 1949, just about the time that Quik was being released to the public. Joyse, a physical education teacher at the old Oswego Teachers College, was also coach and manager of the school's golf team. Bart, a Long Island native, was golfing at Battle Island State Park on a day when Joyse happened to be there, with her team.

"We met at the '19th hole,' and the rest is history," Joyse said.

Kim Siebers Cornetet grew up in the Fulton of the 1960s and 1970s. She recalls how Bart often traveled to Switzerland, Trinidad, or Tobago to study chocolate in all phases of production. She recalls how he was honored nationally with the 1977 Stroud Jordan Award, which is given annually to one person who exemplifies vision and devotion for "candy technology."

"He was also very humble," Kim said of her dad. "He used to remind me he was part of a team. He'd say, 'It wasn't just me who invented Quik.'"

Maybe not, but somebody deserves credit for figuring out how to mix the stuff with milk. As every American child quickly learned, the more you mixed in behind your mother's back, the better it got—eventually paying off with spoonfuls of exquisite chocolate mud on the bottom of the glass.

Even after retiring, Bart did not give up on chocolate. He and Joyse moved to Hilton Head, South Carolina. They ran an upscale sweets store called "The Chocolate Plantation," until Bart developed Alzheimer's disease. He died in 1988, and Joyse eventually retired from the store.

She last visited Fulton in the late 1980s. Not long after that, in 1991, Nestlé stopped producing Quik at the Fulton plant. Two years later, the company pulled out the historic Fulton research lab where Siebers did his work.

Even so, Joyse and Kim can't imagine Fulton without Nestlé's, or that warm, sweet smell.

"I guess you can't stand in the way of progress, if that's what you call this," Joyse said. "But to me, this is kind of going the other way."

Joyse Siebers died in 2004, at 81. As for the Nestlé plant in Fulton, the oldest milk chocolate factory in the United States, Rainer Gut—then-international chairman of Nestlé—said in a 2003 letter to the Post-Standard *that "a very tough competitive environment" forced Nestlé to shutter the operation. Fulton has now gone more than a decade without the smell of chocolate in the air.*

Springsteen on the Verge

A Syracuse-Born Photographer
Captured an Iconic Rock Moment

Saturday, December 3, 2005

Eric Meola knew he had it. That is what stands out for him, even after 30 years. He had Bruce Springsteen and Clarence Clemons in his studio, a couple of young rock musicians nearly finished with a legendary album, and Meola had a chance to take the photo for the cover.

His visitors were in a great mood, Meola recalls, glad for a break from the toil of recording. Springsteen brought a leather jacket, an Elvis Presley button, a floppy hat. Clemons, of Springsteen's E Street Band, had his saxophone. They were playing around with a song Meola doesn't quite remember when "Bruce kind of leaned and put his arm on Clarence's shoulder."

Later, in the darkroom, Meola realized that he nailed the moment. The image went into a pile of photographs that he brought to Columbia Records, where graphic artists John Berg and Andy Engel needed only a few days to create a cover even better than Meola had imagined:

Expansive, jubilant, the design wrapped around both sides of the album. It featured Springsteen on the front, smiling at some secret joke while he leaned on the shoulder of Clemons, whose image covered the back.

Born to Run.

That cover would be tacked onto the walls of countless baby boom bedrooms and dorm rooms. Springsteen himself, in a recent DVD made to celebrate the 30th anniversary release of an album that's sold more than 9 million copies, said the cover did all that he could ask.

23

"I always thought it was one of those records that you didn't have to hear," Springsteen said. "When you saw the cover, you said, 'I want that one.'"

Meola, who bottled that lightning, is from Eastwood.

By any standard, he is a world-class photographer. Eastman Kodak includes him on its list of "legends." His work has appeared on three covers of *Time* magazine. It's almost guaranteed that at some point you've seen one of his photos, such as a famous shot of a shirtless Haitian boy walking past a red Coca-Cola sign.

As for Springsteen and *Born to Run*, the album evoked the same emotions for Meola in 1975 that it would go on to evoke for millions of others: it was about raging youth, feeling trapped, what's lost and gained by breaking free.

"I literally remember Clarence saying to me one day: 'We'll be interviewed about this 30 years from now,'" Meola said.

For Meola, the only question was whether he'd be part of that legacy. Even when he took that shot in 1975, for a fee that he remembers as about $1,500, there was no guarantee it would make the cover. Meola was a young photographer in New York City, seven years removed from Syracuse University, where he graduated with an English degree.

Yet he'd wanted a career in photography since he was a boy in Eastwood.

His father, Dr. Frank Meola, was a general practitioner with an office on James Street. Among the patients was an engineer who had his own darkroom. One day, the engineer brought young Eric along to watch as he developed film.

Meola's dad hoped his son would decide to be a doctor. But in the instant Meola saw an image appear from nowhere in the dark, he knew what he wanted to do with his life. That faith, he said, helped to carry him through those early years in Manhattan.

He shared that creed on his last trip to address students at SU. "I tried to impress on them that your dreams, your passion, is the most important thing you have," Meola said.

Looking back on it, he was drawn to those same qualities in Springsteen, a rock prodigy from New Jersey who was renowned, more than anything, for his tireless live shows. In the early 1970s, at a nightclub called Max's Kansas City, Meola watched Springsteen perform for the first time.

"I was blown away," he remembers. "I was completely hooked. And I knew I wanted to photograph him."

Their first meeting was by coincidence, during a concert at Central Park, when Springsteen and Meola took refuge from a downpour under the awning of the Plaza Hotel. That was the beginning of their bond. Meola gradually came to understand that Springsteen was working on an album "that would be an historic moment in the history of rock and roll."

Meola was young enough, and naive enough, to believe he was the best choice to shoot the cover.

Essentially, he said, he talked himself into the job. He showed up so often that Springsteen grew to trust him. He was welcomed into studio sessions and even into Springsteen's house. Meola has a powerful memory of Springsteen—seated at a piano while a breeze lifted the curtains in the window—playing an early version of "Meeting across the River," a ballad that would show up on the album.

Through Mike Appel, Springsteen's manager at the time, Meola kept scheduling specific times to take the cover shot. On at least four occasions, Springsteen canceled, until Meola told Appel, "Look. Get him in here."

On June 20, 1975, Springsteen and Clemons appeared at the door of Meola's Manhattan studio.

Many photos from the session remain famous, including shots of Springsteen in the shadows of a nearby fire escape. But the cover photo— two friends in the foreground, against an all-white background— has become an iconic image in rock and roll.

Berg, the Columbia art director, said Springsteen wanted a different photo for the cover, a shot by Meola in which Springsteen struck a more self-conscious kind of "street poet" pose. "The reason I went with (the other one) is because it was so charming and so unusual and to get the horn player on the back was revolutionary, to say the least," Berg said.

To make it happen, Berg had to win over Columbia executives, since Berg said a "double jacket" cost maybe an extra quarter per album to produce. It was worth it, Berg said. A major part of the cover's appeal, he said, was "the fact that (Springsteen) was looking off into the gutter and you didn't really know where he was going."

"It's all in his face, and it's not what he was after (for the cover), not the way he saw himself, but it's the way he really is," said Berg, who remembers Springsteen as an unassuming guy who found time to make small talk with secretaries. In other words, to Berg, the cover represents what was happening musically: Springsteen was shedding rock pretensions and finding his own way.

For Meola, the issue of race added elemental power. Springsteen is white. Clemons is black. There had been racial violence near Springsteen's hometown in New Jersey, and Meola said he is confident that Springsteen—by posing only with Clemons—intended to send a message.

All of that was part of a more fundamental theme. "That cover sort of said it all before people even bought the record," Springsteen says, on the anniversary DVD. He was out to make an album filled with great and epic songs, "something that was explosive," and the cover provided the way to pull you in:

You had to pick it up to learn what was making Springsteen smile.

While the rock star and the famed photographer remain good friends, Meola hasn't shot original art for another Springsteen album cover. That was never the point, Meola said. Thirty years ago, he sought only to capture what he felt was Springsteen's growing sense of promise.

He got that picture and moved on, keeping faith with *Born to Run*.

Clarence Clemons died on June 18, 2011, two days shy of the 36th anniversary of the session in which Meola captured the cover shot for one of rock's most enduring albums. "The way I look at it, what's monumental to me is the camaraderie and friendship," Meola said in the Post-Standard. *"I was lucky to get that photograph, I'm just glad I was there and I'd give anything for Clarence still to be alive."*

He Changed Tipp Hill and
While Doing So, His Own Life

Sunday, March 17, 2013

The anniversaries we celebrate aren't always the ones that mean the most. Certainly, there will be many toasts raised today at Coleman's Authentic Irish Pub on Tipperary Hill in Syracuse, where owner Peter Coleman will be celebrating the 80th year of his establishment.

The place was opened by Coleman's father, Peter A. Coleman, and a partner, Bill Behan, whose parents once lived on the same second floor that now provides a lush setting for parties or meetings. In 1934, the elder Peter Coleman bought out his partner. He ran a corner saloon that catered to factory workers packed into the homes and flats of Tipp Hill.

Yet that beginning, maybe, is not what matters today. The anniversary that matters goes back 35 years to late 1978, when the younger Peter Coleman had taken over the place. He looked out at a changing city and a changing clientele—nearby industries almost gone, working families from Tipp Hill often leaving for the western suburbs—and Coleman knew he, too, had to change.

Part of it was business. The other part involved who he was. "I'd spent too much time whacked out," said Coleman, at the time a heavy drinker. He never saw his father take a drink; as for the son, he rarely let a drink go to waste. A moment came, just around that time, when Coleman was sprawled in bed, sick with another hangover, and one of his young daughters looked at him and said:

"Is Daddy drunk again?"

4. Peter Coleman in the meeting room of his Tipperary Hill restaurant. The painting shows his mother, Josephine. (David Lassman/*Post-Standard*)

The words haunted Coleman, who was ready for a major turnaround when he invited an architect named John Rose to stop by the saloon. Rose was in the early stages of his specialty: he would later design dozens of restaurants and taverns in Central New York. Coleman talked about his wish for a different kind of setting, and Rose looked around at the old walls and the worn floor and made a simple observation:

"What about doing an authentic Irish pub?"

Coleman paused and asked one question: could it be done?

Rose was intrigued. He began studying Irish taverns, including the ultimate field trip: with a friend, Egon Heil, an owner of Danzer's restaurant, Rose traveled to Dublin and spent a few days on a "pub crawl." He came home with a vision for what such a place could be, and Coleman was willing to invest in it.

The Coleman's known today to thousands upon thousands of visitors—the place of stained glass and dark wood built around a gleaming bar—grew directly from those meetings.

That new philosophy also came with a new Peter Coleman. "I'd spent half my life living one way, and I wanted to spend the next half living another way," he said. He recognized his own dependence on alcohol and set aside the drink. With the help of friends, he stepped into recovery.

While Coleman still lent his image, as a cartoon, to advertisements about St. Patrick's Day and his green beer, he created an atmosphere where customers could get a sandwich or coffee as easily as they could get a shot. And if any regulars came to the knowledge that enough was enough, that beer and whiskey were causing nothing but trouble in their lives?

"When they've needed help," Coleman said, "I can tell them where it is."

As for John Rose, he's never been surprised by the great success at Coleman's. He said Syracuse was ready for a tavern and restaurant of that style, and he sensed that customers would travel a long distance to enjoy it.

What surprised Rose is what Coleman did next. "He basically created the whole notion, as we have it today, of Tipp Hill as an Irish neighborhood," Rose said. "He didn't want to just let it go to hell."

Indeed, Peter Coleman—the tavern-running son of an Irish-born mother, a guy who never went to college after graduating from the old St. Patrick's High School—showed an intuitive grasp for urban planning principles that over the decades was too often missing in City Hall.

"Now that I had this business going," he said, "I had to protect it." He saw signs of decline in adjoining neighborhoods, and he set out to reinforce Tipperary Hill. That approach not only represents a wise plan of business; it is a core element of civic vitality, said Andy Maxwell, the city's director of planning and sustainability.

Coleman began restoring nearby houses. All in all, he estimates his family bought about 20, including one that became the Cashel House, a store offering Celtic gifts. Remembering Ireland, and the way travelers love striking memorials, Coleman pushed, cajoled, and reached into his own pocket to have a Celtic cross, straight from Ireland, erected at a main gateway to Tipp Hill, and to have a statue of his old friend, Jerry Wilson, put on a Tipp Hill bench.

Most important, he was a primary force in getting the statues of an Irish family, known as "the Stone Throwers monument," set beside the famed green-over-red traffic signal at Milton Avenue and Tompkins Street.

"What he did," said Tipp Hill native and former Syracuse mayor Tom Young, "was to take ownership of that saloon and extend it, figuratively, to ownership of the neighborhood."

Jerry "Bones" Roesch, owner of George O'Dea's tavern and a mainstay in the Tipperary Hill Athletic Club, described Coleman "as the best self-promoter Tipp Hill has ever had. He took a place that had plywood floors and sawdust and turned it into a palace, and what he does trickles down to the rest of us. Who knows what Tipp Hill might be without him?"

Coleman, 76, doesn't spend much time on might-have-beens. A developer is converting the old St. Patrick's school into upscale residential units, and Coleman predicts it will bring an influx of residents into the neighborhood.

"I've never been so excited," he said, which leads him to describe an attraction he wants to see happen in his lifetime, although he knows there might be rules or regulations in the way:

The green-over-red traffic signal is the only one of its kind in the nation, said Coleman, who proceeds to make an offer: if city and state officials say OK, he'll come up with the money to buy a new traffic light of brass, and he'll put green lights on top in the images of shamrocks, and—with the city's help—he'll hang that light at the Milton-Tompkins corner.

Once that happens, he said, it might kick off another ripple of profound change, which in Coleman's mind would include a winding piece of Burnet Park Drive done in cobblestone, leading past a tree-lined block of Irish-style shops. It would be a slice of Ireland, in Syracuse.

That dream, some might say, sounds absolutely whacked, except Coleman knows what that word really means. Long ago, he left the "whacked" part of life behind him. That's the anniversary that matters. It gave birth to our Tipp Hill.

Peter Coleman's 80th birthday is in 2016. His Tipperary Hill establishment continues to thrive in a neighborhood he helped transform.

How a Caring Adult, for One Child, Made All the Difference

Sunday, April 20, 2014

Calvin Corriders is spending much of Easter weekend in New York City. His daughter, Sydnee, will do her graduate work at Columbia, an Ivy League school. Calvin and his wife, Sandra, are helping Sydnee find an apartment close to the university.

Early Friday, before they left, Calvin did a morning workout at a gym in downtown Syracuse. Then he walked to the corner of Jefferson and Warren streets, near a storefront that now holds a Subway restaurant.

At 51, Calvin is a vice president of Pathfinder Bank and a former president of the Syracuse Board of Education. This month, when the Syracuse Housing Authority celebrated its 75th anniversary, it pointed to Calvin as proof of what a child can accomplish with vision and perseverance.

Calvin appreciated it, but he saw another level to the story.

"Before I met him," he said Friday, "I never saw myself as anything special."

The reference was to Mike Zaretsky, the guy everyone called "the colonel." He was the final owner of Wally's Smoke Shop, a South Warren Street newsstand that closed in the late 1980s. Today the building holds a Subway, but Calvin vividly recalls the most dominating feature of the place:

There was a "crow's nest," a little balcony that allowed the colonel to look down on his store.

Calvin was six years younger than his brother Larry, his absolute hero. In the early 1970s, when the New York Knicks were the class of basketball,

5. Calvin Corriders outside the building that once held a newsstand where Corriders worked as a child. (Ellen Blalock/*Post-Standard*)

Larry became a big-time Knicks fan. The Corriders lived in Central Village, the housing complex known as "The Bricks."

On winter days, Larry—his little brother at his side—would walk downtown to buy the New York City papers. He and Calvin would spread them out and read all they could about the Knicks.

The colonel noticed. One day he said to Calvin: "When you're old enough, if you want it, you've got a job."

On Calvin's 14th birthday he was there, working papers in hand.

"You've got to understand what this meant," Calvin said. "I grew up in a place where I saw a lot of things I never should have seen." His mother, a single mom, held the family together. Life in the Bricks could be harsh, day to day, and it was easy for a child to feel lost or overwhelmed.

Before long, the colonel put Calvin on the cash register, a gesture of unspoken magnitude. "He was an older white guy, and I was this young black kid from the projects, and he was trusting me with his money," Calvin said.

In the summers, Calvin would show up at 5:30 a.m., even before the colonel. The smoke shop became a refuge, almost a second home: the Zaretsky family occasionally took Calvin on excursions to the Saratoga race track, a spectacle that was a glimpse of an entirely new world.

The colonel is gone now—he died in 2010—but a son in Cleveland with the same name as his father vividly remembers Calvin's presence at the store:

"How could you forget him?" said the younger Mike Zaretsky. "A young kid with bright eyes, always ready to work."

Mike's widowed mother, Helen, now lives with him in Ohio. Decades ago, the elder Mike retired from the Air Force as a lieutenant colonel. He bought the Smoke Shop in the mid-1970s from longtime owner Paul Bonner. The place still carried the nickname of Manuel Wolnstein, the founder and the original "Wally."

Like Calvin, Mike can close his eyes and see the store: A comic book rack. A big selection of regional and national newspapers. Harlequin romances and other paperbacks. The standard "men's" magazines, with index cards discreetly covering any cover photos the colonel felt were too revealing.

Calvin worked as many hours as he could during the school year, and he'd be there five days a week in the summer. The colonel was often at the young man's side, teaching him the business, making suggestions about dealing with customers, about nuances of grammar.

Soon, Calvin grew familiar with the stream of regulars passing through the store: horse players, stockbrokers, the big shots of downtown business.

This went on while Calvin was at Henninger High School, until one day the colonel asked: "What are you doing after you graduate?" Calvin told him his plan: he intended to ask for a full-time job at the newsstand. He was happy there. The place made him feel good about himself.

"No," the colonel said. "I'm firing you."

The kid, hurt and stunned, asked what he had done. "Calvin, don't you see?" the colonel said. "You're a diamond. You've just got to smooth out the rough edges." The colonel told Calvin he needed to go to college—that some school would be lucky to have him—and then Calvin would go on to greater things.

"I get a little emotional thinking about it," Calvin said. "He saw something in me."

It was good advice. Calvin earned a business degree at SUNY Brockport. He was hired for his first job by a local bank because, in part, the guy doing the hiring remembered him as the polite, efficient kid from the smoke shop.

Calvin achieved success as a banker, as a leader on the school board. He and Sandra raised two children: Sydnee will soon be at Columbia, while their son, Calvin, studies at Syracuse University.

Their dad often reminds them of the difference one caring adult can make in a child's life.

Calvin recalls a day, about 15 years ago, when he was delighted to see a familiar face at the bank: it was the colonel, there to do some business. Before they parted, the young banker made sure the older man knew a simple truth:

"None of this," he said, "could have happened without you."

Friday, Calvin told that story in front of the old smoke shop, before he drove his daughter to the Ivy League.

In 2016, Calvin Corriders, a bank executive, still makes the same point: even on hard streets in the middle of the city, one kindhearted grownup can change everything.

Passing of Bill Carey

Faced with Hardest Choice,
Great Reporter Stays in Form
Monday, August 10, 2015

Bill Carey followed a code. For more than 40 years, he was a television and radio journalist in Central New York, a guy who quietly became a regional legend—but a guy who never believed he ought to be part of the stories that he told.

That didn't change in 2013, when Carey learned he had lung cancer. He dedicated himself to finding a way past the disease. He gave up smoking, a habit he started as a teenager, when some hard-boiled guys in Auburn told him cigarettes could help create a great radio voice.

When his treatments caused most of his thick hair to fall away, Carey—a senior television reporter for Time Warner Cable News—chose not to appear that way, on camera. You'd hear his voice, but you couldn't see him. Carey feared viewers would be preoccupied with the illness of the reporter out in front, rather than focusing on what he saw as most important:

The story.

"He always deals with facts," said an old friend, Channel 9 coanchor Dan Cummings, "even when they lined up against him."

That was Carey's measure last week, in New York City, where he faced a choice none of us would want to make.

Carey was born in 1953 as William Snee, in Auburn. Early in his career, he decided to use "Carey," his middle name, as his broadcasting identity. His family says he made that choice because a journalism colleague had a name that sounded a bit too much like "Snee," on the air.

35

Bill Snee became Bill Carey, whose career took off in Central New York. He won many awards at local radio and television stations. He eventually settled at Time Warner, where he remained passionate about his work as he moved into his 60s, where the rich Upstate tenor of his delivery led many to agree:

If Syracuse had a voice, it would sound like Bill Carey.

He never talked all that seriously about retirement. When he mentioned it, he'd speak of how he'd like to register at least 50 years in the business, a milestone that would have taken him into 2024. Even when he learned of the lung cancer, he kept his sights locked onto that long-range goal.

In 2013, he began an aggressive schedule of radiation and chemotherapy treatments. For a time, his medical scans came back clean.

This year, the doctors said the cancer had returned. Carey settled on a strategy. In mid-summer, he and MaryEllen, his wife of more than 40 years, would visit their son Bill, who had a newborn daughter, Kallie, in California. From there, Carey planned to travel to the Memorial Sloan Kettering Cancer Center in Manhattan, where he'd undergo a new therapy that he hoped might roll back the disease.

Carey was optimistic. In a phone conversation just before he left, when a friend expressed admiration about the way he was coping with his illness, Carey shut down the praise. He insisted it was no big deal. The story really wasn't about him.

The trip, however, did not go as planned. For months, Carey had endured nagging pain in his arm. In California, it intensified to the point of the unbearable. He spent a lot of time with Kallie—the family has beautiful photos of the infant in his arms—but the pain was relentless, even as he headed to New York.

At Sloan Kettering, a doctor took one look at his neck and said, "What's that lump?"

Both Carey and his wife were stunned. They hadn't noticed a fist-sized growth that seemed to come from nowhere. Carey moved into intensive care. Tests showed more tumors, along his spine. The tumors were causing fierce pain that spread from one arm to the other, then began shutting down his legs. By Sunday, August 2, Carey could no longer write a message on a pad.

With MaryEllen's assistance, he got in touch with Cummings, a guy Carey had hired in 1978 when Cummings, as a young man, was still finding his way in the profession.

Carey explained the situation. He said "things had taken a turn," and he told Cummings:

"I just wanted to say I love you."

With that, Cummings knew. Bill Carey was funny, tough, whimsical—but rarely sentimental with his friends. The next morning, Cummings broke away from a family vacation on Cape Cod. He flew to New York. At Sloan Kettering, he and Carey had several long conversations.

"He made it clear to me how much friendship meant to him, that we ought to celebrate our friendships," Cummings said. From intensive care, Carey also made a point of thanking his Central New York audience.

MaryEllen had already helped her husband to get through what might have been the hardest call of his life. Together, they contacted Ron Lombard, a longtime friend and Time Warner's news manager. In classic fashion, Carey said he had good news and bad news.

The good news, he said, was that he was "still breathing."

The bad news was that his broadcasting career—his center of gravity since he was a teen—was almost certainly over.

Still, Carey held onto hope. At Sloan Kettering last week, he went through accelerated chemotherapy and radiation treatments. Cummings told Carey to count on what they both convinced themselves would happen: they fully expected to see each other again in September, back in Syracuse, at the state fair.

When Cummings left, he paused to kiss Carey on the forehead.

A few hours later, the hospital staff was forced to intubate Carey, taking away his ability to speak. But he was alert. He remained optimistic the tumors could still be brought under control.

That Thursday, several doctors came into his room. As Carey and MaryEllen listened, joined by their grown children—Jennifer, Bill, and Joelle—the doctors said the treatments weren't succeeding. Carey's options, essentially, had narrowed down to two:

He could let go of any extraordinary treatment, and accept what that meant. Or he could endure a tracheotomy, which would put him on life support and keep him alive indefinitely—but would mean he'd spend whatever time he had left in his bed, with no way to communicate.

Carey, fully aware, had a day to think it over. As Cummings said, Carey always relied on facts: he knew how he'd approached life for 61 years, and he knew how he wanted people to remember him, and he knew exactly what each choice would represent.

Friday morning, at his request, the doctors removed the tube.

For a brief and precious time, he shared a few words with his wife and children. Eventually, quietly, he drifted out of consciousness.

After maybe three hours, Bill Carey died.

Put to the test, he'd made his choice. Love and courage: one great story.

He didn't tell this one. He lived it. Either way, he did it best.

In February 2016, six months after his death, Bill Carey was posthumously nominated for a New York Emmy Award for his work with a Time Warner Cable News team that covered a prison break by two convicted killers, at Dannemora.

PART TWO

Honor

Another Bout Won, with Help

Wednesday, February 10, 1993

A week or two ago, Dick Tobin rode the bus downtown on what he describes as "a cold, cold day."

He is right. That day reminded Tobin how cold it can get.

Tobin is 86, and as a young man he was a boxer in Syracuse. Later on, after the end of his fighting career, he became ring announcer for the regular bouts out at the state fairgrounds.

For six decades or so, he's done some training at the downtown YMCA, and he still takes the bus there a few times a week to swim 10 or 11 laps in the pool, then to sweat off in the sauna whatever is left. When he feels up to it, Tobin will even take a few swipes at the heavy bag.

On this winter day, the coldest of days, he took advantage of the chance to warm up in the steam. After a while he showered, put on his coat, and hustled to catch an afternoon bus at Salina and Jefferson.

He missed it. Tobin saw the back of the bus sliding away, and the schedule on the wall said the next one he wanted wouldn't come for 36 minutes. That was a problem, since that gave him no time to return to the Y, and it was too cold for an old man to stand outside for long.

So he decided to wait in the doorway of a drug store, until an employee came over and told him, "Beat it. No vagrants."

Tobin went outside, breath rising up like mist in a freezer, and he went to get some coffee at McDonald's. Yet it seemed he had hardly bought a cup before he saw his bus on the street. He rushed out of the restaurant and started to run, worried that he would again miss his ride, forgetting for a moment about the ice.

41

His legs shot out from under him. Tobin fell, face-first, onto the sidewalk. The impact shattered his glasses, and he could feel the blood running from where he'd been cut. For a while he lay motionless, staring at the concrete, the wind knocked out of him.

It was cold along the city's busiest sidewalk. Some people walked past, ignoring the old man who got up on his knees, bleeding on the ice, calling to the bus driver to let him get on. "A drunk," the driver said, looking away. He would have driven off, if not for Bernard Hogans.

Hogans is 35, and he had just moved to Syracuse from Georgia to help raise his stepdaughter. He had been looking without luck all day for a job, and he was waiting on the bus for a ride to St. Joseph's Hospital, where he was going to get a tooth pulled. Hogans, like everyone else, was short on time.

He told the driver to wait. He got off and pulled Tobin up from the sidewalk, and he stemmed the bleeding with a handkerchief, and then he pushed and dragged the stunned man onto the bus. The driver tried to shoo them away.

Hogans, broke and looking for a job, handed over the change to pay for them both. "He's no drunk," he said, "and he's going to the hospital."

The driver didn't like it, and even his dispatcher told him over the radio that a drunk with a cut wasn't their problem.

But Hogans is a big man, and he was getting a little mad, and finally the driver backed down.

Not that they got a ride to St. Joseph's. The bus dropped them at State and James, and the two men had to work their way up the slippery hill, arm in arm, until Hogans finally pulled Tobin into the emergency room. It took eight stitches to close the gash, and they discovered Tobin was covered with bruises.

Hogans got his tooth pulled, went back to his job hunting. When Tobin's grown children found out what happened, they got together and sent $100 to the man who helped their father. Hogans didn't expect it. That's not why he stopped. He likes to think that if his own child was down and bleeding in the snow, someone might be willing to offer a hand.

"It's the way I was raised," Hogans said. "How could I walk past that man? Back in the old days, everyone helped. There's not that kind of love these days."

Not always. But once in a while it still shows up, even on the coldest of days.

Richard Tobin died in 1996. He was eulogized in the Post-Standard *as a legendary boxer, ring announcer, vaudeville dancer, and ballpark usher whose face was known to many throughout Syracuse. Yet Tobin never forgot the day he fell on a downtown sidewalk, no one recognized him—and a total stranger stopped to help.*

Simmons Prepared Boxers
for Ring and for Life

Wednesday, August 24, 1994

John Mastrella grew up in Rochester. He was the son of poor immigrants. When the Great Depression came, the teenager went to work digging holes for the Civilian Conservation Corps, a relief project for thousands of desperate young Americans.

College? Mastrella would have been happy with a job. But the CCC had a boxing program, and he often blew off steam by going a few rounds. One night, a dapper man walked over and asked Mastrella if he was interested in a scholarship.

It was Roy Simmons Sr. Mastrella fought as a lightweight on Syracuse University's only national champion boxing team, in 1936. When he graduated, Simmons took him on as freshman coach, which covered Mastrella's tuition for the Syracuse University College of Law. The kid with no dream would become a state Supreme Court justice.

"Everything I have," Mastrella said, "I owe to that man."

Simmons died Friday at the age of 93. The news moved quickly through a grapevine of his white-haired boxers, especially those Simmons rescued from the worst of the Depression. The coach prowled gyms and clubs in the urban Northeast, searching for young men with fighting potential. The story goes that he looked for kids with no scars on their faces, features that proved they knew how to dodge a blow.

"We were so proud of him," said Americo Woyciesjes (Woy-SEE-chess), 78, who was NCAA light-heavyweight champ in the Eastern region. "We'd call him the 'Errol Flynn of the boxing world,' when he'd dress up in a tuxedo and go out after a fight. Even at the end he was still young, an optimist, never a loser. He fought to the last minute, and that's the same way he coached."

As a 14-year-old, Woyciesjes earned Simmons's attention at the downtown YMCA. "Rico" beat the daylights out of a star SU recruit. The coach didn't forget. Woyciesjes, who often ran to the Y from a job at a Solvay steel mill, got a full scholarship. He made the most of it. After college, he began a career as a research scientist and discovered a new kind of antibiotic.

"I think the great reason for (Roy's) success was that he wouldn't change your style," Woyciesjes said. "He'd help you make it better. Some of these schools, they all (trained their fighters) the same way. You learned to fight one of them and then you knew how to fight them all."

In 1942, Salvatore "Toots" Mirabito became Simmons's first NCAA heavyweight champion. Mirabito, a retired educator, is now 75. Yet, when he ran into Roy Sr. last year in Vero Beach, Florida, Mirabito respectfully referred to the old man as "coach."

"He had the greatest impact on my life of just about anyone," Mirabito said.

Simmons's experience went much deeper than just his heyday in the ring. During his undergraduate days at SU, Roy Sr. roomed with Charles Brannock, the man who invented the famous device used by shoe salespeople to measure people's feet. Simmons often laughed about how Brannock kept him up late in their frat house, tinkering with the idea.

Syracuse lacrosse grew into a tradition under Roy Sr., whose son has now coached the Orangemen to five national titles. After playing football in the 1920s for SU, the elder Simmons served as an assistant coach for 40 years. He also served as a Syracuse city councilor, hardly a typical choice for an SU coach.

But no contribution is more striking than what Simmons did in boxing, where he clearly and profoundly changed young men's lives.

Under Simmons, SU had eight Eastern team champions and one national champion. Crowds of 3,000 used to show up to watch. Before the program was phased out in 1957, he coached seven fighters who won individual NCAA crowns. Another of his pupils, Tom Coulter, is one of the premier coaches in U.S. amateur boxing.

"Without a doubt, Roy Simmons affected everyone he worked with," said John Granger, a welterweight who was Simmons's last NCAA champion in 1955. "He was able to quietly get into your life and get the most out of you."

Granger remembers himself as a "wild kid," fighting for space within a family of 12 children. "I found out if you're going to get along in this world with people, you better be more like Roy Simmons, or you wind up dead," said Granger, who is a retired U.S. Air Force major. "My father died when I was five, and I always said (Roy) was the father I never had."

Ord Fink had never boxed a single round when Simmons spotted him shooting baskets in the Archbold Gymnasium. That was in 1935. The ring was set up near the court, and the coach asked Fink if he wanted to spar with some fighters. Fink boasted he could handle any of Simmons's "punks." The coach simply smiled and gave him the chance.

Within a year, Fink had earned a spot as an alternate on the 1936 Olympic team. "He put all that time into me," said Fink, who would become NCAA middleweight champ. "He was one of the greatest men I ever knew in my life."

Woyciesjes still lives in Syracuse. He made a point of seeing Simmons from time to time until his health made it hard to get around. A year ago, several of his toes were amputated. He couldn't attend Roy Sr.'s funeral Monday. Instead, he pulled out a worn rosary and said a few prayers.

The fighter received the rosary as a childhood gift from his mother. He always carries it in his left-hand pocket. It was with him when he survived hand-to-hand combat in the Pacific during World War II. It has been with him for a string of serious operations.

He has it because of Roy Simmons Sr.

The story goes back to his days at SU, when the boxing team traveled to Michigan State. Woyciesjes knocked down his opponent six times in the first round. They stopped the fight, and the winner casually slung on his long boxing robe. The fighters were in a cab, heading back to the hotel, when Rico reached in his pocket and the rosary wasn't there.

"Turn the cab around," Simmons said.

The coach rousted a janitor, who opened up the darkened gym. They found a way to switch on some lights. Then Simmons got down on all fours, in the sand beneath the ring, and started searching. "He could have left," Woyciesjes said. "He could have said we didn't have time to go back."

They found the missing rosary. Fifty years later, the old fighter used those beads when he missed the funeral. But he knows SU is planning an open memorial service for Simmons.

"I'll be there, if I have to crawl," Woyciesjes said.

In April 2001, during a visit to Syracuse University with filmmaker Spike Lee, football great Jim Brown stopped to contemplate a bust of Roy Simmons Sr. in the Manley Field House. Brown called Simmons the most influential coach he encountered at SU. "He was a great man, a gentle man, who always helped me," Brown told the Post-Standard.

"Missing Piece" Now Honored Guest at Closing of Developmental Center

Wednesday, June 17, 1998

Margie Valentino is ready. She has rehearsed her brief speech, three or four short sentences, and she knows exactly what she will say this morning when the Syracuse Developmental Center is officially closed.

But you have to hope they'll give her time to add a few things from the heart.

She is the symbol, the living reason, for why the doors are being closed. Margie, 36, was born with cerebral palsy. She weighs, as she puts it, "70-something pounds." She uses a motorized wheelchair because she cannot walk, and it is difficult for her to make use of her hands. When she speaks, she does it carefully to be sure she's understood. She is the kind of person, in our culture, who is often written off at first glance.

When she was 14, Margie went into the developmental center. She lived there for nine years. She lived in a unit with 17 profoundly disabled residents who—unlike Margie—could not communicate.

"It was like a puzzle," Margie said. "I didn't fit anywhere. I was the missing piece." She would pass the time with little children on the pediatric floor, or she would sit alone on a terrace, looking down on the city.

"I didn't think I was ever getting out," Margie said.

Today, when the oldest American institution for the "mentally retarded" is symbolically shut down, Margie will be one of the honored guests.

She left the developmental center in 1985, liberated by the movement to return the disabled to their own communities. Margie now lives in her own apartment, with the help of a therapy aide. At SDC, in the same way

48

as a child, she was told when to get up in the morning and told, at 8 p.m., to hit the lights and go to sleep.

Thirteen years after what she calls "the greatest day of my life," the day she left SDC for the last time, she often stays up late simply to prove it remains her own choice.

A crowd of 1,000 is expected today, although the last residents actually left SDC two months ago. The ceremonies will reflect on a mixed history of progress and despair. When the cornerstone for the original institution was laid on the site in 1854, it was hailed as the first building constructed for the care and treatment of the "retarded" in the Western Hemisphere.

Over the years, state institutions devolved into a kind of walled exile, where the disabled were lumped together despite the extent or differences in their particular conditions. It was not until a series of embarrassing scandals erupted 30 years ago in similar centers across the nation that government agencies became serious about cleaning up the system.

That leaves Margie and Michael Kennedy—another former resident expected to address the crowd today—as the echo of countless thousands who were locked up for no reason.

"She never lost hope," said Bob Ciota, who helped manage the developmental center for the state. "She represents the strength and will of a person who can live in solitude and remain hopeful. She always had a strong will to be free."

Because of that insight, Ciota said, Margie agreed to join the steering committee for the ceremonies.

"They should have closed the place a long time ago," Margie said. She remembers, vividly, the years of dead hours inside SDC. Lacking companionship from other adult residents, she spent much of her time in the pediatric unit. One young child, who never showed facial expressions and rarely even moved, would open his mouth to eat when Margie spoke gently to him.

"He needed me," she said, and that kept bringing her back.

That child represents Margie's one fear about the SDC shutdown. In the state's rush to empty the building, she said, she worries that profoundly disabled residents will be relocated to places that cannot meet their needs.

Margie wishes the medical unit of SDC had remained open, at least for a while.

Outside of that, philosophically, she is thrilled by the shutdown. She works each day at Consolidated Industries of Greater Syracuse, doing light industrial piecework for Crouse Hinds. At home, her favorite hobby is building a collage. She takes baby photographs from magazines and carefully pastes them on a poster on the wall. "I love babies," Margie said. "They make me feel calm."

From time to time, she confronts ignorance and cruelty. Often, when she wheels into a restaurant with a friend or a health aide, the waitress will look past Margie and ask out loud, "What should I get her?" Always, simply to drill home a point, Margie will interject, "I'd like a cup of coffee."

She hates the word "retard," which she still hears too often. She has been mocked and ignored and offered pity she rejects. She has also met countless people who sense her dignity, who respect her independence, and admire her fierce will. That is why, for this historic ceremony, someone had the good sense to invite a pioneer.

She remains a little nervous, but she welcomes the chance.

"You know how a flower blooms?" Margie asked. "I'm blooming, today."

Eighteen years after its closing, civic officials in Syracuse are still trying to decide what to do with the long-empty Syracuse Developmental Center—whose one-time residents are doing fine on their own.

Brothers-in-Arms Fulfill a Mission

Wednesday, August 26, 1998

Normandy, France—

The trip was a mistake. Tommy Niland was convinced he should not have come back. He fought in the D-Day invasion 54 years ago, and then his son, Tom III, became his guide on this return to Normandy. They had some laughs in France. Tommy was glad for that. He was glad for the time with his older brother, Joe.

But it was a mistake, Tommy told himself. What was the point?

The journey made him tired. He is 78, and he was worn down by the journey from Syracuse. He is having trouble with his short-term memory, and the hectic pace of the whole visit began to get to him.

A mistake, Tommy told himself, at least until Monday, when he walked with Joe through the gate of the American Military Cemetery at Omaha Beach.

Tommy stepped into the hush of rustling trees and perfect gardens. Led by Michael Green, the assistant director of the cemetery, the two brothers walked along a line of marble crosses.

"Hey!" Tommy said. "I knew this guy!"

The name on the stone was that of Ira Hamblin, who had served in the same army regiment as Tommy. Hamblin was a "guy who seemed too old to be in it over here," which Tommy meant as both a compliment and an epitaph.

For the most part, young men lie under the white crosses.

"Hamblin," Tommy said, as if saying the name brought the face back into focus. Until that moment, he had forgotten Hamblin. He found the grave by accident, among 9,000 crosses.

51

6. Tom and Joe Niland at the graves of their cousins, Normandy American Military Cemetery and Memorial. (Frank Ordonez/*Post-Standard*)

"When you think about it, when you think about what each one of these crosses represents . . ." Tommy said. He spoke of young lives cut short and lost potential, of unborn sons and daughters.

Tommy stopped, looked around, and said, "I've got the chills."

The memories blew in from the surf pounding nearby Omaha Beach. You could stand on the cemetery bluff above the beach, a high point where the Germans waited with big guns, and it made you realize why those crosses stand in rows. Tommy wanted to find the grave of Warren Stubblefield. He asked Green to bring along his pail of sand, to rub a handful of sand across Stubblefield's white letters. The sand makes a name stand out, shining like gold.

Stubblefield was an older man, a major from Texas in the National Guard. He became a kind of father figure to Tommy, a guy who would listen and offer some advice. Tommy remembered how Stubblefield had a sports car and a beautiful wife, how all the young guys dreamed they would someday be like him.

On the day before he visited the cemetery, Tommy had walked a dirt road near the French town of Carentan. There, amid swirling cattails and stone cottages that seemed to rise out of the ground, Tommy recalled how Stubblefield walked ahead in 1944, too close to a ditch. Some U.S. scouts had spotted Germans in the field. Tommy called for him to stop. Stubblefield kept going.

This was a hard story for Tommy to get out. The spray of a machine gun caught Stubblefield in the neck. Tommy crawled 30 yards in the dirt to drag back his good friend. Too late. He was gone. Another white cross.

"He was a good guy," Tommy said. He wondered what Stubblefield might be doing now. There were other men he wondered about, a captain shot to death on a patrol, a lineman who had blocked for Tommy in high school football before dying in the war. Green, the cemetery administrator, abruptly broke in. He had found the graves that brought the Nilands to France.

Tommy and Joe took off their caps. They made the sign of the cross and began to mouth silent words, Catholic prayers from their youth.

Preston Niland and Robert Niland. Green rubbed the sand and the letters turned to gold. Two brothers who survived crossed the ocean for two brothers who did not. Bobby and Pete, as they were called, are now stepping into legend, their deaths a model for Steven Spielberg's film *Saving Private Ryan*.

Tommy and Joe, in the graveyard, were not thinking of a movie.

They were thinking of first cousins, of an aunt burdened with grief. They were thinking of Pete, whose dream was to help run a steel mill. They were thinking of how Bobby was a good guy at your side in a fistfight. "We hung around with each other, played together, dated the same girls," Tommy said. They were much the same. If God had snapped his fingers, the whole thing might have reversed.

Before he went to the cemetery, Tommy went to a place where a wooden bridge once stood. He had been a lieutenant, and he drew a short stick in a lottery with some officers. Tommy and his men crossed the bridge, under fire.

They made it, but Tommy heard bullets hissing past him on the bridge. He was a kid. He can still remember the feeling when everything calmed down, the way his heart pounded over what he had survived.

Somewhere else, doing the same thing, both his cousins died.

Tommy came home after the war to another funeral. His older brother had been killed in a steel mill accident. He stood in the receiving line at his brother's wake. He found himself face to face with Bobby's fiancée, a young woman Tommy had known since kindergarten. They were friends. They remain friends today.

But his cousin's fiancée was out of her mind with grief. She screamed at Tommy, "Why Bobby? Why not you? Why did you get to come back?"

He did not get angry, because he wonders the same thing.

All he knows for sure is the meaning of good luck, an old man with old friends underneath white stone. "I came for them," Tommy said. The trip was no mistake.

Tom Niland Jr., longtime Le Moyne College basketball coach and athletic director, died in 2004. The athletics complex at Le Moyne is named in his honor.

Veteran Returns Iwo Jima "Souvenirs"

Sunday, February 21, 1999

It is not a campaign. That would be too strong a word. It is a quiet suggestion for other veterans made by Martin Connor, a guy honoring the anniversary of hell.

It gets more bearable, he said, without the "souvenirs."

Connor, of Onondaga Hill, survived Iwo Jima. He was a marine private in World War II, in the third wave sent ashore on February 19, 1945. The island was wide open, a piece of volcanic rock. Japanese defenders dug deep caves and connected them with tunnels.

More than 6,000 Americans died during the 36-day siege. The Japanese lost about 20,000 men. No one was thinking about prisoners. Connor was 18. He remembers running past clusters of Japanese bodies, only to have those "bodies" rise up and attack. "They played possum," Connor said. Eventually, the marines would bayonet corpses just to make sure they were dead.

Connor remembers how shrapnel shredded the pack he carried on his back. He remembers a guy named Hayes who died in his arms. Connor remembers how the Japanese often attacked at night, how they'd come on you in silence wearing rubber-soled shoes, how you could hear their movements in the darkness in underground tunnels.

"I never thought I'd walk off the island," Connor said.

He survived to return to Syracuse. He married, raised seven kids, and went on with his life.

He remains close friends with Fred Head and David Osborn, two Syracuse buddies who lived through Iwo Jima, and they always get together for the anniversary.

7. Marty Connor. (James Commentucci/*Post-Standard*)

But Connor, for years, kept some things locked in his trunk.

"Everyone wanted souvenirs," Connor said.

During the war, the nation remained outraged about Pearl Harbor, about the Japanese treatment of prisoners of war. On Iwo Jima, amid the carnage, many young marines stopped being squeamish about what they saved for home.

They took souvenirs off bodies. They unbuttoned shirts to get the Japanese flags many soldiers wore around their waists. Connor still has a lot of military bric-a-brac—a Japanese rifle, hand grenades, volcanic sand from Iwo Jima. But he also took a diary, some photographs, a military paybook.

The Americans, during lulls in combat, would rifle through the packs of dead enemy soldiers. The photographs, Connor said, fell from Japanese helmets. They were family photos Japanese soldiers would carry into battle.

"We carried pictures in our helmets, too," Connor said. "We were just like them."

That understanding slowly grew on him. Twenty-five years after attacking Iwo Jima, Connor returned for an anniversary remembrance. That was the first time he met soldiers he had fought. He struck up a friendship with Tsunezo Wachi, a Buddhist monk who was president of the Iwo Jima Bereavement Association of Japan.

Connor told Wachi about the diary and photographs, and Wachi told him how much they would mean to grieving families. Most Japanese soldiers on Iwo Jima did not leave alive. Few relatives had any idea how their sons or husbands died.

"He told me anything personal would be important, very valuable," said Connor, who went home and thought about it. The Pacific theater was savage. It was hard for many American veterans to forgive their enemy. But Connor had respect for the Japanese foot soldiers, these men completely willing to keep fighting to the death.

"There are wives and brothers and sisters and children and grandchildren over there who to this day have no idea what happened," Connor said. Bit by bit over the years, as he unpacked these personal "souvenirs," Connor started mailing them back to Japan.

Wachi responded. He found the widow of the man who wrote the diary. "She was very pleased to hear this news and eager to get these items," Wachi wrote. Connor sent off the last of those "souvenirs" in 1984.

His fellow vets from the Pacific are now in their seventies and eighties, retired guys with too much time for remembering the war. Some of them, Connor said, still keep Japanese family photos, or diaries, or paybooks they brought home.

He said there is a purpose, a kind of freedom, in sending all that back.

"I looked at those things and I asked, 'What do I need with these now?'" Connor said. "No matter what you think about the war, those guys had families. For us, this can be a final link."

Marty Connor's campaign gradually attracted national attention. Many veterans sent him personal artifacts they'd brought home from Pacific battlefields: photos, notes, battle flags, and other items Connor was able to return to grieving Japanese families—including, in one especially powerful instance, a human skull. In 2005, Connor and an old friend and fellow marine, Nick Zingaro, played a central role in a ceremony of remembrance at Iwo Jima, where American and Japanese delegations came together on the 60th anniversary of the battle.

A Longtime Friend Is Waked at Home

Monday, July 3, 2000

Mary Carr never talked about the details of her wake. The old Irishwoman died Thursday, at the age of 93, but she fought to stay alive until she slept for the last time. Planning a funeral ran against her nature. "Mary always thought young," said her friend and caregiver, Betty Moeller. "She did not want to leave this earth."

Still, she was gone, and there had to be a wake. Mary had no children. Her only surviving relatives live in Ireland and England. Her closest friend was the Reverend John Smegelsky, pastor of St. Michael's Church in Central Square.

Left up to him, the decision was easy.

"I knew we'd bury her from home," Smegelsky said. "That's what we did in my family."

Calling hours were Sunday. Mary was laid out in an open casket in the living room of St. Michael's rectory. A custodian set up some folding chairs around her. Smegelsky placed a bouquet on his door. "A door badge," he explained, recalling his youth, when working families used flowers to announce a wake at home.

Mary's Irish rosary, which she often recited through the day, was wrapped around her fingers. Her husband, John, died in 1976. Smegelsky placed one of John's funeral cards in Mary's casket. Then Smegelsky lighted some candles, stepped back, and looked down on his friend.

"I'll miss the whole of her," Smegelsky said. "I'll miss everything about Mary."

Smegelsky's mother, Kitty, was raised in Ireland. Like Mary, she never lost her brogue. When Kitty was 45, she told the doctor she was pregnant.

59

The doctor gently told her it must be something else. "If it is," Kitty said, "then it's got two feet."

She had a son. Smegelsky's father died when he was 20. Kitty wasn't sure she wanted her youngest boy to be a priest, although she was certainly proud at his ordination. Smegelsky built his ministry around a theme he credits to St. Francis of Assisi: "Go out and preach the Gospel, and sometimes use words."

Kitty died in 1979. She was a teller of fine tales, a believer in the little people. Smegelsky sighed and moved on, figuring he'd meet no more like her. Three years later, he was pastor at St. Margaret's in Mattydale. He walked past a knot of gray-haired women. They were chatting near the pews. Smegelsky heard a familiar brogue. "One of you," he said, "comes from Ireland."

Mary Carr looked straight back and said, "How did you know?"

That started the friendship. Mary came to Syracuse as a teenager to help support an aunt, essentially ordered to move here by her family. For a year, she cried for Ireland every day. She worked at General Electric, and she married John Carr. When he died, she was alone. They never had a baby. "It wasn't for a lack of trying," Mary used to say.

Mary loved eating out with Smegelsky, at Coleman's or Friendly's. They stayed in touch, even after Smegelsky was transferred to a parish in Taberg. Gradually, Mary's health began to fail. Smegelsky was transferred again, to St. Michael's. For the last three years, after Mary broke her hip, he would drive every day to her home in Mattydale. He was often accompanied by Moeller, a parish volunteer who helped him care for Mary.

"She could be stubborn," Moeller said. "I still believe—and these are just my thoughts—he's the reason she didn't want to leave. (Smegelsky) was the one, the son she never had."

Mary never stopped loving life. She watched Larry King. She tended flowers in her garden, and she tended her cat, Penny. She was not beyond taking a nip from a bottle of Black Velvet. She hardly ate anything, no matter how much Smegelsky begged. She had dropped to 55 pounds when she died.

And if Smegelsky forgot to call her, he would get an earful.

Three months ago, Mary had a heart attack. It was clear, this time, that she could not recover. The doctors wanted her to go into a nursing home. Smegelsky, 62, had problems of his own. He had high blood pressure and high cholesterol. In the midst of Mary's crisis, he went in for a checkup. The tests came back fine. He took that as a sign.

He brought Mary and her cat to his rectory, in Central Square. For a while, it was a struggle for Smegelsky and Moeller. Mary was fading. She hated being trapped in bed. Last week, quietly, Mary came to peace. As she died, Smegelsky sat with her, singing "Danny Boy."

She had no kin to claim her. They will bury her, from home.

The Rev. John Smegelsky is now retired, in Oswego. But he does not forget a promise to his old friend. Whenever he says Mass, he includes a prayer for Mary Carr.

Donnie Fielder

They're Still Playing in His Name

Monday, August 9, 2004

Dorothy Fielder kept her promise. She told herself she wasn't going to cry—not when she saw the kids wearing shirts carrying her husband's picture, not when she saw the gray-haired men she once knew as little boys, not when her son called her to the stage at the Southwest Community Center.

She never wept. She maintained her composure throughout Sunday's finale of the 25th Donnie Fielder Basketball Tournament, an annual event named in honor of her husband.

The tournament, to her, is a living monument, more important than a statue or some plaque upon a wall. She wanted to be sure her voice was strong enough to make that point.

"Twenty-five years!" she said softly. "Usually things like this go by the wayside and disintegrate after five years or so. But my husband always had a way of transferring his enthusiasm to other people."

She is the widow of Donnie Fielder. She met him when they were both physical education majors at Tuskegee University, long before her husband went on to become unit director of the old East Genesee Street Boys Club and camp director at Camp Zerbe in Williamstown.

He would be 70 this year, if he were still alive.

Donnie was an athlete, although basketball was hardly his best sport. "My father was a baseball player, a tennis player, a wrestler," said David Fielder, an Atlanta businessman who ran the awards ceremony Sunday. "He came out of Alabama, from an impoverished neighborhood, and he was very street conscious—very aware that kids needed something better to take up their time."

His dad died from cancer at 46, in 1980. In the way of so many strong-willed men, Dorothy recalled, Donnie waited too long before going to the doctor. Yet he lived long enough to see the first tournament played in his honor.

It was organized by many of the young men he'd once helped or worked with at the Boys Club: Joe Godley. The Neal brothers. Richard Brooks. Ron Legette. Donnie's great friend, Ron Fagan, now a retired math teacher.

"What I remember," said Roy Neal, who played major college basketball at New Mexico State, "is that all I had to do was say 'Donnie Fielder,' and (sponsors) would say, 'Yes.'"

He is a teacher now at Elmwood Elementary School. He remembers when Donnie took some Syracuse kids to a tournament in Endicott, and they got crushed by a bunch of teenagers who looked suspiciously old for the age limit. Donnie's players tried to grumble that they'd been cheated, but their coach wasn't having any of that:

Go home and work, he told them. That's the only way you win.

As for Joe Godley, he would go on to become a super vendor, a guy who travels the nation to sell concessions at such events as the Super Bowl and the Olympics. "I came from a fatherless home," Godley said. "Donnie Fielder was like a second father. Without him, I'd probably be in jail."

Julius Anderson, who coached a team in this year's tournament, shared a boyhood memory of how his family had nothing to eat, and Donnie Fielder regularly showed up with food.

"That was the kind of dude he was," Anderson said.

Those stories explain why Donnie's tournament, sponsored by the city and the community center, gets stronger as time goes by. James Jackson, a tourney coordinator, said the mission remains bigger than basketball.

"We have 32 teams, 320 players, from 5 to 18 (years old)," Jackson said. "It brings them together in a common place, with a common goal. It's no one's turf, no one's territory. And the more of a role we can play in these kids' lives, the better."

Dorothy Fielder and Ron Fagan both said Donnie saw sports only as a vehicle. Fagan remembered how his friend started a program to make sure that young men who went away to school had enough money to buy books.

"He thought everyone should go to college," Dorothy said. "Use sports as a way to get there if you want, but go to college. That was his life."

Years ago, after her husband's death, she moved to North Carolina. Her four children are now scattered along the East Coast. But her sons David and Dale were in Syracuse for the tournament finale, and they talked their mom into being the guest of honor.

Dorothy clapped as Andray Blatche, a young man from Syracuse with big-time aspirations, was among the players to receive special awards. She looked down from the stage at little kids in tournament T-shirts, which put Donnie's photo just above their hearts.

"We'll do this again," said his son David, "when we get to 50 years."

David Fielder's dream reunion is not so far away; the summer of 2016 will bring the 37th annual Fielder Tournament to Syracuse. Andray Blatche, one of the teens from Syracuse mentioned in this piece, went on to a career in the National Basketball Association. And Dorothy Fielder, Donnie's widow, is pleased and honored that tournament organizers carry on.

Running on the Emptiness of Senseless Loss

Wednesday, November 22, 2006

Ten days ago, John Fredette ran the Harrisburg Marathon in strong winds and a cold Pennsylvania rain. At 62, he is a veteran of several marathons, but Fredette said he stuck it out for one reason:

"Josh was with me," he said. Throughout the run, behind the jagged rhythm of his own breath, Fredette maintained a conversation with his boy.

That's what helped him finish. That's how he finishes each day.

Fredette is a social studies teacher at Nottingham High School. He and his wife, Rita, raised six children. The youngest, Jessica, a former high school oratorical champion, is now a fine student on full scholarship at Seton Hall University.

She was especially close to her brother Josh, who was the next youngest in the family. He graduated from Corcoran High School. He tried college for a while, didn't like it and came home. He was drifting, but his father had no doubt he'd find himself. The last time John Fredette saw Josh, in July 2005, the father pointed to a circular rug on the floor.

Fredette said: "Your life is just like that. You're walking in circles, when you could get out."

Josh gently punched his father on the arm. "That's a new one, dad," he said. "I haven't heard that one before."

They both laughed. Josh left the house. A few hours later, he was shot to death in an apartment on South Avenue.

Jermaine Nowell, 27, of North Carolina, would eventually plead guilty to murder.

The killing was shocking, even for residents of a city accustomed to street violence. What John Fredette says about his 21-year-old son is

65

8. John Fredette (right) runs with Adrian Dunuwila, a friend. (Chrissie Cowan/*Post-Standard*)

quietly validated by police officers who knew Josh as a teen, and by teachers who had him in their classrooms, and by the sheer grief of the crowd that spilled out the door and into the street at his calling hours.

"He just needed time," Fredette said.

To cope, Rita Fredette said, her husband runs.

"That has given him a way to pull through," said Rita, who has her own ways of seeking out her son. For a while, she'd go to the cemetery and sit in a chair next to his stone, until she could sense his presence wherever she knelt and prayed.

A year ago, she said, the Fredettes had no Thanksgiving. This year, as a family, they will have a turkey dinner. Rita said she sometimes takes messages from dreams. Four days ago, she awoke to the fading words of a clear voice.

It told her to celebrate Thanksgiving for Josh.

Rita said Josh had a close bond with his father. They looked and acted alike, she said. Rita can close her eyes and picture the little boy on his dad's shoulders, memories that make John Fredette "cry every day."

When he can, to find relief, he gets outside and runs.

"It taught me humility, it taught me perseverance, it taught me you don't quit," he said. He is a recovering alcoholic, and running became his therapy once he put down the bottle.

The father recalled how he woke up one morning, savagely hungover, to see the shaken face of Josh, then 4 years old. The boy was tiny. At birth, he had barely weighed more than 2 pounds.

Despite the hangover, caught up in a wave of shame, Fredette realized what he was doing to his child. "He wanted his daddy," said Fredette, sober since that morning.

Often, he goes for long runs at Green Lakes State Park, where churning out the miles gives him time to think. At a time when our nation focuses on dangers abroad, Fredette sees deeper threats in the heart of our own cities. He used to operate a tavern on South Avenue, and he witnessed what crack cocaine did to the neighborhood.

"It changed everything," he said. "People would sell their souls for it. Women would walk out on their children." He came to believe in a simple truth: our children are caught in a clash of good and evil, but the sides are not as clear as people would believe, and the dangers do not end at our city's borders.

"If we're ever going to be a community," Fredette said, "everyone had better get together and start to recognize their responsibilities."

He was speaking of generations of lost children. He was speaking of a culture in which civility is dead in music, in entertainment, in the home.

He was speaking of boys and girls who endure violent lives of dog-eat-dog before entering classrooms where they're told to show respect—rules that lack all sense when you return each day to madness . . .

A madness that can claim even children from solid homes.

Those realities help Fredette define his goals in education: "The purpose is to allow a kid to look in the mirror and like what he sees. It's to teach a kid that you have to learn to take care of the people you care about, that you can live a good life without hurting anyone else."

That's up to teachers, Fredette said, when there's no one else to get it done. Kids need to learn about real work, about finishing hard jobs, he said. They need to learn that rewards sometimes don't come to us for years. And when good things happen, the best ones don't involve fine things or money.

They might involve the way a little boy feels on his dad's shoulders.

You'd like to help Fredette be thankful? Above your turkey, think of that.

As of this writing, John Fredette—now retired as a teacher—was helping to organize an annual meeting in greater Syracuse for the families of murder victims. He finds all too many reasons to stay busy: in 2015, there were 23 homicides in Syracuse.

Faithkeeper and a Nation's History

Wednesday, August 8, 2007

Oren Lyons remembers it well. He was on one of his international trips, talking about the environment to a group that included corporate executives. Once Lyons gets rolling, he gets rolling, and the stories fall easily into one another, and finally a baffled listener asked a question.

"Look," he said to Lyons, "what's your bottom line?"

Lyons laughed quietly as he told that tale, hands on a cup of coffee— decaffeinated now—that he sipped at the Coffee Pavilion in Hanover Square. Lyons is a faithkeeper for the Onondaga Nation, whose people go to sleep at night on a piece of land that never left their hands, a piece of land that was never deeded to the United States or the British or to anyone else.

What is Lyons's bottom line?

"I told him, 'You think in lines,'" Lyons said. "We think in circles."

Answers like that are either profoundly wise or maddening, depending on whether you agree with Lyons. They help explain why he has become one of the most famous people in Central New York. Lyons considered John Lennon a friend. When anthropologist Jane Goodall came to Syracuse, she greeted him with a big hug. He speaks casually of conversations with actor Jon Voight or guitarist Carlos Santana or author Peter Matthiessen.

Thursday, Lyons flew to Los Angeles for a screening of Leonardo DiCaprio's *The 11th Hour,* an environmental documentary in which Lyons offers prominent narrative.

Even the message on Lyons's phone conveys that image of traveler-as-philosopher. "Gone again," Lyons says on the machine. "Who knows where, or for how long."

9. Oren Lyons in downtown Syracuse. (Dennis Nett/*Post-Standard*)

Yet that image might need some delicate retooling. For decades, when you thought about the elders of Onondaga, you thought of men like the late Leon Shenandoah, former Tadodaho—or spiritual leader—of the Six Nations.

Lyons, for his part, seemed to have a perpetual role as a younger, bemused diplomat to the world beyond the nation. But Shenandoah died in 1996. He is gone, as is Lewis Farmer, as is Paul Waterman, as are so many of the gray-haired men who for so long formed the collective face of the Council of Chiefs.

Now Lyons is 77, an elder himself. He is recovering—quickly—from hip-replacement surgery. And he finds a need, at this point in life, to set a few priorities.

"I can see the end of the road clearly right now," he said. "Years are important, and you want to see what you can do."

One major goal, he said, is elevating the relationship between his people and the immediate world around his nation. Yes, he still travels the world to attend United Nations gatherings on indigenous peoples. He still worries out loud about the environment and the ever-growing human population, and he is especially passionate about the question of global warming.

But he will speak of issues closer to home when he offers a public address at 4:30 p.m. Sunday in Hanover Square, as part of the "Honoring the Haudenosaunee" celebration. There are certain things Lyons would love to see in Syracuse. They begin, he said, with a simple revelation. What he wants is a deeper community appreciation of the Onondagas for their "history, instead of fighting about taxes."

That focus is shared by Irving Lyons, Oren's nephew, who is putting together Sunday's festival. To Oren and Irving, it makes no sense that Onondaga County tourism officials do very little with what is probably the best-known historical event in the region: the birth of the Iroquois Confederacy on the shoreline of Onondaga Lake, where the people of the longhouse believe a tree of peace grew from a hole filled with discarded weapons.

Oren Lyons dreams of an environmental center alongside a lake recovering from centuries of pollution and abuse. He dreams of a lake-front Haudenosaunee museum. He dreams of Syracuse as a place that would attract indigenous people from many countries for conferences and forums, which in itself would become an opportunity.

"People around the world love Indians," said Lyons, recalling a European fascination with visits by the Iroquois Nationals, a lacrosse team from the Six Nations. He sees the extraordinary kinship between the Onondagas and greater Syracuse as a bond that we could market. He speaks of a time when the city might fully remember why its lake is considered a sacred place.

In that revelation alone, Lyons said, there would be a transformation.

Above his coffee, message sent, Lyons dropped into what he does best, which is weaving together many stories. His extended family has been wounded by alcoholism, and he remembers his own youthful days as a hard drinker.

"Nothing good really happens until you sober up," said Lyons, who has stayed away from alcohol for many years.

That led into lessons learned during his days as a young artist in New York City. He bought a house in New Jersey, he said, and for a while he took a shot at leading a typical homeowner's life. Then he grew to know a neighbor, a nice enough man who worked long hours to try to get ahead. The neighbor spent the little bit of free time that he had "always taking care of his house and always cutting his lawn and always taking care of his flowers."

"One day I went by there," Lyons said, "and there was a wreath on the door."

The guy was dead from the stress. Lyons sold his house and went back to Onondaga. The clan mothers asked him to be a faithkeeper, to serve on the council of chiefs. Lyons hesitated. He did not know the Onondaga language in the easy way of many elders. He told one clan mother, Rita Peters, that he did not feel qualified enough to do the job.

"Do the best you can," she replied.

Decades later, that is both his circle and his bottom line.

Now well into his eighties, Oren Lyons keeps the same message on his answering machine—because he still isn't slowing down. In 2015, in one of the highlights of his life, the Onondagas hosted the World Indoor Lacrosse Championships on their territory, south of Syracuse, where the United States was listed as a visiting team. And he was pleased to witness the 2015 opening of the Ska-nonh, or the Great Law of Peace Educational Center, which offers a Six Nations perspective on their own origins and history from a building near Onondaga Lake's shoreline.

PART THREE

Faith

The Touch of Her Sister's Unseen Hand

Monday, December 23, 1996

She had not planned to stop. Mary Menapace was driving from Skaneateles toward Otisco Lake, and her only real choice was taking Route 20. It was a quiet Tuesday afternoon, and she was alone.

She decided, abruptly, to get it over with. She parked near the spot where she lost her youngest sister.

"It was something I knew I'd have to do," Mary said. "I worried I was being morbid, but I had to see the place."

This was last Tuesday, not quite a month since the night when Kara Spaulding died in a Marcellus collision. Kara, 27, lost control of her eastbound pickup truck on blacktop slick with snow. Police said she veered into the westbound lane, colliding head-on with a car.

The other driver was injured. Kara's truck rolled over. She was dead at the scene.

Kara had four older brothers and sisters, who babied and mothered their littlest sister.

"She was so beautiful, but she was very unaffected," Mary said. "We all got such a kick out of her."

Mary, nine years older, said she felt like "both sister and mother" to Kara. Ten years ago, when Kara graduated from high school, she went to live in Hawaii with Mary and her husband, John.

"She was so crazy, so wild," Mary said. Kara, with her first taste of freedom, loved to go out to parties. The Menapaces also had an infant daughter, and they sometimes felt as if they were raising two girls.

But Kara was a bright presence, a free spirit, and the bond grew even tighter between the two sisters. Four years later, Kara left Maui to settle in

10. Mary Menapace wearing her sister Kara's ring.
(Stephen D. Cannerelli/*Post-Standard*)

the Telluride mountains in Colorado. She did not return to Skaneateles until two years ago, after Mary and John also had moved back.

Kara was a doting aunt to the three Menapace children. On the Saturday before she died, she went to their house to wash her truck, to take her niece for a ride in the country.

She had the brightness, the innocence, of the well-loved youngest kid, and the rest of the family was always glad to see her.

That left Mary desperate for comfort in the days after Kara's death. At the Ryan Funeral Home, Mary searched for a silver ring Kara bought in Colorado, a ring engraved with images of the moon and stars. But funeral director Mary Carlton said it wasn't on Kara's finger.

"She loved that ring," Mary Menapace said. "She was so proud of it. I even lifted up her hands in the casket to see if she had it on."

It was gone. Mary had to find other ways to make her peace.

She felt a pull toward the place of the collision.

Mary isn't sure, even now, why she had that need. "I used to consider myself agnostic," she said. But she retained a strong sense of destiny. And somehow she believed she'd find her sister on the roadside where she died.

Last Tuesday, almost four weeks after Kara's death, Mary decided it was time. She left her car and started to walk along the gravel. She found bits and pieces of a fender, and it turned into a trail of parts toward the point of impact. Mary finally came to a place with a bent and broken mirror, and she thought, "This is it. This is where she left."

She saw an object in the dust, and bent down. It was the ring.

There had been rainstorms, snowfall, since the day that Kara died. Plows and tractor trailers had careened along Route 20. The ring could have been washed away, or packed down and buried deep. Mary threw her head back and began to laugh, and then she clenched the ring against her heart and cried beside the road.

Wednesday is Christmas. She'll be wearing Kara's gift.

Mary Menapace eventually gave the ring to her daughter, Nancy, who was nine when her aunt died. Mary had copies of the ring made for every woman in the extended family; in that way, all of them now have Kara's ring. It is a constant reminder, Mary said, "of the connection, and of the thread."

Lockerbie Mists Up under the Burden of Its Memories

"I Take Some Comfort Here"

Sunday, December 13, 1998

Lockerbie, Scotland—

The flower shop was tiny, one small room with a big window, where three old women in sweaters told tales of their grandchildren. It was unclear who ran the place and who was visiting. Marion Alderman Jablonski stepped inside to browse through potted plants. She has an American voice, and an American voice in a Lockerbie flower shop almost always means one thing:

Pilgrims. Marion, 10 years later, moves ahead by going back. Her daughter Paula was returning home to Clay on December 21, 1988, when a terrorist's bomb blew Pan Am Flight 103 from the sky. The bomb killed all 259 passengers and crew members, including 40 students and residents from Central New York. Eleven townspeople died when a fireball of jet fuel ignited on the ground. It took Marion eight months to gather the courage to visit Lockerbie, to find the place near a sheep pasture where her daughter fell to earth.

Since then, she has returned at least 10 times. She and her second husband, Ed, were married in a Lockerbie church. "It always feels," Marion said, "like I'm coming home."

Two weeks ago, in the flower shop, Marion bought a small Christmas wreath. The women insisted she accept a yellow flower as a gift. "That's how they are," Marion explained, as she walked toward Paula's cross on a trail of crushed red gravel, walking so fast it was hard for a companion to keep up.

11. Marion Alderman at the place where her daughter Paula fell to Earth, Lockerbie, Scotland. (Dennis Nett/*Post-Standard*)

Marion, 71, survived tuberculosis as a young woman. The disease left her with one good lung. She is not a big walker when she's at her home in Rome, New York.

In Lockerbie, she said, she somehow gets a second wind.

The trail cut between grazing sheep and a golf course, where old men in patterned caps hit balls into the fog. Passengers on the plane fell onto these fields from a height of six miles. Marion, as is her way, shies away from nothing. She knows of the lingering fear in Lockerbie that some passengers were conscious as they fell, a belief that makes it hard for residents to find much peace.

"I know she didn't suffer," Marion said of her daughter, knowledge based on the forces that ripped the plane apart, and that confidence survives each trip to Lockerbie.

She has trouble explaining, exactly, why she comes back so often. She recalls the day nine years ago when the mailman came to her door outside of Rome with a cardboard box. Marion knew the box contained some of

Paula's clothes and luggage. She asked the mailman to stay with her while she opened it.

"I just wanted someone there," said Marion, and someone's there in Lockerbie.

The clay trail took her to the place where Paula fell. In 1989, Marion and her daughter Laura put up a simple cross to mark the spot. Marion later hired a carpenter to build a cross of oak. Every year, when she returns, Marion finds that strangers have tended to the cross, leaving flowers or tying ribbons on pine trees by the trail.

Marion raised four daughters in Central New York, and she used different colors of thread to distinguish their childhood clothing. The yellow flower matched the thread for the third daughter, Paula, born in 1959. "She was a good girl," Marion said, crouching by the cross.

Paula and her husband, Glenn Bouckley, were together on the plane. They had a storybook romance, meeting as teenage pen pals brought together by a rock music newsletter. Years later, on a vacation to Great Britain, Paula worked up the courage to stop and visit Glenn.

They fell in love. They got married. They moved to Clay. Paula took a job as a supermarket clerk. Glenn, an electrician, often did household favors for his mother-in-law. In November 1988 Paula hosted the family dinner at Thanksgiving, cooking the family turkey for the first time in her life.

A few days later, Paula and Glenn flew to England for the wedding of Glenn's brother. Marion expected them home by Christmas.

"I never cried," she said, not even on the night when her family heard the news, when frantic calls to Pan Am kept raising busy signals. Crying is not her way. Marion's father died when she was a toddler. She survived TB to marry a dentist, Gordon Alderman, whose health was up and down. Marion nursed her husband and her ailing mother-in-law for years in her own home, and they both died less than 10 months before Pan Am 103 went down.

On Marion's first visit to Lockerbie, a policeman led her to the place where she now always finds the cross. "I don't know why," Marion said, "but I take some comfort here." She can sense her daughter's presence more clearly at the cross than she can at Paula's grave in England, where Marion feels only brutal finality.

She prefers Lockerbie. She kept coming back as the residents rebuilt from the disaster, as places of charred horror became garden monuments. She also follows, with little hope, the international stalemate over prosecuting the suspected Libyan bombers.

"I'm not a murderous person," Marion said. "But I think I could walk up and shoot them between the eyes."

She stopped this month to leave a separate bouquet at Park Place, a narrow lane of packed-together homes. A boulder marks the place where the fuselage crashed down. The people of Park Place, at dawn, found dozens of victims in their gardens. That is where Glenn's body was recovered.

Marion allows herself no choice but forward motion. "Nothing else for it," they say in Lockerbie, and Marion agrees. In 1993 she married Ed Jablonski, a guy from Rome who knows what makes her laugh. The wedding was held in a church in Lockerbie, which to Marion was the right place for another lifetime bond.

Ed is not a traveler. Marion journeys to Lockerbie alone. She always stays at the small inn of Ann and Bobby Wilson, who live maybe a block from where the fireball went up. Ann cannot speak of it without starting to cry, and Marion hugs her before turning to the town that tends her cross.

After many trips to Lockerbie, Marion Alderman—now 89—doubts she'll go again. The memory sustains her. While she has reached a point where she's simply weary of international travel, she still feels deep kinship with Lockerbie and its people. "For me," she said, "it was always a very peaceful place."

December 21, 1988

For Lockerbie Farmer, Fire in the Sky
and "Folk" in the Field
Wednesday, December 16, 1998

Lockerbie, Scotland—

The father knew. Richard Temple Sr. owns a farm high on the Tundergarth, on the hills and green pastures rolling up from Lockerbie. Dawn came and the helicopters circled Richard's fields, above stone walls that legend says were built by French prisoners during the Napoleonic Wars.

"You don't know what you're going to find up there," the father told his son. Richard Temple Jr. nodded and climbed onto his all-terrain vehicle. His father had gone to a window in his house the night before, when the sky turned orange and the earth shook and a fireball rose up, and the father at first feared a nuclear attack.

December 21, 1988. The son was sitting in a pub in Lockerbie, and the road that took him home carried him by the pasture where the nose of Pan Am Flight 103 crashed into the earth. It took him a long time to get back to the family farm called Wylieholl, and in the morning the son got up to go and do his job, because the cattle and the sheep must be tended in the fields.

That is how the Temples, father and son, first came to know about "the folk" from Syracuse.

The son made the trip once again two weeks ago, his ATV turned almost sideways as it climbed steep and rutted paths, climbing hills where all you heard was the lowing of his cattle. The son loves to read, but he speaks only when it matters. He made the decision, as a teenager, to someday run the farm, and now his father's health is poor and young Richard tends the place.

A livestock farmer in Scotland has plenty of trouble. The scare over mad cow disease has wounded the cattle industry, and the price of wool is also plummeting. A young man with no brains or creativity would stand little chance. "You diversify," said the son, 32, who plows roads in the winter and builds prefab barns in his spare time and always climbs from bed very early in morning.

Constant work helps him move past what he saw upon the hill. "He doesn't talk about it," said Richard Sr., 72, who had an inkling of what his son might find.

The ATV kept climbing, past the place where a scorched luggage carrier slammed into the earth, a carrier filled with the bags and packages of students from a place called Syracuse. "What I remember," said the father, "is a pair of hiking boots."

His son did not remark on that as he rode up the hill. He gunned the ATV until it climbed a good two miles in the fields, to a point high above the pastures and the town, a place where all you saw were green hills, stone walls and sheep. Then Richard Jr. climbed off and stood alone.

"What you have to imagine," he said, waving his arm, "is that the cattle stampeded and they all went over there." He spoke with pity of the terror of his livestock, of fire in the sky and objects plummeting . . .

Objects that fell, said the son, in a long path, a straight line of debris for as long as he could see, and in that swath upon his land were what he called "the folk." That morning, seeing them, he half-believed they were asleep.

"Seven or eight," he said. "Over there, right there, were two wee little bairns. Right together, they were," and then he was silent. "It makes you think," he finally said, "that they were holding each other for dear life."

He stopped again, and you could hear only the cattle. "Aye, a hell of a thing to think of," said Richard Jr., and it came to him often as he worked the fields each day, on this hill beneath a big sky with its constant vapor trails. "One minute you're up there, and the next you're sky diving."

It was the children who bothered him the most. It took two days for investigators to remove the bodies. Every morning, Richard's mother June would bundle up and walk to the peak, and then she would kneel by each of "the folk" on the hill, and she would say a prayer while her son did his work.

Richard Jr. walked over to a stone outcropping, a nook at the very top of the hill. Yes, he said, they found a woman there, and the son's Scottish was soft music as he spoke of her, the way she seemed to be in such absolute peace. On a quiet day long after the crash, he discovered that someone had painted a neat message on the stone: "JFK—Dec. 21, 1988."

The initials are those of Julianne Frances Kelly. She was a junior, a political science and communications major, at Syracuse University. The Temples have never had contact with her family. At first, said Richard Jr., he was troubled by the shrine. He went past it every day. It would not let him forget.

But he found himself tidying up the loose rocks when his livestock jarred the place, and the shrine is now a quiet part of caring for his flock.

Julianne Kelly's sister, Janice, lives in Massachusetts. Reached by telephone, she said her family hadn't known about the painted letters. It is a comfort, she said, to learn that someone tends the place.

"I have this dream," Janice said. "Someday I want to go there and lie down and look up at the sky."

Years later, I interviewed Elizabeth Philipps, whose daughter Sarah was one of the 35 students from the Syracuse international study program who died in Lockerbie. The call involved a road race in Syracuse being held in Sarah's honor. During our conversation, Elizabeth explained how she and her family often journeyed to Lockerbie to climb a steep hill, where they tend to a cairn at the remote and beautiful place where Sarah fell to Earth with a close friend, her London roommate . . .

Julianne Kelly.

Yes. Elizabeth knew the Temple farm.

She said, "People say to me, 'Where was God when the plane exploded and crashed?' I tell them, 'He was in the hearts of all the people of Lockerbie.'"

OCC Commencement
Just a Start for "Lost Boys"
Friday, May 14, 2004

Majak Dut will receive his associate's degree Saturday at the Oncenter War Memorial, where Onondaga Community College holds its graduation ceremony. Except for two close friends of Dut's, also from Sudan, it is hard to believe that anyone else in the building could possibly share such a celestial sense of pride.

Dut doesn't see it that way. He said his diploma is intended as a gift for the rest of us, in Syracuse.

"We want to prove to everyone that we are friends to them," he said Thursday. "We want to show that we are good neighbors."

At 23, Dut is one of the "Lost Boys," the Sudanese children set adrift in 1988 when a bloody civil war tore apart their families. The ruling Muslim government targeted the Christian and animist people of the south. Parents and grandparents were murdered. Children were killed or taken into slavery.

Dut remembers the day troops swept into his village. He was playing in the street with other boys and girls. He could not get to his mother. Village elders grabbed the children, gave them a push, and told them:

"Run!"

Dut, Gabriel Dit, and Gabriel Bol Deng—the three young men receiving OCC diplomas Saturday—were among thousands of children who spent weeks running hundreds of miles toward refugee camps in Ethiopia. They ran naked, with bleeding feet. Children died of exposure, of starvation. Some were picked off by snipers.

To find water in the desert, they tried to follow flocks of birds.

12. Gabriel Dit (seated) and Majak Acuoth Dut, Onondaga Community College commencement, 2004. (Dennis Nett/*Post-Standard*)

Today, as young men, they play down the trauma. "If there was an attack in Syracuse, and you knew if you could run to Scranton you'd be safe, you would go," said Dit.

"If you think about bad things all the time, it makes you thinner and thinner, until one day there is nothing left and you die," Dut said.

Over the last few years, Catholic Charities and the InterReligious Council of Central New York helped about 200 of the Lost Boys come to Syracuse. They remain close-knit, often living in clusters. Dit and Dut are cousins, raised in the same village. Once they got here, quiet stories began to spread among their group: many Central New Yorkers, it was said, were hostile and wanted them to go away.

"They say, 'Lost Boys! These kids must be dangerous! Where are their parents?'" Dut said. "They don't want Lost Boys! They think we will be like the boys downtown, the boys with their pants falling down, selling drugs."

The diplomas, then, become an offering, a statement. Since they were little, these young men have cared only about an education. Sitting on a couch in Dut's Butternut Street apartment, wearing expressions that were almost painfully sincere, Dit and Dut said they understand why some people can't appreciate their story.

"When you are a child, and you face a difficult situation, you want your life to get better," Dut said. "But if you have never faced these situations, you don't have to think about it. We saw people killed. We heard the sounds of the bullets and the bombs. We know what is good and what is bad.

"We know you need education to make your life better. This is what you have to do."

The idea drives them. They no longer cry over the mothers they haven't seen in years, even if they dream of meeting them again. In the camps, when the little boys wept about everything they'd lost, Sudanese elders would say to them: "There's nothing you can do. You have no power. You have no choice. All you can do is study and learn, and then someday you can go back and help your people."

The boys listened. Learning turned into therapy, an act of grief and love.

The passion for education stayed with them when Ethiopian civil war again turned them into targets, when soldiers attacked the refugee camps. The boys fled and were forced to swim a river, where Dit saw his little cousins drown, not far away. They finally made it to a new camp in Sudan. From there, they traveled to Kenya, the last stop before the journey to Syracuse.

Once in Central New York, they looked for jobs and for ways to go to school. Ann Mayes, a Catholic Charities of Onondaga County volunteer, helped them fill out the OCC paperwork. Penny Kim, director of international studies at the community college, took roughly 70 Lost Boys under her wing.

Saturday, Dut, Deng, and Dit will be the first members of that group to graduate. When they started at OCC, they had never even touched a computer. They remember, during their first computer class, how the instructor used such terms as "desktop" and "booting up."

Dit raised his hand and asked, only half-joking, "Teacher. Is this a language class? Because you might as well be speaking Spanish or French."

They learned. They sought out tutoring. They put in extra time. Away from school, they all held at least one job apiece, and sometimes two. After all that, it might seem as if they've earned a little rest, but they don't even plan to celebrate their graduation.

"This is nothing," Dut said. "We're just getting started."

He has already been accepted at Syracuse University. Dit will study medical imaging at University Hospital. Deng, in the fall, will be attending Le Moyne.

They will keep running, always seeking, until someone says they're home.

In Syracuse, those three graduates were only the beginning. Dozens of young Sudanese men and women have gone on to college in Central New York. Many share the passion of Gabriel Bol Deng, who created a foundation—Hope for Ariang—dedicated to creating opportunities for education in Gabriel's home village.

John Dau, a "Lost Boy" who established a foundation to create a medical clinic in his homeland, once told me that education always held a sacred place in the way he and his friends saw the world, especially after they arrived in Syracuse:

"In New York, the wintertime was very cold, but we had no mom or dad," Dau said. *"Where could we find help or protection? Only in education, and what it could give us. In that way, it became our parents."*

On Two Swings, Two Winners

Monday, June 18, 2007

Alfonzo Whitehurst and Henry Sullivan ride the same bus to Danforth Middle School in Syracuse. A month or so ago, they made a little bet. No money was involved. It was purely for bragging rights.

"We bet on who was going to hit a home run first," Alfonzo says.

The two boys, both 12, play in the South Side American Little League at Wadsworth Park. As a columnist, allow me to make this aside: I am an officer with that league, which is how I learned the story.

I think you'll understand why I want to tell it.

Alfonzo is an outfielder and a third baseman for the Valley Men's Club Blue Jays of coach Don DeJohn.

Henry plays first base for the Durr Law Firm Cardinals of coach Milt Vazquez. Henry and Alfonzo, in their final year of Little League, share something in common:

Until a few years ago, they did not know how to play baseball.

They were introduced to Little League as pupils at Elmwood Elementary School. Alfonzo joined first. Henry joined a few years later. At tryouts, Henry recalls, everything felt awkward. But he loved the game, especially hitting, and he vowed that he would learn.

"I saw how the other kids played," he says, "and I wanted to be like other people."

Alfonzo, a big guy, had particular trouble with hitting. Swinging ferociously, he often missed the ball. That disappointment did not stop him from loving the sport. Before any game or practice, he would show up early. He helped the coaches line the field and drag out the equipment.

Mary Carr, Alfonzo's grandmother, describes baseball as an outlet for "the hurt he has inside." In 1999, when Alfonzo was four, his mother—Carla Whitehurst—was found dead in a house on McLennan Avenue. Police said it was a homicide. The killer has yet to be caught, Mary says.

After Carla's death, Mary raised Al and two of his siblings, 10-year-old Marcel and 11-year-old Oliesha, who was born with profound cerebral palsy.

Henry Clemons, Alfonzo's grandfather, says Alfonzo routinely shovels sidewalks in the winter, and then gives Mary what he earns to help pay for groceries. Mary recalls how her grandson once saw an elderly woman drop $80 in cash. Alfonzo picked it up and returned the money.

He is also a dedicated older brother for Oliesha, who uses a walker. "Al's always been her arms and legs," Henry says.

To Alfonzo, then, baseball is both a passion and an escape. Mary says she recently found her grandson crying in bed. Little League was almost over, he explained. He can't imagine life without it.

Like Alfonzo, Henry Sullivan—one of six siblings—is in his last season at South Side American. A year ago, he had trouble even fouling a pitch off. It would have been easy to quit. Instead, he came up with a way of getting better. He taught many of his friends to play baseball. He organized games in an empty lot. Seven of his cousins, because of that, signed up for Little League.

Quickly and steadily, Henry improved.

"I believe in myself," he says.

His mother, Janet Roberson, says Henry covered his bedroom wall with baseball posters and cards. He even stopped playing his beloved video games in favor of playing catch or throwing a ball up in the air.

Around Harrigan Field at Wadsworth Park, people took notice. Henry evolved from a baseball novice into a solid first baseman. He barked and chattered in the infield. He hit the ball often and hard.

Still, as the season neared its end, it seemed as if the bet on the bus would have no winner.

"I'd be walking to the field, and I'd pray, 'God, please let me hit a home run tonight,'" says Alfonzo, who also prayed for games where everyone had fun.

That brings us to a recent Friday night, when Alfonzo's Blue Jays took on Henry's Cardinals. Alfonzo got up in the second inning with the score tied, 1-1. On the second pitch, he took that big swing and for once—totally—got his body into the ball. It was barely off his bat when he heard a teammate, Ryan Suddaby, screaming: "It's gone!"

It was a moon shot, a home run that landed near a playground, far beyond the fence. The jubilant Blue Jays spilled out of the dugout. As Alfonzo rounded first base, Henry offered a half-smile and said, "You got me," referring to their bet.

This story, however, ends with a pair of winners. The Blue Jays carried a big lead into the sixth inning. With two outs, the Cardinals fought back. They tied the game at 7-7, and the bases were loaded for Henry Sullivan. He got up and worked the count to three balls and two strikes. Then he got the pitch he wanted, a fastball on the outside of the plate.

He hit a grand slam home run of such majesty that it almost cleared the flagpole in center field.

Henry's mom, overjoyed, watched him jog around the bases. She took him home, where her usually quiet son sat at the kitchen table and replayed the moment, deep into the night.

As for Alfonzo, he cried a little about losing the game, until Mary Carr—his grandma—found the right thing to say:

"I told Al when he hit that ball, his mother jumped up and down in heaven."

Alfonzo Whitehurst is now attending Utica College. Henry Sullivan transferred his passion to basketball, and became one of the better high school players in Syracuse.

Coughlin's 2nd Family Celebrates His Victory

Wednesday, February 6, 2008

Tom Coughlin and Judy Manfredi Cooley are not related by birth.

Yet to Judy, in many ways, Coughlin is her second brother.

She felt that Sunday as she watched the Super Bowl. Judy and her husband, Harvey, were "jumping up and down," she said, while Coughlin coached his New York Giants to an epic victory over the heavily favored New England Patriots.

As Coughlin and his players celebrated, Judy said, one thing was on her mind:

"Deep in my heart I knew, if my brother were still alive, he would have been at Tom's side," said Judy, 64.

She was 18 months older than Terry, her only sibling, who was an inseparable childhood friend of Tom Coughlin. Both boys grew up in working-class families in Waterloo. In high school, they played together on the football, baseball, and basketball teams.

Waterloo coaches remember Terry Manfredi as a big, quick guy who stood about 6 feet 2 inches and weighed close to 300 pounds. Coughlin was smaller and leaner. In football, Terry was a tackle who blocked for his friend. In basketball, Coughlin was a guard who fed the ball to his buddy at the post. In baseball, Terry was a first baseman; Coughlin, the fiery catcher.

Mike Ornato, the Waterloo football coach at the time, and Bill Carey, who coached baseball and basketball, both vividly recall the tight bond between the boys.

"The whole team was close," Ornato said, "but those two in particular."

That extended beyond the playing field. Coughlin, Judy said, was a regular overnight guest at the Manfredi home. The teens would often swim together in the nearby Cayuga-Seneca Canal. For dinner, they would eat big plates of spaghetti made by Laura Manfredi, Judy's mom. At night, the boys would fall asleep on the front porch.

On quiet summer days, Judy said, they would use fresh vegetables from Laura's garden to make what they called "lettuce sandwiches"— sandwiches they would eat for what they described as lunch, which was really the waiting period before they could sit down for more spaghetti.

College would eventually separate the pair. Terry, a class ahead of Coughlin at Waterloo, went to school in Virginia. He later settled in Florida, where he became a high school teacher and a coach. Coughlin, who went to Syracuse University, spent the years after college leading the often nomadic life of a career football coach, on the rise.

They stayed as close as possible, Judy said. They served as best man in each other's weddings. They would get together when they visited family in Waterloo. All the while, Tom was continuing his ascent in football, and Judy has no doubt that Terry would have been there for every important game his buddy coached.

He didn't get the chance. In 1984, Terry went fishing near St. Augustine, Florida. The boat hit a buoy, Judy said. In what Harvey Cooley describes as "a freak accident, a terrible thing," Terry was thrown from the boat and killed.

Coughlin was a pallbearer. Once the funeral was over, he sat down with Terry's parents. He made a promise to Laura Manfredi, who had always been so happy to fix him a home-cooked meal, who had always been agreeable when Terry asked if Tom could spend the night:

"He told her he would be her second son," Judy said.

Coughlin kept his word. Every time he returned to Waterloo to see his own parents, he would also stop in to see the Manfredis. After Judy's father died in 1991, the bond between Coughlin and Laura Manfredi grew even stronger.

When Laura eventually moved into a nursing home, Coughlin made regular visits. By that time, he was an accomplished coach, a national figure. If people wondered why Tom Coughlin was walking through the door, Laura made sure they knew the answer.

"He would come to see her, and she would be so happy and so proud to be a celebrity for the day," Judy said.

About six years ago, the doctors told Laura she had cancer in her throat. They sent her to Strong Memorial Hospital in Rochester for a tracheotomy. Coughlin, Judy said, called every day in the weeks leading up to surgery. On Laura's birthday, he sent flowers to her room.

After each conversation, Judy recalls, "my mother would just glow."

Laura Manfredi died in 2003. For Judy and Harvey, who live near Buffalo, it might seem as if Coughlin's triumph in these last few days would be difficult to watch, a reminder of all too many could-have-beens.

The effect is the opposite. Judy has been thinking about her father, John Manfredi, and how he'd sit on the side porch talking baseball with the boys. She has been thinking about the hours her brother and his best friend would spend shooting baskets in the driveway, or the sound of their voices from the front porch, before they slept at night.

Those memories come to her when she turns on the TV and sees Tom Coughlin, a Waterloo kid who has reached the pinnacle. While she cannot help but wish that her brother was also there to celebrate, her sadness is tempered by one guarantee:

With utter certainty, she knows Coughlin is making the same wish.

Tom Coughlin went on to win a second Super Bowl with the Giants. He resigned in 2016, after his twelfth season; many observers expect he will someday be inducted into the Pro Football Hall of Fame. As for Judy Manfredi Cooley, she overcame a long sequence of medical problems before she died in 2015, from a virus in her lungs. "Any normal person would have given up," said Harvey Cooley, her husband. "My wife was very, very strong."

How the Lunch Ladies Saved Graduation Day

Nottingham High, a Beloved Student, and a Race with Time

Monday, May 26, 2008

Paula Nottingham teaches chemistry at Nottingham High School in Syracuse. A few weeks ago, there was a knock at her classroom door. Beverly Whelan and Carol Salvatore had come calling. While they are officially listed as food-service workers, they are known throughout the school by a universal title.

"The lunch ladies!" thought Paula, whose visitors had a message to convey:

Veronica Claire, they said, needed a graduation ceremony.

Paula is close to Veronica, a 19-year-old senior who has endured three years of treatment in her abdomen for desmoplastic small-round-cell tumor, a rare and aggressive form of cancer.

In 2006, Veronica began taking a Regents chemistry course from Paula. She seemed as "healthy and happy" as any student in the class, Paula said. One day, in a matter-of-fact way, Veronica told her teacher about the cancer. Paula was stunned. She can appreciate the observations of Brittany Lyles, a friend of Veronica's throughout high school.

The girls often did sleepovers at each other's houses. They were both in Girl Scouts. They enjoyed the same music, notably Mariah Carey.

As for the cancer, Veronica seemed to treat it the way some teens treat a trip to the orthodontist.

"It was never really a problem," Brittany said. "It was just something she had to deal with."

In March, it reached a point where she no longer could cope with it in school.

Her stepfather, Mike Elderbroom, is reminded of her absence every day. He is a maintenance worker at Nottingham. He and Veronica's mother, Rebecca Elderbroom, are intensely proud of the way their daughter keeps going, despite relentless pain.

"We always tell her, 'Don't give up,'" Rebecca said. "Sometimes, sure, she gets down, and we tell her, 'Keep fighting. Don't get down in the dumps.'"

For three years, Veronica brought that attitude to Nottingham. Despite the barrage of treatments and surgeries, Veronica kept up with her schoolwork. She was also a regular volunteer for Edye Bonanni, who teaches special needs students with developmental disabilities.

"I just noticed they didn't have many friends and they needed someone to talk to," Veronica said. She would take the time to paint the nails of Burnese Lloyd, a freshman in the class. Burnese recalls how Veronica reassured her during her first and overwhelming days of high school.

"When you say 'Hi' to her, she says it back," said James Estanford, better known as "Pic," another special needs student who is close to Veronica. "Not everybody does. When she says 'Good morning' to you, she means it.'"

He misses Veronica. He has barely seen her since early spring, when her worsening condition took her out of school.

All of that came up during a conversation between Mike Elderbroom and the lunch ladies. Usually, their relationship is built on barbs and wisecracks. When there are spills in any school cafeteria, the lunch ladies will pick up the phone and ask for "Mike Get-A-Broom."

Once he arrives, they make sure to ask about Veronica.

A few weeks ago, Mike told them how his daughter would not be back to school. He told them how much she had looked forward to graduation day, and how it looked as if she would miss the celebration.

That afternoon, on behalf of the entire cafeteria crew, two lunch ladies sought out Paula Nottingham.

The ball started rolling. Paula went to school Principal Debra Mastropaolo, who received permission from district officials to put together a ceremony. The original idea was to keep it relatively small, with maybe 70 or 80 guests.

They did not reckon with the way teenagers communicate.

The word went out by instant message and by cell phone. Seniors Zelda Thomas, Riley O'Neill and Nicole DeSalvia heard of the ceremony in their classrooms or through word of mouth. Krissie and Katie Oja, twin 12th graders, learned about the event on Facebook. They showed up, and were stunned to see students pouring into the auditorium.

Tuesday, at the end of the school day, Rebecca wheeled her daughter from behind the curtain, onto the stage.

The place was almost full. The seniors came out in full force.

"I went out and saw (the crowd), and my breath just left me," said Rosanne Dempsey, a secretary in the main office.

Veronica started crying, as did just about everyone in the place. Someone turned on a tape of "Pomp and Circumstance." Paula read an essay that Veronica had intended to include with her college applications.

"There are a lot of people that may have an impact on you," Veronica wrote. "There is one person that influences you the most. My mother is the person that has taught me so much. I'm me and that is all that matters to her the most."

As cameras flashed, Board of Education President Ned Duell gave Veronica her diploma. The crowd rose as one, a sustained standing ovation, before everyone went into the cafeteria. The lunch ladies had baked some cakes and strung balloons, all part of the big surprise of the day:

Veronica had been named prom queen. Two of her many favorite teachers presented her with her tiara and her sash. The prom is June 7 at the Landmark Theatre. Before she left, Veronica promised to do her best to be there.

At Nottingham, they've learned this much: When she says something, she means it.

Veronica Claire died on June 23, 2008—less than two weeks after she walked the red carpet at her senior prom.

Celebrating a Native Saint

To Her Faithful, Kateri's Status Was Never in Doubt

Monday, January 2, 2012

Theresa Steele went to Crouse Hospital on Friday to pray at the bedside of Sarah Hassenplug.

Steele said her old friend, hospitalized with severe pneumonia, kept drifting in and out of sleep. Steele went through some prayers that she knew were Sarah's favorites, before offering one they'd said together many times: in a quiet voice, Steele prayed for the Catholic Church to canonize a native woman known as Blessed Kateri.

This time, Steele could recite the words in gentle thanks, rather than as a plea. When she finished, she told Hassenplug, "We need a new prayer."

Their bond was built upon that quest, finally achieved last month. Hassenplug, 67, is a Mohawk, born into the Six Nations. She used to drive a school bus in Liverpool. Steele, 73, is a Canadian-born Algonquin who lives in Clay.

More than 25 years ago, Steele saw an article about a Catholic Mass in Syracuse that would be celebrated at St. Lucy's Church. The Mass would be held in honor of Kateri Tekakwitha, whose Mohawk name is pronounced melodically as "Gad-a-lee."

As an organizer of the event, Hassenplug's phone number was in the paper. Steele called, and a few minutes of conversation turned into an enduring friendship. They shared a reverence for Kateri, a 17th-century Upstate figure of such spiritual force that Native American Catholics across North America sought for years to convince the church to make Kateri a saint.

Two weeks ago, it finally happened.

Pope Benedict XVI announced that Kateri, in October, will become one of seven new Catholic saints. She will be the first Native American to achieve such exalted status in the church.

Native Catholics in greater Syracuse speak of relief and a sense of vindication. Still, many elderly Mohawks who labored at the cause—such as Anna Dyer, Eleanor Edwards, and Harriet Ellis—have trouble rejoicing while Hassenplug is seriously ill.

As for the announcement itself, they say the pope only affirmed what is common knowledge within the Six Nations:

"To us, she was a saint long ago," said Edwards, 80. "What the church did, it's just a formality."

In 1936, as a 15-year-old, Edwards became part of a native migration to Syracuse from Akwesasne, the Mohawk territory that straddles the border of New York and Quebec.

"The reservation had no electricity, no paved roads," she said. "It wasn't the life for me."

She settled in a Mohawk enclave near Adams Street, where Kateri was already a presence. Stories about the "Lily of the Mohawks" were handed down for generations: Edwards heard accounts of Mohawk hunters, lost in the woods at night, who were guided home by a light sent by Kateri.

Native Catholics, as children, learned the tale from their mothers: Kateri, born to an Algonquin mother and a Mohawk father in a settlement near what is now Fonda, was nearly lost as a child to the smallpox that killed her parents. The disease scarred her face and damaged her eyesight.

The trauma turned Kateri into a solitary and contemplative girl, who eventually embraced the Catholic faith.

At 19, she was baptized by the Rev. Jacques de Lamberville, a Jesuit missionary to the Mohawks and Onondagas. When her conversion led some Iroquois to shun her, Kateri left on a long journey to Kahnawake, in Quebec. While she practiced self-mortification—the notion of self-inflicted pain as a means of communing with God—she was best known for a selfless humanity that created growing reverence after her death, at 24, in 1680.

"She taught that you must share, and that's being Indian," said Dyer, 84, a Mohawk who spent much of her life in Syracuse. "She was always Indian. She never forgot."

Within the Six Nations, Kateri was quickly regarded as a saint. It took the church more than 300 years to reach the same conclusion.

Local efforts to work toward her canonization were organized by the Rev. James Carey, then-pastor of St. Lucy's, on the Near West Side of Syracuse. In the late 1970s, he established a Blessed Kateri committee whose members were dedicated to the quest for sainthood.

Kateri "symbolized courage," said Carey, now based at St. Leo Church, in Tully, where he presides over three parishes. He said the committee strengthened the bridge between the church and native Catholics in Syracuse.

St. Lucy's soon opened a Kateri chapel, whose stained-glass windows commemorate the family connections and natural symbols of each Iroquois clan. Carey, 71, was also supportive of an annual "Falling Leaves" Mass that uses native traditions to honor the souls of the dead.

"We love him," Dyer said of Carey. "He let us bring our drums to Mass. He's more Indian than white."

Following the practice of many elders among the self-described "city Indians," Dyer recently left Syracuse to settle again in Akwesasne.

"I wanted to come home," she said.

The St. Lucy's committee is coordinated by another Mohawk, Emily Garrow-Stewart. The members hand out pamphlets and religious medals, speak to Catholic youth groups and try to guarantee that Kateri retains a high-profile presence.

They remain amazed that their work finally paid off, Garrow-Stewart said.

"It could get disheartening," she said. "There were times when you'd wonder, will it ever happen?"

The disappointments were offset by generations of belief.

Those who loved Kateri felt she was a saint, regardless of whether the church made it official. Such faith brought together Steele and Hassenplug, who grew into close friends. They served as volunteers at a Fonda shrine that honors Kateri. Hassenplug also wrote a one-person monologue about Kateri's life that Steele—in traditional garb—has performed many times.

In July, Kateri devotees from around the nation will convene in Albany, Steele said. She is guessing that Kateri's canonization ceremony at the Vatican will be held in the fall, and she expects the conference to focus on planning nationwide celebrations. Until then, for Steele and others who are close to Hassenplug, their business with Kateri is far more immediate:

At Crouse Hospital, they seek the intervention of a saint.

Sarah Hassenplug died on January 7, 2012, at Crouse Hospital. Ten months later, Kateri Tekakwitha—the seventeenth-century woman to whom Hassenplug offered lasting devotion—was formally canonized and made a saint by Pope Benedict XVI.

PART FOUR

Courage

Dark Past Haunts Lighthouse

Thursday, October 31, 1996

Haunted. Ed Brown, the U.S. Coast Guard chief in Oswego, hears the tales less often these days. His outfit installed a solar-powered lens in the old lighthouse in 1994, and then locked it up because the place was packed with asbestos.

Until that day, some regulars at the Oswego Coast Guard station dreaded going to the lighthouse. It is lonely, windy, often banged by waves. They would speak of putting a lightbulb in a socket high above the floor, only to find it set down on the ground the next time they went there.

They swore they could hear footsteps in the tower and would ascend to find no one there but themselves. Sometimes they'd look out from the shore toward the lighthouse, across the churning lake, and it would seem a light was burning in a window.

Haunted. These were not the tales of children but of grown men, who knew how six men died at the lighthouse 54 years ago. And while you can laugh off the stories as a legend or a myth, the simple truth is that some things were never put to rest.

Not all of them concern the spirit world.

In Syracuse, David Ginsburg doesn't fret much about ghosts. He is 98 years old. He sits in his small apartment in DeWitt, near the shelf that holds a portrait of his son, Irving. Haunted? Ask David about the stories and he smiles, lifts his hands. He has not gone near Oswego in perhaps 50 years, but the lighthouse still haunts him every day of his long life.

"He was quite a guy," David says of Irving. He lost him at the lighthouse on a date David often says out of the blue, a date he repeats in a singsong, rhythmic way.

13. David Ginsburg holds a photograph of his son, Irving.
(John Berry/*Post-Standard*)

December 4, 1942.

Ginsburg, 21, died along with five other Coast Guard crewmen. They were attempting a rescue. The lighthouse, in those days, was still manned around the clock by a Coast Guard keeper. A savage gale came up on Lake Ontario, and the keeper—Karl Jackson—was cut off from the shore. The only possible rescue by foot was on a narrow spit of breakwall. Ice covered the wall and giant waves washed over it.

Jackson went three days without relief. Lt. Alston Wilson, the Coast Guard chief, kept waiting for the chance to relieve his weary keeper. Finally, when the winds dropped from 65 to 30 mph, he set out with eight others in a 38-foot boat. They made it through rough waters to the dock at the small lighthouse.

The Coast Guard crew helped Jackson get into the boat. Two new lighthouse tenders got off and went in. The worst seemed over. But as Wilson and his crew of seven backed off from the light, the boat's engine gave out. That had been their only protection from the storm.

A wave picked up the boat, smashing it against the foundation of the lighthouse. The boat overturned. Six of the men, including Ginsburg, fell into the water. Two others, Fred Ruff and John Mixon, were trapped on the boat. They both survived. They plunged deep into the lake and dragged themselves onto the wall.

Exhausted, helpless, they watched their six friends being swept off by the waves. "They were fighting to beat the devil, trying to stay up," remembers Ruff, now 86 and living in Erie, Pennsylvania.

All six died. Ginsburg, a strong swimmer, was last seen trying the back stroke to stay up in the frigid water. Ruff and Mixon crawled on their bellies over blocks of solid ice. One slip, and they knew they would go into the lake. Finally, they got close enough to shore to get picked up by a boat. They were treated for exposure and then called on to help search for the bodies.

"I never went out there again," Ruff says of the lighthouse. "I wanted nothing more to do with that."

Molly Ginsburg, Irving's mother, learned the news in a hard way. The Coast Guard sent a telegram. Irving often wired money to his parents, and Molly thought the envelope contained a Hanukkah gift.

Irving was the oldest boy, the pride of the family. In the aftermath, the Ginsburgs took comfort in tentative plans by the Coast Guard to build a monument in Oswego. It never went up. "Not a darn thing," says Ruff. "I've often thought about that."

David Feigin is second in command at the Coast Guard station in Buffalo. During his years in Oswego, he was intrigued by stories about the disaster. He heard accounts of the accident and tales of the haunting. So he went back and did some research.

His theory is that national trauma over World War II prevented the Coast Guard or the city from putting up a monument. He still thinks the most appropriate spot would be the public parkland at Fort Ontario.

"If (the tragedy) happened today, it'd be all over CNN," he said. "Back then, with everything that was happening in Europe and the Pacific, who was going to pay attention to a handful of Coasties who get smashed against a breakwall? But something should have been done. It should have been acknowledged."

The Ginsburgs waited. The war ended and America went back to its business. Molly died 15 years ago. No monument was built. Even now, if you walk the Oswego shoreline, you will find no reminder of the six men who died. Over the years, the accident became less a story of heroism than a ghost story of such lonely power that it bothered grown men at the Coast Guard station.

Until that changes, until his son and the five others are given public honor, David Ginsburg has vowed to stay away from Oswego.

"They said it would happen," he says of a monument. Until he retired, David was a milkman. The old man can remember delivering milk by horse and wagon on the streets of Syracuse. Irving would often sit by his dad's side. The boy grew into the quarterback at the old Central High.

David knew about war. He was a marine. He saw combat, too much of it, in World War I. He went on to become a marine drill sergeant.

In 1941, after the Japanese bombed Pearl Harbor, Irving wanted to emulate his father. He planned to enlist in the Marines. His dad talked him out of it. He knew the kind of warfare the Marines would be facing. He convinced Irving to instead enlist in the Coast Guard.

Even now, at 98, the old man shakes his head. "The Coast Guard," he repeats. He figured it was safe.

After Irving died, David and Molly and four surviving children slowly went back to their routines. David has lived a full life. He is proud of his family. He has letters on the wall that proclaim his status as the nation's oldest drill sergeant. But a day never goes by without him thinking about his oldest son.

Haunted. Six men died as heroes and have no monument. David Ginsburg, 98, says he intends to see one built. As for ghosts, legend says they have business left undone. If a spirit haunts the lighthouse, the old man shares the watch.

In the months after this column appeared, the U.S. Coast Guard put together a memorial service to honor the men killed in 1942 at the Oswego lighthouse. On December 4, 1996, the 54th anniversary of the disaster, a boat carrying David Ginsburg, his daughters, and Andrew Cisternino, a Coast Guard veteran who nearly drowned while attempting to recover those thrown from the boat, traveled to the place in the harbor where the tragedy occurred—and the passengers dropped a wreath into the water. The following year, David was there when a plaque honoring the victims was unveiled on the Oswego waterfront. The coverage of the ceremony led to a phone call from Gene Lee, a Marine Corps veteran of World War I; he was stunned to learn a fellow survivor of the battle of Belleau Wood lived in greater Syracuse.

The two men remained close friends until Ginsburg's death in 2000, at 101.

Win Speaks Volumes of Orator, Her Fans

Wednesday, November 20, 2002

My-Kellia McShan had her own rooting section Saturday in the Lincoln Middle School Auditorium. Her mother, Linda Dreher, was there. So was Kate Palumbo, one of My-Kellia's teachers at the Delaware Elementary School on South Geddes Street, and Milagros Escalera, Delaware's principal, and many other relatives and faculty members.

They were there to watch My-Kellia—all 48 or 49 pounds of her—compete in the third- to fifth-grade finals of the Syracuse school district's citywide oratorical contest, organized by the National African-American Parent Involvement Day committee. My-Kellia, nine, wore a new red-and-black outfit, with a butterfly theme that made her particularly proud.

She had already survived two nerve-racking qualifying rounds, competing against some fine young orators, before it all came down to this last chance.

Yet she said she wasn't nervous. Not one bit.

As for her fans? "We were dying," said Palumbo, who stood amid a fist-clenching, lip-biting squadron of adults.

In one way, the whole thing started with Palumbo, although maybe it really started with My-Kellia's mother. Dreher, 30, was once a little girl who loved to read, but life can move as fast as a freight train. Dreher was pregnant with her first child by the time she was 15. College became a lost chance, a fantasy.

My-Kellia is the fourth of Dreher's five children. They live in an apartment on Delaware Street, next door to a boarded-up house with spray paint on the walls. My-Kellia, whose father lives in Florida, said she's

14. Oratorical champion My-Kellia McShan with one of her teachers, Kate Palumbo, and her mother, Linda Dreher. (John Berry/*Post-Standard*)

never traveled beyond Syracuse. Until she entered the oratorical contest, the greatest moment in her life was a children's party on Halloween.

Still, she learned an important lesson very early: if you can't leave town by airplane, you can leave town by book. My-Kellia embraced reading at a young age. "My mother told me that reading gives you courage," My-Kellia said.

Tuesday, as Dreher stood on the front porch of her apartment, she offered a blunt explanation of why she gave that message to her daughter. "I want her to have the courage to make it someplace and to be something in life," Dreher said.

The oratorical contest was a step toward getting there. It started with qualifying rounds in classrooms filled with attentive, note-taking adults. It meant standing in front of them, all alone, without coaching from teachers or from friends. But My-Kellia said she was way beyond the need for coaching.

Her journey to the finals began two months ago. Escalera had directed the staff at Delaware to watch for any potential orators. "My-Kellia had a real strong voice, and her expression was great," said Palumbo, who asked My-Kellia if she wanted to take a shot at the contest.

My-Kellia said sure, and her mom offered support. Palumbo and Kristi Ruthig, another teacher, drove the child to evening practice sessions each week, because Dreher doesn't have a working car. The biggest challenge was choosing a topic. The child was required to in some way speak about the Bill of Rights. Palumbo and My-Kellia went online, where they didn't see anything that seemed quite right for a fourth grader.

In the end, they found what they needed in a most fitting place. They went digging through the shelves of the school library, where they came upon a well-worn book by children's author Bill Martin Jr.—the same guy who gave the world *Chicka Chicka Boom Boom*. The book included Martin's poem, "It's America for Me." The poem is 22 lines long. The main theme is how we all get along in this "feudin' fussin' land of liberty."

Palumbo loved that theme, but she worried the poem would be too much for My-Kellia to memorize. The child took the poem home on a Friday. She worked on it, alone, in her mother's bedroom. She had it down when she went back to school on Monday morning.

My-Kellia and Palumbo then tied the whole thing together. My-Kellia told her teacher how the idea of free choice reminded her of *The Giver*, a story she'd read about a place where people live without personal freedom. They added that thought to the conclusion of her speech. My-Kellia, every night, would close the bedroom door and practice.

Saturday, in the final phase of the contest—without cards, without reminders, just a child all alone—My-Kellia spoke her lines with precision and passion. The judges went out back to do their work. All the children in her age group were then asked to go on stage, where Yvonne Young, an assistant superintendent, announced the winner:

My-Kellia.

Her rooting section exploded, clapping, screaming, waving clenched fists. My-Kellia smiled down, not even one bit fazed. Reading gave her courage. Her mother had it right.

Fourteen years after that childhood oratorical triumph, My-Kellia works full time for the U.S. Postal Service; she is a familiar face behind the counter at

Syracuse's West Colvin Street post office. She and her husband, Queshawn Jenkins, are the proud parents of two children; as this book neared completion, they had just been married in a ceremony at the Second Olivet Missionary Baptist Church. Queshawn graduated in May 2016 from Le Moyne College, while My-Kellia has been accepted for readmission to the school. She plans to return to Le Moyne for classes in September 2016, with a goal of earning an accounting degree.

Mom Keeps Waiting for Her Marine's Return
Monday, April 12, 2004

Patty Amidon went to watch her youngest child, Josh, play lacrosse the other day. He is a freshman on the LaFayette High School varsity boys team, and Patty lost herself in the game. She was with some friends, other lacrosse parents who've been her friends for a long time, and one of them told a funny story that made her laugh.

Then Patty stopped. She does not feel she has any right to joy, at least for now. She was surrounded by the life that's made her happy for years, the rolling hills of LaFayette and kids playing lacrosse. But Patty, abruptly, has stepped outside that world.

Her son Matt is a marine, stationed 11 miles from Fallujah.

"I want him home," she said. "That's all I want."

Fallujah has become the garish centerpiece for the bloodshed in Iraq. It is where four American contractors were ambushed and killed, their bodies mutilated by a wild mob. The incident ignited a deadly wave of attacks and reprisals. Escalating violence has brought the U.S. death toll, since the war began, to 663. At least 600 Iraqis are believed to have been killed in recent fighting.

For many Americans, those numbers are still remote, impersonal. Patty Amidon is not so lucky. Her boy is there. His barracks was hit a few weeks ago by a mortar shell. Shards of jagged metal sprayed into his belongings.

After that attack, Matt sent his family an e-mail in which he described consoling a friend who'd been sitting next to a truck driver killed in the shelling. Matt described his fury at some Iraqi men, hired to work for the Marines, who laughed about American casualties.

114

15. Patty Amidon, mother of Matt Amidon, of the U.S. Marine Corps, while Matt was serving in Fallujah. (John Berry/*Post-Standard*)

Matt Amidon, a young man whose mother always admired his "soft heart," expressed fear and rage, the ancient sentiments of war.

"I find," Patty said, "that it's better if I keep busy."

Her husband is Arnie Amidon, a construction superintendent whose family has lived for generations on Amidon Road in LaFayette. Go to their back door, and all you see are wooded hills. It is hard to imagine a more beautiful place for growing up.

"We've been blessed," Patty said, even if the landscape, right now, means little to her. When she comes home from work, she hopes there is no message on her answering machine. Her head jerks up when she hears a ringing phone. She fears seeing a military car in the driveway.

At least three times a day, she checks her e-mail to see if she's heard from Matt. She prays continually. She makes a daily call to a phone line, maintained by the Marines, that updates families on troop movements in Iraq. Her usual springtime routines no longer matter.

"I couldn't care less about getting the screens put in," she said. "I couldn't care less about the yard. I just want my son home."

It is not quite a year since Matt enlisted. After graduating from LaFayette, he attended Herkimer County Community College and the State University College at Cortland. He talked, all that time, about joining the Marines. Finally, last spring, he told his parents he was ready.

"You know what this means," Arnie said to the young man. "You know, if you join up, that you're going to war?"

Sitting at the dining room table, in the same place he'd sat since he was a little boy, Matt told Arnie he understood what he was doing.

For Patty, the biggest relief comes from other mothers in the same place. This is not World War II, when almost every family had someone at risk. Most Americans remain untouched by this war. Patty has regular conversations with three local women who have children in the service. One of them received this recent message from a son, in Iraq:

"Mom," he told her, "I don't know if I'm coming home."

As she says, Patty does her best to stay busy. She is glad for her bookkeeping job in a doctor's office. She looks forward to lacrosse games involving Josh or his sister, Courtney. Every night, Patty puts on headphones and goes for a four-mile walk, often listening to Josh Groban or Toby Keith, music that in some way reminds her of her son.

This weekend she packed Easter baskets for her kids, just as she's done every year since they were small. As for Matt, she often mails him packages. When he said he missed her homemade chocolate-chip cookies, she sent him some that she wrapped one at a time, in hopes they wouldn't melt in the desert heat.

Sooner or later each day ends, and then Patty's forced to think.

"You're under this tremendous amount of stress, hoping that your child will come home, and not in a body bag," she said.

That fear, even unspoken, simmers in the house. Patty described how she recently blew up at Josh because she felt he wasn't studying enough. "A little thing like Josh not being properly prepared for a test is not really about Josh not being properly prepared for a test," she said.

Josh, who wears a set of Matt's dog tags, said he knows what was really eating at his mom.

As for politics, Patty doesn't want to hear it. She appreciates when people tell her they're thinking about Matt. But she can't stand it when some stranger learns Matt is stationed in Iraq and goes into a long analysis of how American troops should never have been sent there in the first place.

All Patty knows is that Matt is in the middle of a war, and that the faster the Marines succeed, the faster he comes home.

He has told her that he wants to bring a few friends to see LaFayette in the fall. Patty "lives for that," she said. While she waits, she tends to her "patriotic tree" in the living room, a little tree with red, white, and blue ornaments. She has a sign near her driveway that reads "Support the troops." The Amidons fly both the American and Marine Corps flags from a pole in their front yard.

Matt came home and saw those flags last Christmas. It was an emotional visit. The family knew he was going to war. Patty can't even talk about the good-bye at the airport. She prefers to think about the way her son kept a long stick near the door. Whenever the winds of LaFayette wrapped the flags around the pole—and that could happen five, 10, even 15 times a day—Matt would go outside, with his stick, and set them free.

For Patty, right now, that's all the politics she needs.

While Matt Amidon would eventually return from Iraq, Patty never forgets all the families waiting quietly, day by day, for the homecoming of those who serve in Afghanistan and other points of danger—a vigil she came to fully appreciate during the endless days when her son was stationed near Fallujah.

Matt Amidon

At Home, Marine Says Americans Are Clueless
Monday, November 1, 2004

Matt Amidon is a marine. He spent almost eight months in Iraq stationed near Fallujah, one of the strongholds for the anti-American insurgency. Matt returned to the United States in September, and he just finished a 20-day visit with his family in LaFayette.

He agreed to do an interview, but he had one request: No questions about the presidential race. What he wanted to say doesn't involve politics.

"You go over there, and you learn about war, and you learn about yourself, and you learn about America," Matt said. "I just wish people over here wouldn't take what we have for granted."

This is what he means: Matt is stationed now in California. Not long after he got back from Iraq, he stopped at Pizza Hut. He watched a man buy some food and then throw his pizza box and other garbage out the window of his car. Matt was stunned. He wanted to chase after the man. He wanted to take him by the shoulders and ask him what he was doing.

Matt had just returned from a place where the streets are thick with filth, a place where the sanitary systems are broken down, a place where men and women would lean over and kiss the ground if they could spend one day without the stench of human waste.

He thought of that as this guy dumped his trash from the car.

"Sometimes," Matt said, "I just want to grab people and strap them into a parachute and push them out of a plane over Iraq."

Matt is 23. He spent his teenage years in a house near Amidon Road, which runs in the shadow of the hills of LaFayette. It was an idyllic way

16. Matt Amidon of the U.S. Marine Corps after his homecoming from Iraq. (Chrissie Cowan/*Post-Standard*)

to grow up, but Matt was restless after he left high school. He went to college, where he said he was "doing things I knew I shouldn't do." Acting on a boyhood dream, he decided to enlist in the Marines, a choice that soon put him in combat near Fallujah.

He made it home, where he no longer sounds like a boy.

In the way of many veterans, Matt declines to speak of exactly what he saw. He nodded when reminded of the old expression: If you've been to war, there's no need to talk about it with those who understand. And it's impossible to talk about it with those who don't.

Maybe the worst thing that happened during his recent visit home occurred while he was buying some CDs at a Syracuse store, and the clerk—realizing that he was a marine—began talking to him about Iraq.

"Did you kill anyone?" the clerk asked, in a hungry tone.

Matt knows many people worried and prayed for him while he was away. But the comment from the clerk was enough to make him sick.

"That's the beauty of freedom," he said. "You're free to do whatever you want, as long as you don't break the law."

Even so, Matt sounded tired as he said it.

He will tell you that two marines stationed at his base died while he was in Iraq. He will tell you about a rocket that struck the ground while he was walking back from breakfast, about shrapnel jagged enough to slice through doors with a sound "like a million quarters hitting the deck."

He will tell you about the group of friends that mean the world to him right now, young men who came from wildly different places in America, Marines who watched one another's backs during those long months. He will tell you about an evening just after they got home, when they were standing on a walkway above a parking lot in California, and a garbage truck dropped a big metal container . . .

In that one instant, when the metal crashed, they were all back in Iraq.

No, Matt Amidon doesn't want to talk about politics. He is more interested in discussing a nation that too often, as he puts it, seems to be "clueless." During his time at war, he saw starving Iraqi families who lived day to day on pieces of bread, men and women with little access to clean water, men and women with their teeth literally rotting in their mouths.

The suffering of the children haunts him most of all.

"I feel so bad," Matt said, "for the people who want to get out of there and can't."

He returned into a world of clean water and nice bathrooms, a world where the biggest problem involving food is that so many Americans kill themselves by being overweight. He sees all that and he wishes people here would thank God for what they have, instead of bickering and feuding over day-to-day issues that just don't matter.

"Life is too precious, life is too short, to let the little things get to you," Matt said.

Saturday night, he hugged his family and returned by plane to California. He has 30 months left with the Marines, and there's a good chance he will get sent back to Iraq. Once he's out, he knows exactly what he wants to do: he plans to teach American history and coach high school football.

You get the feeling a lot of parents will want him to coach their kids.

As this book neared completion, Matt Amidon, now 34, had just graduated from Onondaga Community College. He and his wife, Ona, have two children: Lily, eight, and Braylon, five. Matt's next stop is Le Moyne College, where he intends to earn his certification as a chemistry teacher. If you need an example of the perspective he brought home from Iraq, Matt didn't attend his commencement ceremonies at OCC; one of his children had a lacrosse game that day, and Matt felt as if that was where he ought to be.

They Should Have Been Grandpas Together

Monday, May 25, 2009

During the war in Vietnam, Andy Mondo embraced an informal slogan used by soldiers in the 101st Airborne Division. He still makes use of it all the time. It is the ultimate response to any problem involving property, paperwork, or money.

"It don't mean nothing."

In Vietnam, those words were a defiant statement of priorities. Written in big letters on a sheet of paper, the expression hangs on a wall in Andy's Camillus home. He is confident that young Americans who've served in Iraq and Afghanistan would understand. The slogan refers to what matters and what doesn't.

Because of Bobby Donovan, the lesson never fades.

"I think of Donovan every day," said Andy, 62. "If we both made it through, our grandchildren would be growing up together, and we would be grandpas together, and we'd go to each other's parties when our grand-kids had their First Communions."

Andy and his wife, Jeannette, will bring their toddler grandson to this morning's Memorial Day parade in Camillus.

Andy's thoughts will be with Bobby, as they are every day.

They knew each other casually as teenagers on the south side of Syracuse. Their deeper connection began downtown in March 1966, in the old military offices at the Chimes Building.

Bobby had been drafted. As for Andy, he'd bounced around a little after high school. He held a couple of jobs before enrolling at Onondaga Community College.

122

17. Andy Mondo holds a photo of Bobby Donovan, his army friend from Vietnam, at an Elmwood Little League field named in Donovan's honor. They were together when Donovan was shot and killed. (Dennis Nett/*Post-Standard*)

"I flunked out," Andy said. "I spent too much time drinking at the old Club 800."

Short on options, he said the hell with it. He'd sign up for the army. He and Bobby stood in the same line. Andy told the recruiter he wanted to be a paratrooper. The job seemed heroic, romantic. "I grew up watching John Wayne," said Andy, who recalled World War II movies in which the heroes dodged bullets and always made it home.

Bobby made the same choice. He and Andy ended up training together with the 101st Airborne, at Fort Gordon in Georgia. In their free time, they'd rent motorcycles for long rides on dusty roads, or they'd drink beer and wonder about what was coming next.

At 19, they were sent to Vietnam.

Just before they left, they were allowed to spend two weeks in Syracuse. Andy was at the old Hewitt's bar in Camillus, holding two drinks, when a woman walked up and casually took one from his hand. That's how he met Jeannette. He started laughing, until he realized she was hoping he would ask her for a date.

He told her he was going to war.

"I'm going to wait for you," Jeannette said, which led to an exchange of letters that began in September, when Andy arrived in Vietnam.

He and Bobby were assigned to the same gun company in the central highlands. They went on regular missions far from camp, patrols that were known as "humping the boonies."

Andy said that he and Bobby were naive. Around camp, they were known as "cherry boys," a vulgarity that described soldiers who hadn't been in combat.

On November 9, 1966, that status permanently changed.

Their company was doing reconnaissance, Andy said, walking "along a kind of ridgeline," when they heard the sounds of gunfire higher on the hill. "Our adrenaline was pumping," Andy said. "I don't think we were scared at all."

Bobby was about 10 feet ahead of Andy, in a grassy area dotted with young trees. At one point, Andy recalls, Bobby turned around and smiled. They kept going. Andy walked into a patch of heavy brush. He had just gotten down to crawl beneath it when "the world exploded," as Andy puts it.

The North Vietnamese had opened up their guns. In that instant, all childhood fantasies were gone. Andy looked up at a withering fire strong enough to cut down trees. "It was like being in an insane asylum," Andy said. He cannot say how long it continued, or when he realized Bobby had been hit, or when a medic finally arrived to help.

The medic moved on quickly. Bobby was dead.

Days later, when Andy finally got back to camp, Bobby's gear had already been removed from their tent. Andy wrote letters to his parents and to Jeannette, telling them what happened. But nothing changed. There was no respite.

Sick with grief, almost immediately, he was sent back into combat.

"It wasn't like you could run away," Andy said.

For the next 10 months, he kept doing the same job. He would be gone for days, often sleeping in the mud, usually soaked.

"People always think it was like you were fighting all the time," Andy said. "You weren't. It was more like long days of just walking, never seeing anything, with short periods of intense, unbelievable violence."

Andy survived. He looked out for the guys at his side, who did the same for him. They all counted down the days until they left Vietnam. Andy did not really believe he was safe until he was on a jetliner, lifting off. At the moment the plane left Vietnamese airspace, every soldier aboard erupted into wild cheers.

Within days, Andy was back in Syracuse. He remembers going outside to stand in the rain, allowing himself to get completely drenched, just so he could strip down and then savor warm, dry clothes.

That began a lifetime of grappling with the question he still faces every day: Why did he make it out, and Bobby didn't?

"When he was gone, it left a hole," Andy said. "I had good friends in my company, but not like Bobby. It's hard to explain. It was like someone took a leg from under me."

At home, Andy went to Assumption Cemetery and found the graves of Bobby and Andy Stein, another guy from Syracuse who died in Vietnam. With his dad, Andy visited Bobby's parents, Fran and Helen Donovan, trying to explain the unexplainable. He learned that Bobby had been awarded the Silver Star.

In the mornings, Andy went looking for work. He took a job in a factory, and hated it. He felt better when he was hired by the United Parcel Service.

He became a driver. On long drives, then as now, his thoughts would drift toward Bobby. "I can still see his face, I can still hear his voice, I can still see his smile," Andy said. "I worry that I might lose that someday."

Andy eventually retired. He and Jeannette will celebrate their 40th anniversary this year. They've stayed in the same Camillus house for 38 years. That's where they raised two children, where they now build their lives around their grandkids.

As for Bobby, Andy sometimes pulls out a photo of his friend. It goes back to a morning before they went to Vietnam. Andy crept over to the bunk where Bobby slept. He took a flash picture, right in his buddy's face.

Bobby leaped up roaring, seeing only bright lights, demanding to know who played the trick.

Andy hid the camera. He had this one planned out. A day would come when they would be among old friends, maybe after they got out of the service, and Andy would hold up the picture and plead guilty.

He and Bobby would laugh at that photograph, forever.

Instead, on Memorial Day, Andy carries it alone.

Andy Mondo still makes his annual Memorial Day pilgrimage to both the Little League field named in honor of Bobby Donovan, and to Bobby's grave at Assumption Cemetery. Some commitments, Andy said, you don't forget.

Nothing Can Keep This Coach Down

Monday, October 1, 2012

John Hohm showed up Friday at the Corcoran High School stadium for the Corcoran-West Genesee football game. Hohm's 1986 state championship cross-country team was being inducted at halftime into the school's hall of fame, along with such Corcoran stalwarts as the late Janet Bluem, a legendary coach and teacher.

Hohm still coaches cross-country for Corcoran. He spent almost 40 years teaching there before he was moved to Henninger in 2010 as part of a state-ordered shakeup, based on graduation rates. While Hohm liked Henninger, leaving Corcoran broke his heart. Last spring, he retired from teaching. He came to Friday's game on the request of school alumni president Paul Grace, who asked Hohm to make the hall of fame presentation to the runners.

It was a setup. As Hohm stood on the sideline, in a steady rain, announcer Rocco Carbone told the crowd that the hall of fame was about to welcome a surprise inductee:

John Hohm.

"It means a lot," said Hohm, 63. His Corcoran track teams were consistently excellent. His cross-country teams won five state championships, and missed a sixth—in 1981—only because Steve Loretz, Corcoran's top runner, got lost in a blinding snowstorm that caused some race officials to abandon their posts. Loretz finished first, but was disqualified for straying from the course. The Cougars placed second behind McQuaid of Rochester, a ruling so unfair that Bob Bradley, McQuaid's coach, gave the championship trophy to Corcoran.

18. Longtime Corcoran High School cross-country coach John Hohm. (Michael Greenlar/*Post-Standard*)

Loretz settled in Texas. Paul Norman, another fine runner of that era, lives in Virginia. They both attended Friday's ceremony. They said Hohm changed their lives through pure stubborn example.

He was a marathon runner who "could run with any of us," Norman said. Matt Kerwin, a former Cougar who was on the 1986 team, said Hohm often saw more potential in his runners than the teens saw in themselves. Kerwin and many others said Hohm's relentless nature could drive them nuts, but he inevitably helped them call on strength they didn't know they had.

Decades later—as fathers, professionals, and human beings—the idea that you never quit serves them well.

Still, Hohm's greatest gift to his community had nothing to do with trophies. He lives a few blocks from the school, in the same house where his children grew up. In 1993, while his family was away, Hohm was roused from sleep by a strange noise. He climbed from bed and walked into the darkness. A man stepped from hiding and stabbed the coach in the stomach.

Hohm fell to the floor. Three strangers bound and gagged him, then ransacked his house. One assailant choked Hohm until all signs of life were gone. The intruders took Hohm's keys and fled in his car. Hohm, who'd been feigning death, dragged himself to the phone and called the police. Within minutes, the attackers were arrested.

"I was an older guy," Hohm said recalling the brutality of the man who tried to kill him, "and I think he figured I wouldn't last."

His recovery involved two painful surgeries. Gradually, Hohm got himself back into marathon shape. At Corcoran, he continued to teach and coach. "My life was in the city," he said.

The assault sent a wave of panic through a quiet Syracuse neighborhood. Many residents assumed Hohm and his family would move, a decision that could have touched off an exodus. Instead, Hohm stayed where he was. Police told him the attack was a freak incident, the act of desperate men who made a random choice.

"I remember it happened a week or two before we moved into our house," said Sue Fahey Glisson, a neighbor who was at Friday's Hall of Fame induction. "Over the next few months, we got to know John and his family and we grew very close to them. It always stuck in my head that he made a statement by staying in the neighborhood. It was huge. It sent a huge message to everyone."

Joe Serrao, coach of Corcoran's girls' cross-country team and a member of the 1986 championship squad, said he never doubted Hohm would resume his normal life. "He instilled the idea in all of us that you should never be satisfied, that you can always be better," Serrao said. "And I knew he'd have to run again, because when he can't run, he goes nuts."

Nineteen years after the stabbing, Hohm is a very proud grandfather. Hundreds of young people he taught or coached grew into lives of achievement and respect. Many were there Friday, watching in the rain, as Hohm entered Corcoran's hall of fame. The attack, even then, flashed through his mind.

"What it makes me remember," Hohm said, "is everything I could have missed."

While John Hohm is now retired as a teacher, he is preparing for another season as cross-country coach for the Syracuse West High School team based at Corcoran High School. He continues to set the ultimate example for his student-athletes: neighbors remain accustomed to seeing Hohm, in snow or sun, running the streets of Syracuse.

"God Puts People in Your Path"

Pat Wiese, amid Hard Treatments, Finds League of Angels

November 28, 2013

Dr. Mike Wiese speaks of what he calls "cancer angels." He's encountered them many times since last summer, when he had as tough a meeting as he ever faced with any patient.

Wiese is an orthopedic surgeon. He and his wife, Kathleen, who live in Fayetteville, are the parents of four children. Pat, 21, is their youngest son. Baseball is the great passion of his life. He was one of the best high school players in the region when he attended Christian Brothers Academy, and he went on to become an outfielder—and captain—for the Le Moyne College team.

Last season, he batted .333 and led the Dolphins in a slew of categories. But his leg began bothering him toward the end of the school year. The pain grew unbearable during the summer, when Pat was playing with the Vermont Mountaineers of the New England Collegiate Baseball League. He worried he'd torn some cartilage. He came home and asked his father to check his knee.

"A bone bruise," Mike said. "That's all I thought it was." He ran some tests. He looked hard at the results. Then he asked his boy to step into his office. Mike has to stop and gather himself as he recalls the conversation:

The doctor told his son there was cancer in his leg.

"Pretty devastating," said Pat, who learned he has osteosarcoma, a form of bone cancer.

The upshot was clear: he was done playing organized baseball.

19. Pat Wiese, Le Moyne College baseball standout, with parents Dr. Michael and Kathleen Wiese. (Kevin Rivoli/*Post-Standard*)

In early autumn, to remove the tumor, he had knee-replacement surgery. In October, he traveled with his parents to the Dana-Farber Cancer Institute in Boston, where specialists helped to map out his treatment. He would need chemotherapy. They talked about the schedule.

Pat managed to find humor in that destination. Since childhood, with passion, he's followed the New York Yankees. Boston has always been the nemesis, the fierce rival.

Yet at Fenway Park, the Red Sox's ballpark, Pat met another cancer angel.

His parents say it isn't really a surprise. At every stop in this journey, the angels keep emerging.

There was a grade-school classmate Pat hadn't seen in years, a young woman who heard about his illness and sent him a letter. She was praying for him, she wrote, because she remembered so clearly—at a point in her childhood when it meant everything—how Pat was kind to her, every day.

There was the overwhelming response at Le Moyne, where his baseball buddies rallied behind him, where this month's home opener for the men's basketball team was built around three familiar words on campus: "Pray for Pat." Before the game, his friends and teammates presented Pat with checks worth more than $6,000 to help him start a foundation to battle cancer. He walked onto the court. Everyone in the gym rose and cheered.

Cancer angels? Mike and Kathleen Wiese find them in their own house, where Pat's two brothers showed up in crew cuts before Pat began chemotherapy. They saw it this way: if their little brother could look good wearing his hair that way, why let him be the only one?

That outpouring of love has little to do with baseball, despite Pat's considerable skills.

"To me, he's an exceptional individual," said Tom Dotterer, Pat's high school coach at CBA. "He is an individual utterly devoid of ego. He's a leader in every sense of the word: behavior, effort, support of others. It was a tremendous honor for me just to be around him as a coach."

In October, Pat and his parents made the trip to Dana-Farber, where doctors went over the details of his treatments. The family had a different reason to look ahead: Dr. Bob Ashenburg, a Syracuse radiologist, is a good friend of Mike Wiese's. Bob's son Nick has a friend, Kathryn Quirk, who works in the front office of the Red Sox.

Boston was getting underway with its World Series showdown against St. Louis. Through Nick Ashenburg, Quirk heard about Pat's situation. She offered him tickets to a game. Pat was appreciative, but he was dealing with too much pain. He knew he couldn't sit in Fenway for nine innings.

All right, Quirk said: She'd do the next best thing. She told Pat and his folks they could watch batting practice before a series game. After the Wieses finished their appointment at Dana-Farber, Quirk met them at Fenway, a few hours before the first pitch of Game Two. Quirk led them to a spot near the best seats in the ballpark, where they watched as the Red Sox and Cardinals took their cuts.

Then, a surprise:

"Unbelievable, (but) she's opening a gate and taking us down onto the field," Pat said.

He was getting around on crutches given to him by an uncle, crutches with baseball-styled pads on the top. "When I stepped onto the field," Pat said, "I felt like I was floating."

Former Yankees manager Joe Torre walked past. So did Chris Berman, the ESPN broadcaster. Pat and his parents looked at the brilliant lights, the green grass, thousands of fans filling the stands.

Once again, they met a cancer angel.

A man in a Red Sox jacket walked over and made an admiring comment about the baseball pads on Pat's crutches. Pat had no idea who this guy might be, but somehow he immediately felt comfortable. He told his story. The man listened. He said he understood.

As a young man, he told Pat, he'd been a standout pitcher in Ohio. His dream, too, had been to make the Major Leagues. One day, as he walked along a street in a little Ohio city, a driver hit the gas when she should have hit the brakes. Her car slammed into the young pitcher. She almost killed him. The force of the collision shattered his knee.

All dreams of playing baseball disappeared. While recovering, the man remembered how his father died when he was a small boy, how his mother somehow rallied to raise her children.

Lose one great love, he told Pat, and you need to find another.

Thirty years later, Dave Mellor is head groundskeeper of the Boston Red Sox. He'd had so many knee surgeries it's easy to lose count, but the perspective he took from all the pain causes him to embrace a little ritual before many Red Sox games:

He'll find someone from the crowd who seems especially fitting. He'll let them paint home plate, prior to the first pitch.

Before the second game of the World Series, when he looked around, he saw Pat.

"Fenway is unique, and it has an aura unlike any other place I've ever worked, and a great part of this job is helping other people create memories," Mellor said.

He asked the Wieses to stand near a dugout, even as game time approached in the World Series. With almost no one left on the field except for umpires and players, Mellor and Pat went to home plate. From the time when he was a little boy, Pat had dreamed of someday standing at that spot. He leaned down and used spray paint to make the plate a glowing white.

Mellor led him to the mound, where Pat used the white paint on the pitching rubber, and the two men also made a quick check on second base.

"I'm out there thinking, 'This isn't Opening Day. This isn't the regular season. This is a World Series game, and I'm at the center of it,'" Pat said.

For a few minutes, in that place, he had no thoughts of cancer.

The separation is harder to find in Syracuse, where Pat is going through his second round of chemotherapy. Still, his parents say what he experienced at Fenway illustrates how the family finds the strength to cope.

"God puts people in your path to remind you this is all about something bigger," Kathleen said. "We've received so many acts of kindness from so many people, and we're so humbled and feel so connected to this whole community.

"I try to tell Pat this all is happening because of who he is. I tell him I'm so fortunate to be his mother, because he's made me a better person, a better friend, and he's shown me so much about living.

"Thankful? Yes. We're so thankful."

As for Pat, he said his cancer has taught him to take nothing for granted. Anything you love can end without warning, he said, and what he loved—above all else—was playing baseball.

Someday he'll take that passion and put it somewhere else, but for now the one consolation he can find is that when he thinks about baseball, he can tell himself one thing:

"I played as hard as I could every day, every game."

Whatever you love, he said, don't cheat it. You never know about tomorrow.

Mike and Kathleen say that Mellor, the groundskeeper, calls Pat a few times every month, just to check in. "Fenway," Mellor said, "is a very spiritual place," and he's already given Pat a standing invitation: a new season is not so far away, and there's a home plate in Boston that will need some painting.

If Pat could put a game or two on his schedule, Mellor would be thankful.

Pat Wiese did return to Boston for that opening day, and he again joined Mellor in painting home plate. Almost three years later, Pat continues his work with his foundation, which raises money to provide support for families with loved ones who are receiving radiation, chemotherapy, or other treatments. He is also an assistant baseball coach at Onondaga Community College, teaching young players both through wisdom and example. In 2014, when the Syracuse Chiefs had their first home playoff game since the 1990s, Pat threw out the first pitch. It was a strike.

On the Thruway

Fire, Desperation, a Crushed Door . . .
and Then It Opened

Thursday, December 12, 2013

Often, early in the morning, Tom Buckel will add a thought to Twitter that he hopes will serve as a kind of signpost for his day. Monday, just before he left for a drive to Utica, Buckel stood in the kitchen of his Syracuse home and wrote out this tweet:

"Your mission: one act of kindness today. And excellence in all things."

Within 20 minutes, he had to prove he meant it.

Buckel, a former Onondaga County legislator, is now managing attorney for Legal Services of Central New York. He often works from an office in Utica, and he uses the drive as a time of quiet reflection about his family and his job. He was so lost in thought Monday as he drove eastbound, on the New York State Thruway in DeWitt, that it took him an instant to fully register what he'd just witnessed:

A westbound pickup truck, across the median from Buckel, veered off the Thruway and slammed—seemingly at full speed—into a bridge that carries I-481 above the interstate.

Buckel pulled into the median, stopped his car, and sprinted across slick and snowy grass toward the truck. He was aware of others coming behind him.

"I ran to do what I could," said Buckel, who looked through a shattered driver's-side window and saw a man, pinned and unconscious, his head pressed against the steering wheel. Flames were already coming up from beneath the dashboard and licking at the injured man's shoulders.

137

20. National Guard Captain Tim Neild and his daughter, Catherine. (Stephen D. Cannerelli/*Post-Standard*)

The man wore military fatigues beneath his jacket. One side of the vehicle was pushed against the bridge. The driver's side door was crushed in the fashion of a can, smashed from the bottom: the upper edge projected out by a few inches, while the base was pushed in, toward the truck.

Buckel grabbed the door and started pulling. He was vaguely aware that several others had joined him and were tugging, as well.

The door wouldn't budge.

It was maybe 8:20 a.m.

Kevin Harrigan, a Syracuse adoption lawyer, was also driving eastbound, on the way to Albany. He was in his car with his legal assistant,

Sherry Kline. They were going to meet with a birth mother at an Albany hospital. She was ready to sign the papers that would allow an adoptive couple to take a baby home.

Harrigan and Kline saw the truck already pressed against the bridge. They realized the collision had just happened, that emergency crews had yet to arrive.

"I think I'll see this for the rest of my life," Harrigan said.

Like Buckel, Harrigan pulled his car into the median. He and Kline ran to help a little knot of men, maybe three, who were already gathered by the pickup. Harrigan and Buckel are both Syracuse lawyers.

They have known each other for years.

They looked at each other and said nothing. There was no time.

About five people, by that point, were pulling at the door. It was wedged tight. The flames were closing in on the unconscious man. One of the rescuers, Kline said, ran to his car, found a fire extinguisher, ran back, and tried to spray it on the flames.

It was empty.

"I've never felt so helpless," Kline said. "For the rest of my life, I am always going to keep a working fire extinguisher and a crowbar in my car."

That desperation bound them all. "It occurred to me, as we're trying to open (the door), that we're going to have to watch this poor guy burn to death," Harrigan said. A man he described as "a little guy," another rescuer, climbed onto the roof of the truck and started pushing against the lip of the damaged door with his feet. The flames grew more intense.

Someone screamed that the pickup might explode.

They already knew it. They stayed put, and kept pulling.

Five minutes into the attempt—"Maybe more," Buckel said—a man appeared behind them, as if from nowhere, carrying a fire extinguisher. He hurried to the window and did his best to hold back the flames, until the extinguisher was empty. Then he took a good look at the unconscious driver. He reached in and examined the name tag on the man's military jacket.

"That's my captain!" he shouted. "We have to save him!"

The newcomer was Raymond Presley, a truck driver who is also a sergeant first class in the National Guard. Presley recognized the driver as

Capt. Timothy Neild, a veteran of duty in Afghanistan. Neild and Presley are in the same platoon of the 27th Infantry Brigade Combat Team, based at the Thompson Road Armory at Hancock Field.

Presley was bringing his tractor-trailer back from Connecticut, where he'd dropped off a load of furniture. Typically, he said, something would have been delayed at some point in the delivery, and he would have gotten home at least 15 minutes later.

On this particular run, everything went exactly on schedule. He was ready to drop off his rig and then to go to his house and get some sleep. But he saw the smoking pickup jammed against the bridge, saw the little group of people frantically working at the door.

Presley stopped. He grabbed the extinguisher. He ran to help.

Inside the pickup, he saw his captain.

At any minute, the entire pickup might explode.

"Don't you leave him!" Presley screamed to the others. No one did. The man on top of the vehicle kept pushing with his feet. The smell of smoke, of fumes, was sickening. Kline, looking at the bent plastic and metal near the driver, realized the damage would make it impossible to unsnap the driver's seat belt. She shouted that someone had to cut him loose.

Presley had a knife in his pocket. He was pulling at the door with both hands, but he told one of the other men to grab it. The blade was so sharp "it went through the seat belt like butter," Harrigan recalled.

Minute by minute, without much hope, they kept pulling at the door. Presley estimates they gave it "four or five big yanks," falling into a fierce, unspoken rhythm.

Finally, with one great effort, they moved the door. But the opening was only 18 or 20 inches wide, Presley recalls. It hardly seemed to be enough space to extract a human being.

"It's time," Presley shouted. "We need to get him out of here!"

A sea of arms reached in and grabbed Neild. The dashboard was pressed forward, toward his body. He appeared to have fractures in his legs and feet. Flames had caught onto his jacket, near his neck. As the men pulled him out, Kline did her best to pat out the fire with her hands.

The little group dragged him about 15 feet away from the pickup. Presley "wouldn't let go of his hand," Buckel said. They had just set down

Neild when Sgt. John Tirinato, another guardsman, ran toward them to help. Like Neild, he had been on his way to a drill at Hancock. He saw the wreck. He stopped his car. Only when he reached the scene by foot did he realize the victim was a captain in the same brigade.

As Tirinato watched, flames exploded in the now-empty pickup with such force that Buckel was thrown onto his face.

"I've seen a lot of accidents, but this was completely crazy," said Tirinato, who called Presley a great soldier. "Every second counted, every decision that was made. It was God's good grace that saved the captain (and) will allow his wife to have a Christmas with her husband."

Patrick Parker, another man who'd stopped, shouted that they still were too close to the truck. Everyone came together to move Neild behind a concrete pillar. Tirinato jumped in to carefully support Neild's neck and head, and the little group dragged the captain another 20 feet.

A second explosion rocked the pickup, kicking metal into the air. The vehicle was consumed by flame.

Neild was safe. They'd brought him out of danger. The pickup burst into flames, Buckel estimates, "probably 30 seconds, 45 seconds after we got him out."

Presley wept and held the captain's hand, vowing that he wouldn't leave.

Memories, at that point, become muddled: One of the men in the little group had medical knowledge. Some witnesses say he was a doctor; others said he was an emergency medical technician. Police and firefighters arrived at the scene. Neild was transported to Upstate University Hospital, where he remains in critical condition.

Yet "the prognosis is very good," wrote Neild's father, Rick, in a note sent Wednesday to the *Post-Standard*. Rick Neild said his son has a young daughter, and his wife, Beth, a schoolteacher, is expecting another child. The captain's injuries will demand a long recovery, Rick Neild wrote, "but the key word is recovery."

If not for the efforts of every rescuer, wrote the father, "this fine young man . . . would have perished."

At the scene, once Neild was safe, a bystander warned Harrigan he'd better move his car before someone ran into it. Harrigan and Kline got in and kept going to Albany, where the impending adoption was too important to skip. Their thoughts, the whole way, were with the injured driver.

Caked with mud, they finally walked into an Albany hospital. The birth mother looked at them, astounded.

"I know," Harrigan told her. "It looks like I just crawled under a truck."

As for Buckel, he was stunned, overwhelmed. He stayed and told investigators what he'd seen, before he finally prepared to leave. Already, he was thinking how every person on the scene was meant to be there, how different it could have been if another minute had gone by, how "fate means everything, and we never really have control of our lives."

He found his way to his car. It was still running.

In the weeks after this story appeared, the identities of other rescuers were made public. The man who climbed atop the burning pickup was a Connecticut physician, Dr. Christopher Sewell. Kevin Shier, a young Canadian hockey player on his way to a college visit, also stopped to help with pulling the driver from the truck. All of those who put themselves at risk—including Kevin Harrigan, Tom Buckel, Sherry Kline, state trooper Joseph Krywalski, Sgt. John Tirinato, Sewell, and Shier—eventually received Conspicuous Service Medals from the National Guard, while Sgt. 1st Class Raymond Presley received the Soldier's Medal, the army's highest award for heroism in a non-combat situation. The guest of honor at the medal ceremony was Capt. Tim Neild, the man they rescued with barely a half-minute to spare.

After 25 Years, Fierce Devotion for Slain Investigator Wallie Howard Jr.

Thursday, October 29, 2015

If you seek living memory of Wallie Howard Jr., the little house on Ashworth Place in Syracuse is a treasury. As a child, Wallie saw it as a second home: there is a stump, in a garden near the front door, that's all that's left of a tree planted by Wallie and a cousin, Ricky Howard, when they were little boys.

Nate and Edith lost their original home on Ashworth to the 1960s demolition that claimed much of the old African-American enclave in the 15th Ward. Forced to move, they went a half-block away, and then stayed put. Nate is a navy veteran. He and Edith left Georgia in 1953, traveling with a friend—another veteran named Frank Donaldson—who told them there were jobs in Rochester and Syracuse.

They wanted to find a place where "if you wanted to work, you could make a living," said Nate, 89. By the time they reached Syracuse, the universal joint was shot on Nate's car, and they had to leave it at a garage on East Fayette Street.

They took a room for a few nights in a nearby hotel. That did it. The Howard family decided to stay in Syracuse. Nate soon found a job. Relatives from the South began joining the couple in the 15th Ward.

Among the newcomers was Nate's brother, Wallie Howard Sr. He'd soon meet and marry a young woman named Delores Hill. The couple had four children before the marriage broke up; their oldest son, Wallie Jr., was born in 1959. How close was that child to his Uncle Nate? When

143

21. Delores Howard at the grave of her son, Investigator Wallie Howard Jr., of the Syracuse Police Department. (Dennis Nett/*Post-Standard*)

Delores faced complications after giving birth, Nate and Edith say they temporarily brought the infant home.

Nate was the patriarch. He was basically a grandfather to an army of nieces and nephews. "He has the biggest heart you'd ever want to see in your life," said Larry Brown, 56, another nephew and a retired Syracuse police officer who joined the department on the urging of Wallie, his cousin and close friend.

Twenty-five years ago Friday, Nate was at work with a paving company when Wallie stopped by to see him in the morning. The young man was working as an undercover narcotics investigator. He told Nate he was on the brink of a big-time bust. The two men were fishing buddies, confidants. Nate remembers he'd dreamed of Wallie the night before, a vague and unsettling dream, and he simply told his nephew:

Be careful.

It was a gorgeous day, blue skies, warm for late October. Within a few hours, Nate was hurrying in disbelief to Upstate University Hospital, where Wallie was on life support. He'd been shot in the head by a 16-year-old, Robert Lawrence, a teenager from Brooklyn who tried to turn the drug buy into a robbery.

Wednesday, on a raw and rainy afternoon, Nate sat on his couch at Ashworth Place. His voice dropped as he recalled seeing his nephew in the intensive care unit, fragile life sustained briefly by tubes and cords. For a moment, Nate lapsed into silence.

Then he broke out of it, turning to the comfort that sustains him: he willed himself to see Wallie as he knew him for 31 years, a smiling presence of such luminescence that Nate and Edith said Wallie could change the feeling in a room, simply by walking in.

They remember how Wallie and Ricky, playing one day, planted a tiny pine in a small garden. Whatever childhood visions they had for that tree actually came to be: it would grow so big its roots pushed under the sidewalk and got into the sewer, until Nate finally had to bring it down, leaving the stump a few feet from their front door.

"I dream about him many nights, about what should have been and what should not have been," Nate said. When he wakes up in the morning, he often believes—for a few seconds—that his nephew is nearby.

A ceremony in Wallie's memory will be held at 2 p.m. Friday, exactly 25 years after he was killed. Law enforcement officers will assemble at the Public Safety Building and march to a police memorial at Forman Park, where they'll observe a moment of silence at 2:24 p.m., the time when Lawrence fired the fatal shot.

Much of the preparation for Friday's event was handled by Rebecca Thompson, a Syracuse deputy police chief. In 1990, she was part of a federal detail that established surveillance around a parking lot at South Salina Street and Brighton Avenue, the spot where Wallie planned to arrest several dealers who'd promised to sell him $42,000 worth of cocaine.

Instead, when he was shot, it was Thompson who reached him first, who put out a frantic call that an officer was down. To her, remembering Wallie is a lifetime responsibility. She can quote the taped conversation Wallie had with the men who tried to rob him as he sat in a parked car, how they asked for the time—and then demanded cash.

Gunfire erupted in the parking lot. Wallie wounded one assailant, Anthony Stewart, before Lawrence fired from close range through an open window.

Lawrence would be convicted of murder and sentenced to life. That sentence was changed last year to a possibility of parole in 2020, based on a Supreme Court ruling that mandatory life sentences for juveniles are unconstitutional.

A quarter-century later, the October afternoon is seared into the memory of those who loved Wallie, "an all-around good guy," Thompson said. Gwen Dowdell, retired after a career with the police, recalls how she'd often see Wallie at the front door of the Public Safety Building as they were changing shifts.

Sometimes she'd be tired, worn down by a hard day. She said Wallie had the ability to lift her spirits through sheer presence, through a smile that was akin to hitting a light switch in a dark place.

Larry Brown and Ricky Howard, the cousins who were two of Wallie's closest friends, speak of him as if they saw him yesterday. Brown recalls an excursion when the three cousins went fishing in Phoenix—fishing as the gift, the passion, learned from Uncle Nate—and Wallie hooked an enormous carp. He battled for a long time to drag it in, before he finally headed for the water to finish off the fish . . .

It was strong enough to knock him off balance. He fell in. Brown began laughing—a deep, appreciative laugh—as he remembered Wallie rolling around in shallow water, the huge carp swinging its tail and slapping him . . . *Whap! Whap! Whap!* . . . in the face.

Wayne Howard was Wallie's younger brother, by six years. He is a crew leader with the city's Department of Public Works, and he said he measures himself each day against one question: "I always wonder what he'd think of what I've become."

Delores and Wallie Sr., who died in 1999, separated when Wayne was young. Wayne shared a room with Wallie and watched the way his brother handled life, how Wallie got up every day to go to work, to follow through on his obligations.

"I couldn't ask for a better role model," Wayne said. "He was full of integrity."

He remembers how Wallie accepted an opportunity, as a young police officer, to moonlight as a security officer at the old Kennedy Square housing complex. It didn't pay much, but there was an incentive: each security guard was offered an apartment, rent-free. Delores, at the time, worked as a therapy aide at a rehabilitation center.

Wallie took the job—which meant he went from his shift with the police to a shift at Kennedy Square—so his family could use the apartment, at no cost.

"He didn't need the money," Wayne said. "He did it for mom and me."

His brother also loved to race on motorcycles. Wallie would bring Wayne along to watch those high-speed showdowns, and Wayne—as a teen—dreamed of having a motorcycle of his own. Delores worried her youngest might get hurt, but on Wayne's 16th birthday, Wallie showed up with a moped.

"My mother," said Wayne, "just threw up her hands."

He will be at the ceremony today, looking out for Delores and thinking about his brother. He believes, if Wallie had lived, that "things would definitely be better" in the city, that something in Wallie's warm and level personality might have served as a bridge, that he could have made a difference in the bloodshed on the streets.

Wallie's friends and relatives have different visions of what he might be doing today. Some wonder if he'd have "been 20 and out with the police," if he would have retired to his family, his two children, to his fishing. Wayne joins Larry Brown in maintaining that Wallie, always driven, would have felt compelled to take on the madness of city violence, that he might have sought a much higher rank with the police.

"Knowing him, the way he did things, if he had stayed on the force he could have done anything," Wayne said.

As for Delores, at 76, these annual ceremonies are increasingly difficult. Her oldest daughter, Stephanie, died from kidney failure. The tragedy haunted Wallie, Wayne, and another sibling, Shelley. Delores has a wall in her home that serves as a family memorial, photos and mementoes dedicated to Wallie, Stephanie, and Najee, a three-month-old son Wallie lost to sudden infant death syndrome.

Even now, sometimes, when Delores is busy in her kitchen, she'll get an overwhelming feeling that Wallie's about to walk in. A mother knows the footsteps of her children, even when they're grown. She can remember exactly how it felt whenever Wallie came into her house, the way he'd close the door behind him, the way he'd clear his throat before he came into the kitchen and hugged her.

Always, he wore the same expression:

"That smile," Delores said.

After 25 years, eyes closed, that's how she sees her son.

Nate Howard, too, has a wall of family photos. One portrays Wallie as a young officer, just finished with the police academy. Nate and Edith began speaking together Wednesday of Wallie's life. The couple has been married for so long—they met in the 1950s, in Georgia—that their voices meld into a kind of harmony, exclamations and affirmations almost like a song.

They remember Wallie, Larry, and Ricky, upstairs as little guys, firing a forbidden BB gun out of a window. They remember how Wallie, as an adult, was always drinking his beloved Mountain Dew, because—as anyone who knew him will emphasize—Wallie chose not to drink alcohol or smoke.

Nate used to go to high school track meets and watch his nephew set high-jump records for Henninger. Larry Brown recalls how Wallie would run the court in playground basketball, going up so high he could slam a basketball with both hands. Ricky Howard laughed about the last time he saw Wallie, how Ricky slept off a hangover in Wallie's SUV on a long drive to go fishing, until they arrived and Wallie asked in a voice loaded with mock courtesy:

Did you have a nice sleep?

Nate thinks of him "laughing and pulling pranks," while Edith said: "If you needed him, he'd be right here." All of that, all those tales, came together in the image they created of their nephew, gone now for 25 years, a young man Nate still encounters—vivid and alert—in his dreams.

"He did quite a few good things, and he accomplished something you can carry on," Nate said. To the rest of us, that kind of sacrifice equates to legend. To Nate and Edith?

On Ashworth Place, near all that's left of a strong tree, they just miss Wallie.

In a 2013 interview with the Post-Standard, *Wallie Howard III—son of the slain investigator—offered this philosophy as the best way of building a living monument to such warmth, humor and courage: "My father loved life, and he had a sense of responsibility; he knew things could be better. I'm not telling anybody what they have to do. I just think we all see opportunities in life where we know we could do something, and all I'm asking is for all of us to take advantage of those opportunities, and to reach out instead of looking away."*

PART FIVE

Diligence

Midway Mystery

This Vampire . . . Is He Alive?

Friday, August 30, 1991

The public address announcer Wednesday at the New York State Fair had just announced temperatures of 87 degrees—"and that's at the airport!"—when the plastic surgeon from Utica stopped to watch the mechanical vampire.

It stood on the midway, near the "Thriller" house of horrors. It jerked its shoulders and swiveled its torso, while feet and legs stayed locked on a black metal case.

The vampire, white-faced and silent, was hardly different from any of the grotesque mannequins up and down the midway.

But then, somehow, it seemed alive.

The fair has been there 145 years. Few things remain that can inspire real wonder.

Yet Dr. Carl Krasniak, the plastic surgeon, drew back from putting his hand on the vampire.

And behind the doctor and his family, a crowd—sluggish from the heat, eager to push on but compelled, somehow, to stay—also began to gather, heads cocked, curious.

Like they have since the fair's first day, the conclusions lasted seconds, then changed.

"He's not real," Krasniak said. "He doesn't blink."

Richard Morris, the "carny" running the house of horrors from a nearby booth, rested his chin on his hand, oblivious. Sometimes he gave a gravel-pitched call to the midway crowds, asking them to step inside.

Sometimes one hand dipped toward an electronic panel in his booth, and the crowd wondered if those controls made the vampire turn and scowl.

Still, there was something about the folds of skin beneath its chin, or the long lashes on the sightless eyes . . .

No. The legs were spindly, rigid, metallic. They seemed locked to the case.

"Look, he blinked!" shouted Sarah Krasniak, 14, the surgeon's niece.

"No," said her aunt, Lidia Krasniak, a professional anesthetist and the doctor's wife. She walked up to the mechanical vampire, stared at its neck, its profile. The crowd watched. Many had sweat dripping down their faces.

She shook her head again. A dummy. Her husband agreed.

"He's got a good jugular," she said of the vampire. They both laughed.

By now two ambulance paramedics in a golf cart had joined the crowd, equally uncertain, caught in the spell. The doctor, in turn, moved to within a few inches of the vampire. It jerked past him, mechanical scowl flexing in and out, fingers extended inside rubber gloves.

Krasniak waggled his hand inches from the vampire's face. Nothing. He ran back to make a final prognosis to his brother, Mike, Sarah's father.

"He's not real," the doctor said. "He doesn't blink."

Morris, in his booth, stared into space.

The vampire jerked again, to its left. It took a step off the platform. It began walking up the ramp, toward the doorway to the house of horrors.

It wanted a cigarette.

"Time for his break," Morris said.

The crowd released a collective sigh.

"Look at that," said the astounded plastic surgeon, voice soft.

The vampire's name is Cheyene Diamond Bear, a longtime street performer in Syracuse until he moved away five years ago. He is of native descent, he said: "The only Native American I know of who's doing mime."

Amid the humming machinery behind the house of horrors, built atop a tractor-trailer, Diamond Bear drew at a cigarette and said his parents were both carnies with the midway shows of James Strates.

He began doing mime in 1959, at the age of four, gradually expanding his act to include more than 200 characters. On his business card, he calls himself "the Legendary Mechanical Man."

The name fits.

Last year, after returning to the area, he went looking for work while the fair was being set up. His talents convinced the owners of the "Thriller," who hired him to stand near their facade for 11 or 12 hours a day.

He wears a cape, a high collar, a heavy tuxedo. His hair is slicked back and his skin is hidden beneath white powder.

A golden ring hangs from a pierced ear and his hands are encased in plastic gloves.

There is no cup on the ground, no open hat, no invitation for tips. There is no clue about whether the vampire is alive.

That is why Morris, behind his casual demeanor, never stops watching.

"A lot of people try to touch him," Morris said. "Late at night, when you get people who've had alcohol, we can have some problems."

It is Diamond Bear's apparent immunity to the heat that particularly astounds onlookers, who are themselves weary of steaming blacktop, relentless sun, of a fairgrounds pinned down by the humidity.

"I try not to think about it," Diamond Bear said. "I try to put it out of my mind."

The plastic surgeon looked again at the vampire, smiled, and turned to leave. Another niece, 11-year-old Michelle Krasniak, offered a parting summary.

"He's very good," she said, "but he's alive."

Cheyene Diamond Bear's "mechanical man" performance on the midway would gradually turn him into one of the legends of the New York State Fair.

To Jim Brown

Fear Must Follow 44

Tuesday, November 21, 1995

Here's some good news for Rob Konrad. The greatest running back in the modern history of football, the guy who began the whole legend about the number Konrad wears, enjoys the way the freshman Orangeman carries the ball.

But Jim Brown also lays down a formidable challenge.

"I like him," said the 59-year-old Brown, who was in the Carrier Dome Saturday for Konrad's big game against Boston College. "But I haven't really seen him run yet. It wasn't the true test for me."

Ask Brown to describe that true exam for a great back, and his answer almost sounds like football poetry. He said it comes when you're playing on some miserable day, and every time you huddle up, they're calling your number. "Your socks are falling down," Brown said, "you're on a drive, and you take over that drive."

Four, five, six times in a row, Brown said in a soft and faraway voice, you take the ball and pound and squirm for extra yards. And every time you go back and line up again, when you look across the line into the eyes of the defense, you can tell they're just praying someone else gets a turn.

Once that happens for Konrad, Brown said, the football world will know. The last guy who did it in a fashion that made Brown use the word "great" was Earl Campbell. Still, Brown sees some real potential for Konrad, although he suggests the young fullback should try and shed "five or six pounds."

"He was usually right on it, but one time he made his cut a little too slow," Brown said. "You don't need to be bigger. You can always get bigger. You need to be quicker."

On Saturday, Brown was in the Carrier Dome both to see SU play and to be honored for his admission into the College Football Hall of Fame. Konrad is a true freshman, a 6-foot-3, 230-pound fullback. As Brown watched from the chancellor's box, Konrad scored three touchdowns and piled up 99 total yards.

From a fan's perspective, Konrad did it all. He ran hard off tackle. He scored one touchdown after he took a short pass and flew 21 yards down the sidelines. "I like the kid," Brown said. "Overall, he's got all the equipment. He's got the team attitude, he's got the energy, I could tell he's always alert.

"It's just a matter of staying with it step-by-step, staying with what the coaches tell you, but always keeping that individuality going." By that, Brown explained, the great backs know when to spontaneously abandon the set nature of a play, understand when it's right to forget about your blocking.

"Sometimes you have to be daring, to make a move that isn't designed, even if you know you'll be criticized if it doesn't work," Brown said.

The legend of No. 44 at SU began with Brown, although the legend very easily could have been No. 33. That is the number Brown wanted, the number he had worn in high school. But SU senior Vince Vergara already had 33 when Brown made the varsity in 1954. Brown asked for anything close with double digits, and 44 was available.

So that was the making of a tradition. The university would eventually change its telephone exchange to reflect that number. SU's zip code includes No. 44. The same number has gained some power of its own in basketball, worn in recent years by Derrick Coleman and John Wallace.

In football, after Brown, it remained famous with such SU greats as Ernie Davis and Floyd Little. Over the past two decades, however, it's been worn by some fine but less earthshaking backs. Brown still believes it carries special meaning. "It isn't infallible, and it doesn't always predict itself correctly, but it's a good thing to have," he said.

He has a hunch Konrad will be a good fit, although he worries about rushing too fast with expectations. "When I talk about the greatness of a player," Brown said, "it's when I see him break four tackles, when I see him explode in the hole, when I see his acceleration. There were times when I scored three touchdowns, but they were all easy. There were times when I broke three tackles in the backfield to gain one yard, but that was a great run."

Konrad, who came to Syracuse a little startled at all the hoopla about his number, said he's grown to appreciate the sense of tradition. He isn't pressured about it by the Syracuse coaching staff, although he said the media always talks about the number. And while he never got a chance to shake Brown's hand this weekend, Konrad was impressed by Brown's presence when the great back addressed the team.

Brown offers the same advice to Konrad he offers all young running backs. In practice, "keep working on how quickly you can get off the ball. Let your peripheral vision work, and really hit that hole with some force. The greatest rush is to accelerate through the hole and really hit the secondary full speed. But the real rush is when you get that determination to break four or five tackles."

When it comes down to it, Brown said, "the sign of a great back is that the defense is scared to death of him. Every time they stop him, they feel relieved." Brown, in saying that, capsulized his own career.

He also mapped the path to greatness, for the newest 44.

More than 50 years after he retired from the game, many analysts and publications—including Sporting News—*still rank Jim Brown as the greatest professional football player in history. As for Rob Konrad, he graduated from SU and went on to spend six years with the NFL's Miami Dolphins. He was in the national news in January 2015 after the Coast Guard reported he fell from a boat while fishing off the coast of Florida, and spent 16 hours in the water, swimming to safety.*

The number 44 has now been retired by the university. No player has worn that football jersey for the Orange since Konrad, although debate continues about whether the policy should be changed.

The Loyal Heart of Rank and File
Saturday, April 20, 1996

The phone rang last Thanksgiving Day. Jim Delmonico had his family there, his grownup kids back home for a Syracuse holiday, and he was thinking about a turkey dinner until he heard the voice. Then he started to laugh.

"Missssster Delmonico," John Stanley said. The word was drawn out, like a taunt. Stanley had said it that way ever since the two men first met as adversaries, opposing field generals in a ferocious labor conflict.

In an era that now seems impossible to imagine, that postwar time when General Electric employed 19,000 Syracuse workers, Big John Stanley was the towering king of its union. More than 10,000 rank and file, at the peak, were in the IUE, an AFL-CIO local representing GE electronics workers. The union says the number now is fewer than 300.

Delmonico, as head of labor relations here for GE, was the company guy who throughout the 1950s and into the '60s battled Stanley one-on-one, often in a sleek GE boardroom in Manhattan.

Stanley was broad-shouldered. He grew up working in the Pennsylvania coal mines, where his father-in-law died when a cave-in broke his back. He stood six foot four. He would look Delmonico in the eye and threaten to close the entire GE works by shutting down one plant at a time. Then he would do it.

He was the master of the one-hour strike, a show of force intended to make a low-cost point. In one strike, he choked off the New York State Thruway by ordering his people to stop their cars and walk away.

The moat between the two sides was filled with acid. Stanley once brought a young son to a GE open house, where father and son encountered

159

Delmonico. The greeting was stiff. Delmonico smiled, held his hand out to the child.

Stanley grabbed the boy and pulled him back.

"We don't shake hands with management people," Stanley said. Delmonico was red-faced, furious. He demanded an explanation the next time he saw Stanley, a couple of days later. "You're poison," Stanley told him, before he teed off.

That was the wildest part of the deal. Away from work, Stanley and Delmonico were golfing partners. Their angry debates in the boardroom sometimes spawned violent clashes—fistfights along the picket line, or the late-night shotgun blast that blew out Stanley's front window.

Then they would get together on the links, where they rarely spoke a word about their jobs. Delmonico doesn't remember how the golfing started. They almost never called each other at home. They would sit at a table for bitter dialogue, then walk into the hallway and decide where to play.

Many of Stanley's union brothers didn't like it. Delmonico, too, used to get edgy comments about the golfing from other GE managers. They hated Stanley's guts. "How can you golf," they'd ask, "with such an S.O.B.?"

Delmonico didn't feel that way. He saw Stanley as a true believer, a man of conviction. He still believed it last week, when Stanley died of cancer at the age of 77. Delmonico showed up at the church. "We were diametrically opposed as far as business was concerned," Delmonico said. "But I had a lot of respect for that guy."

In death, Stanley reinforced his own legend. He had terminal cancer, and the doctors told him dialysis might extend his life for a few months. He turned it down. He was coherent, and in control, and that is how it ended. Three days before he died he wrote his own epitaph, which his daughter, Carol, read at the church.

"Thank you for the opportunity of having served you," Stanley wrote, the same words he told his membership at every union meeting.

Delmonico has a photo hanging in his house. It shows him with Stanley at Electronics Park in 1963. They are smiling. They had negotiated all day. They did not argue about a single detail. It was so unusual for them to get along that Delmonico asked a GE photographer to capture the moment.

"I did labor relations in Ireland and Mississippi and Indiana and Illinois, and I never met anybody like this guy," Delmonico said. "When he worked, he worked like a bull. He'd make a machine sing. His father worked in the mines, and John worked in the mines, and he saw a lot of terrible things. He believed all businesspeople were out to get working people.

"This guy was tough, stubborn as a mule, and you couldn't budge him from something he believed. If he told his people to walk, they'd walk. He could have gone management. I know he had opportunities. He could have been a foreman. But he had a real force of personality, and he believed in what he was doing."

Still, the two men often infuriated each other. Stanley's children remember long strikes like the one in 1960, when their front window was shot out in the dark of night, when grownups on the street would curse and shout at them.

Delmonico, still loyal to GE, recalls going to church one Sunday, where union pickets were waiting for him.

Violence sometimes erupted along the GE picket lines, and Stanley once called for 68 strikes in a single year. Twice, unsuccessfully, GE tried to fire Stanley by blaming him for picket violence. Both times, arbitrators rejected the claim.

Even Delmonico says Stanley wouldn't stand for thuggery. Delmonico said Stanley was a fine, college-educated orator, capable of electrifying an audience, and some listeners took the message too far. Delmonico remembered, during the worst of the tension, how a family friend had a wedding reception at a union hall. Delmonico and his wife arrived to find IUE members parking all the cars. He was recognized. A shout went up.

Stanley was there. He ran to the car. "Missssster Delmonico!" he cried. Delmonico stood over six feet tall, yet Stanley lifted him off the ground in a grizzly bear embrace. Then Delmonico and his wife went inside, to the wedding. No one bothered them. Their car was left alone.

Gradually, year by year, everything changed. GE started to pull out thousands of jobs. In 1963, the company finally succeeded in getting Stanley fired for "disloyalty," claiming he spread false stories that GE military parts were faulty. Delmonico, worn down by all the battles, shifted to a GE vice presidency in 1968, a job that took him out of Syracuse.

Stanley remained union business agent until 1972, when he became a national union consultant. After retiring in 1986, he was elected to represent GE retirees in this region. He wrote regular letters to the editor, warning that industries are loyal to no flag but their own.

Even today, veterans of the union wars debate whether Stanley's hardball tactics caused good jobs to leave town. Delmonico thinks it was a contributing factor. He said GE philosophically rejected a union's place in day-to-day decisions. The union, of course, wanted its strong say.

"It was like two immovable objects, both based on principle," Delmonico said.

He remembers GE meetings where managers spoke wistfully of going to Sunbelt towns without union strife. Eventually, it happened. But Stanley's friends and supporters, such as IUE veteran Art Smith, say it is too easy to blame the union for the loss of jobs. GE left for greater profits, Smith maintains, and because New York state was brutal for business.

As for Stanley, he retired from union work in 1986, but he never lost his fire. His favorite hobby, besides golf, was finding lost golf balls. He would wade barefoot into a lake or pond to retrieve an errant shot. He would wander through woods next to the links, digging out balls, throwing them into baskets in his trunk. He often reached in to grab handfuls for his friends.

Including Misssssster Delmonico.

The phone rang last Thanksgiving, and there was the mocking voice from the past. Delmonico laughed, talked to Stanley for a while. Delmonico knew about the cancer, knew his old adversary was failing, but Stanley still seemed his same ornery self. It was their last conversation before Stanley died.

Delmonico went to the funeral. He stood alone in the church as the casket passed by. There had been no calling hours. Delmonico felt a little empty, wishing for a way to voice his regrets. Delmonico turned to leave, just as Stanley's youngest child, Joe, returned for a few things. Joe is an attorney. Delmonico was glad for the chance.

Without hesitation, he shook hands with Big John's son.

James Delmonico outlived his great friend—and adversary—by 15 years. He died at 91 in January 2013, and he was relentlessly curious until his final days: according to his obituary, only months before his death, Delmonico watched a grandson's wedding on his iPad.

A Chair for Every Man

Friday, January 20, 1997

A barber has to change. Phil Malara understands. His dad cut hair for many years on the west side of Syracuse, and Phil inherited that family clientele. But Phil knew all bets were off when the Beatles came along.

It was the mid-1960s. Short hair was history. Barbers who refused to deal with long-haired kids soon went extinct. Phil changed the name of his place on South Geddes Street. It had been Phil's Sanitary Barber Shop. Phil turned into a "Barber Stylist."

"The guy who says he knows it all," said Phil, 71, "is the guy who knows nothing."

He went to school. He learned to cut long hair. He learned to give curly perms to middle-aged men. The shop survived. Now, the name has changed once again.

Phil still cuts hair, but he no longer owns the shop. It is officially called "Barberito Luis." That is Spanish for "Luis the little barber." Luis Casares is a small man, born in Puerto Rico. He speaks two languages and he is heir to Phil's hair. But Phil still shows up to work three times a week.

Their partnership has created an extraordinary West Side clientele. Phil has a thick white pompadour, Luis a goatee. The Sinatra generation waits in cushioned seats, side by side with kids who dance to fast merengue. Retirees make small talk with tough guys from the mosh pit.

"I come here," said a fierce-looking man named Tom, who wore a big gold earring on his bulldog head, "because it's the one place I know where they give white guys a good fade."

22. Barberito Luis Casares, "the little barber," with friend and mentor Phil Malara. (John Berry/*Post-Standard*)

That is a cut in which a tuft of hair on top fades on the sides. Luis keeps up on all that kind of stuff. Phil, in his 70s, learns from watching Luis, just as Phil taught Luis a lot about the business.

"You've got to keep learning," Phil said with emphasis.

His father, Patsy Malara, left Italy to settle in Pennsylvania. Patsy did not want his kids breathing dust in the coal mines. He moved to Syracuse. Eighty-three years ago, Patsy opened his own West Side shop. Four of his boys, and one daughter, would grow up to cut hair.

Phil had his first place on Gifford Street. In the '60s, he moved over to South Geddes. When his dad died, he inherited many family customers. He rented a chair to Dave Griffin, a good friend, who cut hair despite crippling diabetes. The years went on, and the neighborhood became more and more Latino. One day, through word of mouth, Phil heard about a Puerto Rican stylist looking for some work.

That was Luis. Phil rented him a chair.

Luis, 44, is the son of a farmer in Puerto Rico. He moved to New York City as a teenager. He went to school to be a beautician. Then he and his wife returned to Puerto Rico for 10 years. They moved again, to Syracuse, in hope of finding better jobs.

At first, Luis was a hesitant barber. He wasn't sure about giving up on women's hair. Phil and Dave convinced him. They talked about the Latino influx, the benefits of speaking Spanish. On their advice, he worked for a while as a barber at Shop City, where he learned to handle a stream of men's traffic. When Dave left Phil's shop, too ill to continue, Luis moved back to take over that chair.

Then Phil went through the hardest times of his life. Two of his grandchildren—three-year-old Sarah, and his namesake, Philip, eight—died in a house fire in Seattle. Phil's heart troubles erupted. Diabetes claimed Dave's life. Phil is a devout Christian, but even he needed space to rebuild from all of that.

He retreated into grief. He sold the shop to John Raite, another barber. The Malara lineage on the West Side seemed at an end.

But Raite decided to sell the shop to Luis, who offered Phil an escape from his sorrow. "I couldn't sit around the house all day," Phil said. He returned to the Barberito to cut hair part time. Luis made some changes, beyond just the name. He hired two women, Debbie Wright and Rosa Bedraza, to help as stylists and beauticians.

Old world, new world. Spanish, Italian, Latino, urban funk. Men and women, kids and seniors. The mix worked. "They are so funny," Rosa said of the two barbers. "I wait all week to come here, just so I can laugh."

On a recent Saturday morning, Bob Winn, 76, a retired corporate controller, sat in one chair. Miguel Mateo, 26, a sharply dressed Dominican with beautiful gold jewelry, sat in another. Mateo said he first came to the shop because he saw the Spanish greeting in the window.

Finally. He could tell his barber, in Spanish, exactly how to cut his hair.

"But it is not just for the language," said Juan Marcano, another Puerto Rican regular. "It is for the man." Marcano offers Luis the same loyalty Winn reserves for Phil. When Winn was ill, recovering from cancer, Phil would drive to his house to cut his hair.

Luis is up on all the latest in little boys' haircuts. That brings in young customers from both the West Side and the suburbs. Phil retains his long-time clientele, including many regulars who've left the neighborhood. At any time, in the shop, you will hear men and women speaking in both Spanish and English, and the soft chatter of children waiting for their turn.

"The most important thing to me," Phil said, "was staying in the West End. The West End has been very good to me, and I wanted to keep a true barber shop here."

Luis made it happen. The door burst open and a young Dominican walked in. He exchanged elaborate soul handshakes with a couple of waiting friends. Phil raised his eyebrows, amazed at the technique.

"I want to learn that," said Phil. El barberito knows he will.

Phil Malara died in 2005, although he kept cutting hair for his friends for many years at his Camillus home. As for Luis Casares, "the little barber," he is still busy at his trade at Carbena's, a barbershop on South Geddes Street. He serves as a mentor to young barbers, who treat him with great respect.

The Gravedigger's Art

Monday, May 26, 1997

He is a legend. Stop at a tiny crossroads store in Genoa, ask the clerk for the fastest way to North Lansing, and her face lights up. "Did you know," she says, "there's a man there who still digs graves by hand?"

She refers to Arthur Leonard, or plain old "Arthur" to everyone in town. Once the clerk even piled her kids into the car, drove over the Locke Road through rolling dandelion fields, just to watch Arthur dig for minimum wage in the North Lansing cemetery.

"A grown man with the mind of a three-year-old," says Larry Moore, who runs the dairy farm where Arthur eats and sleeps in return for doing chores. But no three-year-old could do what Arthur does as perfect art. He excavates graves that are beautiful to see.

"Listen, folks," says Arthur, the two words that start his wandering proclamations. "The man says to me he's never seen another grave like that. No machine could dig a grave like that, the man says."

He is right, although he can't exactly remember who said it. Arthur lives in his own gentle world. Cemetery manager Rod Hatfield measures off the dimensions for each new grave. Arthur slices away the grass and digs six feet straight down. By eye, he carves sheer and sculpted walls.

When he gets to the bottom, he reaches up to grab a tombstone and pull himself out.

It usually takes him five hours to dig a grave. He once dug three of them in a single day. Arthur, 58, weighs 160 pounds. He prefers the same long-handled shovel he has used for years. He won't wear gloves because they make his hands "too hot." By autumn, his calloused palms will crack and bleed.

23. Arthur Leonard, gravedigger. (Stephen D. Cannerelli/*Post-Standard*)

His appetite is famous at the dinner table. Sherry Moore, Larry's sister, has watched Arthur wolf down 10 pancakes and some sausage, then ask without blinking for a big bowl of ice cream. He paints by numbers to relax, takes a bath, falls into bed.

He is up at 5 a.m. to feed the rabbits and the chickens, and within a few hours he again is digging graves.

"Four inches and chop down," Arthur says, windy voice more like a song. That was the best advice he ever got. It came from Kenneth Tarbell, who lived in a fine white house by the graveyard. "Listen, folks," Arthur says. "Kenneth Tarbell's a great man."

For years, Tarbell ran the cemetery. He knew Arthur's dad, Harry, who worked on local farms as a hired hand. Tarbell saw something in Harry's quiet child. Tarbell gave the little boy a few odd jobs. Pretty soon, Arthur was learning to dig graves.

After a while, Arthur lived in Tarbell's house. When Tarbell died, Arthur moved to the farm of Elsie Searles, whose family took over the cemetery duties. Now Elsie is a widow well into her 90s, and Larry Moore moved in with his family to run her dairy farm.

As part of the deal, Elsie and Arthur can stay there as long as they want.

Arthur knows almost everyone he's buried. He cried as he threw dirt onto Tarbell's casket, just as he cried as he buried his own father. Arthur rarely stops talking as he digs. He talks to himself, and he talks to motorists who beep their horns as they pass. Often, he talks to old friends all around him in the ground, particularly Tarbell, who brought meaning to his life.

"I miss him," Arthur says. "I tell him that."

Arthur doesn't drive. Hatfield picks him up in the morning and takes him home at dusk. Arthur digs graves and cuts the grass with a hand mower. He wears a torn windbreaker against the cold spring air. "My father's jacket, folks," says Arthur. "My father gave it to me."

Harry Leonard died six years ago. It was Harry who gave his son a fighting chance. Arthur was the first of 10 children. His mother, Florence, is now 74. She quickly knew, as she puts it, that "Arthur's mind wasn't all there." In grade school, Arthur struggled. Other children taunted him.

A nurse recommended one easy solution. "Send him to the farm," she said, meaning an institution for the developmentally disabled. In those days, they locked away those known as "mentally retarded." They packed them into filthy buildings, behind towering brick walls.

Harry wouldn't let anyone touch his son. "His father didn't want him to go away," Florence recalls. Instead, Arthur became his father's shadow while Harry worked at local farms, and that is how Arthur found his way to the graveyard.

He has been there now since just after World War II. He digs graves that are beautiful to see, the final honor for neighbors he has known most of his life. In North Lansing, no one talks about getting a backhoe. They have Arthur, and the job is his until he wants to quit.

"Listen, folks," Arthur says. "No machine can dig like that."

Arthur, now 77, retired from gravedigging more than 10 years ago. He lives with his brother Richard in King Ferry, where Arthur is now recovering from a stroke. He remains intensely proud of his lifetime occupation: when you see him, he'll tell you he must have dug 1,000 graves.

Spilt Milk Brings Tears

One Family Fights a Storm to Save the Farm
Wednesday, January 14, 1998

Rossie—

Linda Whitney was crying. It surprised her because she did not have time for it. She had been talking about the trouble on her farm, a house lost to fire, a herd of cows threatened by ice.

She is a small woman, and the tears rolled down her face, and she gave her head a shake as if to drive them away. Then she knelt down, still weeping, and continued milking cows inside the wooden barn.

"You can't give up," Linda said. "Once you give up on something, it's awful hard to get back to it."

She and her husband, Jimmy, won't accept losing their farm.

Six months ago, their St. Lawrence County farmhouse burned down. They bought a modular home to replace it. They planned to move in this week. Linda, Jimmy, and their son, Josh, 18, were in the barn last Wednesday when the ice storm began.

They have 65 milking cows and some goats. Usually, every couple of days, the Whitneys transfer two tons of milk into a truck. The ice left them without power. They couldn't pump drinking water to their livestock.

Worst of all, they had no way to milk the cows.

Unmilked dairy cows can develop mastitis, an infection of the udder. A bad case of mastitis ruins a milking cow. Without power, the Whitneys couldn't run their milking machine. Linda and Josh, desperate, went from cow to cow, squirting milk by hand to relieve pressure on the udders.

171

Dawn on Thursday brought an absolute dead end. Husband, wife, and son were trapped on the dark farm. They had no food except a few sausages. They drank raw milk Linda drained from the tank. They listened as the ice splintered and destroyed their favorite apple tree.

Linda, abruptly, began laughing out loud.

"There we are, with all these responsibilities, and all we could do was sit," she said.

By Saturday, Jimmy, 42, found a way to share a generator. They milked the cows. Ten were already infected. It got worse. Thirty cows now show signs of mastitis. The Whitneys are milking them twice a day. They hope to cure at least 20 sick cows.

If they can't, the biggest gamble of their lives could come to a sad end.

"We took a chance," Linda said, recalling when they bought the 256-acre farm. As a child, Jimmy watched his dad milk other people's cows. He knew his father always dreamed of his own farm. After high school, Jimmy became a school custodian. It was solid work, but he and Linda had a goal.

They wanted a dairy farm. They bought a small one in 1987. Jimmy quit his day job. He made a living off his cows. In 1992, the Whitneys bought the larger farm in Rossie, about 25 miles north of Watertown. The family moved into the old farmhouse.

Six months ago, on a Saturday, they were up before dawn. The Whitneys call Saturday a "lazy day," their one chance a week to relax after the chores. They used a wood-burning stove. They thought it was safe. From the fields, they saw their house go up in flames.

"We lost a little of everything," Jimmy said. "Pictures, furniture, electronic equipment. I had a collection of old soda bottles. I'd found them here and there since I was a kid. All gone."

Last month, they bought a modular home and placed it on the old foundation. They planned to move in this week.

"Things were going smoother," Linda said. Josh got up at 4 a.m., did his chores, went to school. Jimmy farmed. Linda milked cows, then did her day job in an office.

In 20 years of marriage, the couple has never taken one vacation.

"It's worth it," Jimmy said, "to be your own boss."

They could lose as much as $25,000 from the ice storm. They already pay $2,200 in bank loans every month. They are afraid to even hope for emergency federal aid for the disaster. They've learned, as American farmers, not to set their hopes too high.

For the Whitneys, the latest blow came Tuesday morning. The milk truck arrived to empty their tank. The driver said the milk was bad, impossible to market. It showed signs of mastitis. Jimmy had no choice but to dump two tons of milk from the big tank.

It killed him. His family tried to beat the ice storm, and now he had to pour his milk. Until this week, he said, his cows rarely became sick. Jimmy couldn't watch. It was up to Josh. He opened a spigot and the milk spilled down the drain. It took 45 minutes to get rid of it all.

"We're in trouble," Jimmy said. "This is the worst thing I've ever seen."

Linda, crouched over, was crying as he said it. She knows just one reaction. She kept milking the cows.

The memory of the great ice storm has taken on legendary proportions in the North Country. The storm caused vast damage across a wide swath of New York. Amid the bitter cold, more than 120,000 customers lost heat and power—for weeks, in some cases.

Attacks Burn in Ex-Ironworkers' Minds

Friday, September 13, 2002

Gene Taylor was there, more than 30 years ago, for the symbolic completion of the first tower at the World Trade Center. He stood on the open peak of what was then the tallest building in the world as a crew of ironworkers officially "topped it off."

The workers strapped an American flag to a beam at the base of the project, and slowly raised it more than 100 floors. Two of Taylor's fellow Mohawks, both of them now dead, grabbed the beam at the top and bolted it into place.

"Then we partied," Taylor said, laughing softly. "They gave us the 45th floor (for the party), one whole floor."

Taylor, 73, lives on the Kahnawake Mohawk territory in Quebec. He is among a dwindling number of living Mohawk ironworkers who took part in building the trade center, which at the time was the most extreme "high steel" job in history.

Most of Taylor's time was spent building the north tower, the first one to be attacked one year ago. "That building meant everything to me," Taylor said. "That was crazy, what they did. I was upset a little while for the people who died in there."

In the understated way of his people, he was saying that it shook him to his core. He chose to stay home on Wednesday, the first anniversary of the attacks. He watched the ceremonies on television. He is long retired, and he has not gone to New York City since the day the towers fell, which he described as an almost physical blow.

"Naw," he said. "I don't want to see nothing."

He meant that literally, referring to the hole.

174

Leonard Oakes, another Mohawk who helped build the trade center, lives at Akwesasne, the Mohawk territory that straddles New York state and Canada. Leonard, raised in Brooklyn, was forced to retire about 10 years ago. He was doing repairs on the Williamsburg Bridge in New York City when his scaffolding gave out beneath his feet.

Leonard fell 35 feet. He never fully recovered.

Wednesday, he took part in a daylong sequence of remembrances at Akwesasne. Members of Iron Workers Local 440 set up a model of the twin towers on Route 37, near the office of Iron Workers business manager Mike Swamp.

Swamp's rank and file visited schools and raised American flags across Akwesasne, accompanied by Mohawk military veterans, firefighters and police. The ceremonies climaxed with a flag ceremony at the Mohawk casino, where gamblers set down their cards and chips for a moment of silence.

The only sound, amid bowed heads, was the electronic music of gambling machines. For Leonard Oakes, the setting took him back. His wife works at the casino. He was there a year ago, eating breakfast, when he learned the towers were under attack.

"It hit me like . . ." Leonard abruptly stopped, seeking the right word. "To put up a building like that and then to watch it go down in seconds? No building was built to stand that kind of heat."

Leonard spent one summer in the late 1960s helping to erect the World Trade Center, sometimes under the direction of his father, Arthur Oakes, who died five years ago. Arthur was a construction superintendent on the job, and the attacks caused Leonard to think of his father's role.

"He would have been hurt a lot worse than myself," Leonard said. "He worked all the way from the bottom to the top." Leonard described his father as "a tough guy on the job. He used to say, 'I don't have family from 8 until 4:30.' You work for your father, you've got to be better than anybody."

That paternal intensity, Leonard said, helps explain why the son left the Trade Center for another job.

Still, Leonard is proud of his dad's role in creating history. "These were massive buildings," Leonard said of the twin towers. Like other ironworkers from Akwesasne and Kahnawake, Leonard expressed a kind of spiritual kinship toward a New York City skyline that the Mohawks helped to build.

William Oakes, a second cousin of Leonard's from Akwesasne, also spent a summer working on the towers. He said the height of the project never bothered him. After a while, he explained, fear is relative. There's not much difference between a fall from the 10th floor and one from the 90th.

In his childhood, William set out to conquer any fear of heights. For practice, he would scale the open framework of many Akwesasne bridges. Overcoming an aversion to high places, he said, was ingrained in Mohawk culture, then and now.

The payback was the euphoria of working on such jobs as the twin towers. On warm and sunny days, the ironworkers looked down on the rest of New York City. They had a magnificent view of the Statue of Liberty. Many times, they'd end up even higher than the clouds.

As for Gene Taylor, he hopes that officials in Manhattan will decide to put up significant new buildings at ground zero. Taylor does not see new construction as dishonoring the victims, but rather as a powerful tribute in the sky.

The desecration, to Taylor, is the gaping, empty hole.

In the aftermath of the attacks, plans were made to build a gleaming glass skyscraper near the place where the twin towers once stood. In 2012, media outlets around the world recorded the moment when the new One World Trade Center, also known as the Freedom Tower, officially became the tallest building in New York City—at least for a while. The man who turned the bolt was Steve Cross, a Mohawk of Kahnawake.

For the Leonards, Sap Flows
in Good Times and Bad

Saturday, April 7, 2012

Beneath the metal roof of a long shed at the Central New York Regional Market, amid vendors hawking old CDs or fresh vegetables, Max and Esther Leonard embody one sweet institution: in a voice like an old wind chime, above jugs of maple syrup, Max spends every Saturday chanting, "Free taste!"

"We come here half for the syrup and half for the people who sell it," said Judith McIntyre, of Utica. She and her husband, Pat, have been customers of the Leonards for many years. Like hundreds of market regulars, Judith has trouble imagining the place without white-haired Max and Esther, both 87, who converse gladly about the maple business with anyone who stops.

The Leonards awaken each Saturday into the 4 a.m. darkness of their Tioga County farm, ready for an hour-long drive through a tangle of country roads to Syracuse. At the market, they offer no hint of a wound that's yet to heal:

In January, they lost a grandson who played a critical role in making syrup when Dan Leonard was killed in a snowmobile accident.

At 34, Dan saw the world in much the same way as his grandparents. He had willingly accepted the day-to-day struggles of running the family dairy farm. His four-year-old son, Gunnison, still runs in and out of Max and Esther's house, his footsteps a reminder of the dad who isn't there.

Dan "was the one who wanted to take it over," Max said a few weeks ago, in the kitchen of his home on Turkey Hill Road, in Berkshire.

24. Max Leonard on his farm, Berkshire, Tioga County. (Michael Greenlar/ *Post-Standard*)

He broke away from the conversation to pick up a ringing phone. The caller was a telemarketer. Max told her he was busy at the moment, and the telemarketer quickly asked "if he wouldn't mind" if she called back in a few hours.

"I wouldn't mind if you never called back at all," said Max, in his rolling voice. He offered a pleasant goodbye, then put down the phone and laughed.

Humor, Max said, is often a farmer's only choice.

His forward motion after the death of Dan Leonard is emblematic of a clan that's farmed the same Berkshire hillside for almost 200 years:

You go on, even when you feel your grandson in every rock and fence post on your land.

Max was born in 1924, on the same hill where he makes maple syrup. "If I had a million dollars," Max said, "I wouldn't live in any other place."

His father ran a dairy operation. When Max was a teenager, a hired hand quit and left the father in a difficult spot. Max didn't waste time thinking it over. He told his father he would assume the duties. Once he graduated from high school, Max gave his life to the farm.

The Leonards got started with maple syrup during World War II, when wartime rationing left many families without sugar. Max and his dad, seeing an opportunity, got busy tapping trees. Gradually, as his father aged, Max took over. He kept buying land until the place grew to about 340 acres. By the late 1980s, he was ready for a break: Max leased most of the farm to his son Bill, who would later hand over the dairy business to his son, Dan.

"I can't express how pleased I was that (Dan) took it over," Max said. His grandson appreciated the deep family history. While he had big dreams, he understood the elemental truth that Max says goes with farming:

"If you're in this to get rich, you're going to get discouraged."

Dan and Misty, his wife, made their home on the far side of the hill. From spring through autumn, their days were filled with the dairy operation. In the winter, Dan would go into the woods to check the sap lines to the maple trees. He and Max boiled and canned syrup in a sap house near the road, sweet aroma drifting over the snowy fields.

No one got rich, but their heads stayed above water. In the summers, Dan would host a big dirt bike race on the property, hundreds of bikers camping on the hill. When the snow came, he'd blow off steam on his snowmobile.

This winter brought an unusual problem: not only did the mild days shorten the maple syrup season, Tioga County never got a big snowfall. In January, Misty and Dan traveled to Lewis County for a chance to do some snowmobiling on Tug Hill trails.

On a Sunday morning, Max was jarred from sleep by a call from his son Bill. Dan had been thrown against a tree while he tried to take a curve. He was dead at the instant of contact, the doctors said.

Before his 35th birthday, the grandson who loved the farm was gone.

"Hard to believe," Esther says now, "the kind of void one person can leave in a family."

She and Max met in the 1930s, when she was in the eighth grade and he was in the seventh. Max said he noticed her right away, which makes

Esther laugh, because the courtship didn't happen overnight. During the war, Esther went to Baltimore to work in an airplane factory, but she came home when Max asked her to marry him. They raised two children. From dawn to dusk, they took care of the farm.

That continued until 1986, when Max handed the dairy operation over to his son. He and Esther finally had a chance to travel, and Max vowed he'd never milk another cow.

As for the sap run and the weekly drives to the market in Syracuse? "If I didn't make syrup, I'd sit down in my chair and wither away and die," Max said. Even open-heart surgery in 2001 didn't stop him. In January and February, he was always ready to put on snowshoes and to wade into the drifts, doing what he could to help Dan.

This year, without his grandson, Max steeled himself to keep the syrup business going. Misty, Dan's wife, felt the same way about the rest of the farm.

"I know what it meant to my husband," she said, "and it would break my heart to let it go."

Even so, she and Max were glad for unexpected help.

In January, hundreds gathered to bury Dan. Among those who came to mourn was Mike Leonard, 46, Dan's oldest brother in a family of five. While Mike left home in the 1980s to make a career building log cabins and furniture in Colorado, he and Dan remained close. In Berkshire, Dan and Misty would name their own son Gunnison, after the Colorado town in which Mike lived.

Like Dan, Mike was profoundly influenced by his grandparents. Max, he said, "was the kind of guy who never yelled or screamed or scolded you. But he was always so damn easygoing, and he'd act so hurt and make you feel so terrible when you did something wrong, that he never needed to give you a whack."

After the funeral, Mike did some thinking as he drove along dirt roads in his grandfather's old pickup. Winter is always a quiet time for him in Colorado. His ex-wife had custody of their eight-year-old son, a little boy named after Max. Mike missed the child, but he felt the need on Turkey Hill Road: how would his grandfather prepare the maple syrup without a little help?

Mike told Max and Esther he'd hang around for a few weeks, a time frame that kept getting longer. For more than two months, he and Max worked side by side. Together, they checked the lines in the woods. They did the boiling in the sap house by the road, during a season made short and hectic by the gentlest March that Max had ever seen.

By April, they'd collected about 350 gallons of syrup—a source of deep satisfaction for Mike.

"My great-great-great-great-grandfather got this land (in return) for fighting in the Revolutionary War," he said, "and I was going to do what I could."

Last week, Mike finally headed back to Colorado. He's already planning to bring his son to Tioga County for much of the summer. Mike wants to take the boy on the same childhood walk through the fields that Mike and Dan often made, on their way to classic lessons at Max and Esther's house:

"Think before you speak," Mike said. "Spend less than what you make. And whatever happens, try to make the best of what's going on."

His grandparents didn't lecture. They just lived it. You might call it a free taste.

Esther Leonard died in late 2013, a hard blow for Max. It broke his heart, although he could smile at one of Esther's last bits of advice to their children, words true to their humble philosophy:

"Don't let your dad fool out a lot of money on a casket."

Max responded to that loss with the only therapy he knows: he still seeks out his friends—who feel more like his family—at the market.

For Alf Jacques, Wooden Stickmaker, Legacy of Reverence

Thursday, October 16, 2014

Every day, for Alf Jacques, now brings with it some pain: he especially feels it in his hands, in his elbow, in his back. He still goes each morning to the little shop near his mother's house at the Onondaga Nation, where he uses an axe and a mallet to break apart hickory trees, a raw beginning that leads to polished lacrosse sticks that gleam like bone.

Alf makes about 180 a year, down from the time, years ago, when he worked with his father, when they often turned out that many in a week. The sticks now demand Alf's full attention—he retired after spending 24 years as a machinist—but long years on a plant floor and a lacrosse field have worn upon his body.

He is teaching his skills to two apprentices, and Alf, 65, dreams of scaling back. Yet he has no plans to ever completely walk away. That commitment, he said, comes straight from his parents: while Lou Jacques, Alf's father, died from emphysema almost 30 years ago, Alf's mother, at 86, is still on the move.

Wednesday, Ada Jacques picked raspberries near Alf's shop, then carried several baskets to her house, where she makes jam. She lives out the advice she often gives her son:

"If you sit down," Alf said, "then you're going to get old."

Sunday, at Traditions at the Links in East Syracuse, Alf will be inducted into the Hall of Fame of the Upstate New York chapter of U.S. Lacrosse with seven others: Brian Keith, Bridget Marquardt, Michael Schattner, Tommy Smith, Mark Webster, Frank Welch, and Phil Willard.

25. Alf Jacques, maker of wooden lacrosse sticks, in his shop at the Onondaga Nation. (Michael Greenlar/*Post-Standard*)

That would matter to Alf under any circumstance—he's being honored for years of playing, coaching, and stickmaking—but it has particular meaning because his father is already in that hall.

In that way, again, they will be side by side.

"What he used to say is that nothing is ever easy," said Alf, a message the son sees as imperative for each new generation: Faced with a job, confront it and finish it. The harder it gets, the sweeter the reward.

To Alf, in some way, that is the tale of every wooden stick.

His dad was a Mohawk, from the Akwesasne territory. Lou Jacques married Ada Webster, an Onondaga, and the couple settled at the nation, near Syracuse.

As a boy, like his father, Alf embraced lacrosse. A day came when Alf needed a new stick, and buying one demanded more money than he had. Father and son chose to carve one themselves. They felled a hickory tree. They learned by trial and error.

Many of the craftsmen who made sticks kept the secrets to themselves, but Lou studied the process. He quickly grew in understanding.

Alf emphasized that what he does today is a routine learned from his father:

Select a tree, bring it down, use an axe and mallet to split it into eight pieces. Trim the wood by band saw and then do your hand carving. Steam each stick above a fire, and bend it around a form. Shellac the wood. Weave in the gut webbing.

Alf signs and dates every stick. Typical price: at least $300.

Years ago, before plastic became the norm, Alf and his dad faced a torrent of demand. Now, the orders are far more specialized. There is no need for Alf to use Facebook or Twitter: word of his skills gets around, by itself.

He makes sticks tailored to native groups who play distinct regional forms of the game. There are also customers who simply love lacrosse, people willing to purchase wooden sticks as throwback symbols of their youth. Some, Alf said, will drive hundreds of miles to see his shop.

At the core of it, always, is what the sticks mean at Onondaga, where lacrosse is a "medicine game," a form of reverence. Alf makes tiny sticks that are placed with newborns, in their cribs. Old men, when they die, often go to their graves with Alf's sticks upon their chests.

As for organized leagues, there are some in which the sticks are still used. They were legal, for instance, when the Iroquois Nationals played in last summer's world championships in Denver. Kevin Bucktooth Jr., of the Nationals, said spectators often approached him—as he left the field—to ask about his wooden stick.

He did what he could to explain the meaning. But there was rarely time to get into the full significance, the knowledge that's grown on him since he was a young man. One summer, Bucktooth said, he took a job mowing the lawn outside Alf's shop just for the chance to watch each step of how a stick is made.

"It gave me a deeper appreciation," Bucktooth said. He has several wooden sticks at home, and he makes sure he uses them—even to play catch in the yard—from time to time. Each one, Alf said, retains some essence of a living tree, and he said every stick "has its own energy."

Stickmaking has brought Alf a measure of fame—photographers, writers, and filmmakers are all drawn to his shop. Still, Alf said what he does is no different, really, than when his mother makes jam in the way taught to her as a child, or when their neighbors follow quiet traditions that have been with them since before memory.

Wrapped together, to Alf, it all means being Onondaga.

It's been almost 30 years since he lost his father. The son, now an elder himself, carries on their work. In his shop you'll find raw timber next to polished wooden sticks, and the toil bridging those extremes is the way Alf defines honor.

If it's grown harder, there's a blessing: in each stick, Alf finds his dad.

In 2015, when the World Indoor Lacrosse Championships came to Onondaga, many visitors from around the world arrived with a specific goal: they wanted to visit the little shop just off Route 11A, where Alf Jacques still makes wooden sticks. As this book went to press, Alf was recovering from surgery to remove a cancerous kidney. He is resting now, but expects—soon enough—to return to the shop.

PART SIX

Soul

Simple Set of Rules Means
Messere Simply Rules Lacrosse
Tuesday, June 13, 1995

No university has ever courted Mike Messere. None. On Saturday, his West Genesee lacrosse team won its ninth state championship since 1981. The Wildcats have 46 consecutive victories. Messere's all-time record is 412–20. But he said colleges rarely look to high schools for a coach.

Not that it matters. Messere, 51, is happy where he is. He is glad to be free of the pressures of winning in college. "It's our one small corner of the world," he said Monday, sitting in his office near the Wildcats' locker room.

It is often in small corners where a coach can make a mark.

Yes, Messere said, winning it all still feels as nice. The pewter trophy for the state title leans on a wall in the office, and Messere likes having it around. "It's my carrot," he said, one to dangle for young players. The Wildcats never speak of the state championship when they gather in the spring, but the date of the game is always marked on the team's printed schedule.

What keeps Messere going is the challenge of tough kids. He likes taking some angry, young guy with a wild, mouthy side and teaching him what it means to give yourself to a team.

"It's scary, the way we're dealing with kids today," Messere said. "There's all this disrespect. In some schools, a kid can say anything to a teacher in a classroom—anything—and nothing happens. That's a disaster. That's one thing that won't happen here."

He wears a T-shirt that says, "There's no 'I' in team." He carries a heavy hammer with his players, who are forbidden to even show their faces at a party where beer is being served. The penalty, without argument, is getting kicked off the team.

At one time, if he heard his kids were at a keg party, he would show up unannounced while teens scrambled for the doors. Now, the parents of lacrosse players organize and hold quiet parties for the players, parties that keep the Wildcats safe from the wrath of their coach.

This might sound impossibly cornball, except for the way Messere wins and wins and wins. It has gotten to the point where each state champion becomes like a bottle of champagne, and in memory he can take an appreciative sip from every one. This year's squad, Messere said, was small and cerebral, and it did as much with what it had as any team he's coached.

"We emphasize basic skills," he said. The theory starts in the Camillus youth lacrosse program that he also helped to build, and it continues when those children reach West Genesee. There is no flamboyance, no behind-the-back business. His biggest mission is teaching poise under pressure, and he loves to watch his kids pass the ball when games are on the line.

"Ping . . . ping . . . ping," Messere said, flicking an invisible stick with his hands, closing his eyes and smiling for a moment.

The funny thing is, he almost didn't coach lacrosse. As a kid in junior high, "I was a jerk," Messere said. Sports woke him up. He played three sports in high school, including lacrosse, but wrestling was his favorite. He liked the stark training the sport demanded, the way work and discipline could take you so much higher.

But lacrosse was the sport that he got a chance to coach, and lacrosse became the sport where he built a dynasty. "There's a lot of losing in winning, and a lot of winning in losing," he said. By that he means the final score rarely tells the story. There have been times the team bus would leave the field after a Wildcats victory, only to stop by the steep slope of the Westcott Reservoir. Messere would celebrate by having his players run wind sprints, up and down the hill.

Messere insists coaching is not about love. Love, he said, is something you get at home, or from your girlfriend, or from your faithful dog. Lacrosse is about respect for your coach, respect for your teammates, respect for yourself. He said that, and then he politely broke away because some of his old players had stopped by to shake his hand.

Mike Messere, now 72, continues to coach and change lives at West Genesee High School. He is ranked as the winningest high school lacrosse coach in national history; his teams had captured 15 state championships as of the beginning of the spring 2016 season.

The Last of the Stone Throwers
Saturday, March 16, 1996

Gene Thompson has this St. Patrick's Day proviso. He and his brother Ed are the last survivors from the making of an Irish legend, and he is more than happy to share what he recalls. But he also wants you to understand one thing:

"I deny everything," said Thompson, who then goes on to tell the tale.

Thompson is 85. A "mini-stroke" and surgery have put him in a wheelchair, and it takes a while to understand his speech. But his memory is sharp. His sense of humor remains strong. And he is part of the lore of Tipperary Hill in Syracuse.

He lives on Avery Avenue, in a house built by his parents when he was three years old. He grew up to become an electrician, and he served in World War II, and now he and his wife share a quiet retirement. But his slice of fame is never out of sight. From Thompson's dining room window, you see the traffic signal down the block that flashes "green on top."

On Tipp Hill, he is known as one of the Stone Throwers. They were a group of Irish boys credited—if that is the right word—with refusing to accept in 1925 that red should go above green on a new traffic light at Milton and Tompkins. Their fame is such that a dozen of them, as a group, were grand marshals of the 1987 St. Patrick's Day parade.

But the death of Ken Davis, within the last year, made it official. Gene and Ed Thompson are the only Stone Throwers left—although you'll have trouble getting them to admit it. Gene's own granddaughter, Erin, knew the story of the light before she knew about her grandpa's stake in it.

192

According to Mary Dorsey, whose husband, George, was also in the gang, the boys would stand outside a Tipp Hill corner store, seething at this light with green on the bottom, and when the coast was clear they would start to throw stones.

Smash. Out would go the red light.

The city would always come in to fix it. By the next day, the red light would be smashed again. The joke was that leprechauns were about their work, but the leprechauns in this case were some freckled, hard-nosed teens.

Thompson recalls how the city finally said the heck with it, let the corner go for weeks without any red light at all. The traffic guys figured the kids would forget. One day the city returned with another bulb, and quietly put the red light on top.

Smash.

"They infuriated the boys," Thompson said, carefully declining to put himself into the group. That was enough to make his wife, Loretta, laugh out loud. She speaks of visits from Thompson's brother Ed, and how they will discuss in detail the way Gene would drift up the street to throw the stones, always ducking behind pedestrians coming in and out of shops to be sure any cop would have trouble spotting him.

Thompson listened with a hurt and stunned expression as his wife spoke. "No!" he exclaimed. "That can't be!"

Loretta looked right back at him, shaking her head. "He's always denied it," she said. "He was afraid of his mother."

In 1925, Thompson recalled, traffic signals were brand new in Syracuse. At the time, the *Post-Standard* reported on how the city council was caught up in a big argument: should the lights be only red and green, or should they add a yellow light for caution?

Amid all that, Alderman "Huckle" Ryan asked for green to be allowed up on top on Tipp Hill. Thompson was then a 15-year-old student at Most Holy Rosary High School. The way he remembers it, the city initially put the green on top. But then city officials ruled against any exceptions and switched around the bulbs.

Smash.

Eventually, sick of all the expense and the trouble, the city gave in. The light has become a true Syracuse icon. Onondaga County natives often bring visitors to see it. Even Bobby Kennedy made a point of stopping by that corner.

The light is also the spiritual nerve center of this weekend's St. Patrick's Day celebration, a symbol of humor and mischief and spirit. That is why this spring they are putting up a statue near the light, to honor the Irish nature that wanted green on top. The statue will be on a float in today's big parade.

Ask Thompson if he threw a stone, and he will tell you, "Nah." But he hastened to add that things could get boring in those days. "We had to make our own fun," he said.

The rebellion wasn't limited to throwing stones. He knew of one group of kids who killed time by waiting for trolley cars to stop. The boys knew a way to short out the whole car. Just like that, the trolley would go dead in the middle of the street, while the fuming driver looked around for that bunch of hooligans from Tipp Hill.

Thompson told that story with head tilted back, dreamy-eyed, wearing a small smile. Asked if he took part, his expression turned to shock. "No!" he exclaimed. "Not me!" He and his brother are the last of the stone throwers, or as Thompson says, "Allegedly."

Gene Thompson, the last of the Stone Throwers, died in 2001. He would have been pleased to know that in 2005, Bertie Ahern—prime minister of Ireland at the time—visited the corner of Milton and Tompkins with Rep. James T. Walsh of Onondaga for the express purpose of seeing the famous traffic signal that glows green over red.

Dog Is a Blessing That One Boy Left Behind

Friday, October 3, 2003

Betsy Atkinson raises and trains Australian shepherds in Fabius. She has great respect for the intelligence of the breed. She is not one of those people who ordinarily impose human traits onto the minds of dogs.

In this one case, Betsy can empathize with a dog named Smudge.

The dog in recent weeks has chewed the hair from her own haunches. Smudge, a star performer in agility competitions, will no longer respond when Betsy commands her to do tricks. The dog prefers to lie quietly in a room in the basement, not far from Hunter Atkinson's favorite recliner.

Betsy is president and founder of the Heart of New York Australian Shepherd Club. These are working dogs, she said. Whatever job they learn becomes their sole purpose in life.

"Smudge's job," Betsy said, "was making Hunter happy."

Hunter, Betsy's 13-year-old son, died in July. He grew up on a farm, near Betsy's present home. His first years of life were almost idyllic. From his yard, he could see farmland and rolling hills. Hunter and his younger sister, Mariah, had the chance to raise goats, ducks, and rabbits. Betsy, a single mother, often needed the children's help with new litters of puppies.

Eight years ago, doctors discovered Hunter had Wilms' tumor, a malignant childhood cancer that begins in the kidney. The boy's existence became a war for life. He endured chemotherapy, radiation, and stem-cell transplants. At least four times, Betsy said, she believed Hunter was cured.

Every time, the cancer came back.

Hunter, amid all that, needed space to think. He had a favorite tree that grew alone in a field. When he felt well enough, Hunter would jump

26. Hunter Atkinson with his dog Smudge. (Frank Ordonez/*Post-Standard*)

off the school bus and call for Smudge. Boy and dog would walk to the tree. During Hunter's worst treatments, Betsy would ask him to visualize his walks with Smudge.

The dog was given to them by a close friend, Ann Atkinson, who raises "Aussies" in California. Betsy had told Ann, who is not a relative, how she wanted the right dog for Hunter. He was too sick at the time to raise a puppy. Smudge was an eight-month-old "return," a dog that had been too lively for its first owner. Ann flew Smudge to Syracuse in a crate.

"As soon as he saw that dog, he got down and went nose to nose," Betsy said. "He started training her in agility. He totally took her over. This was Hunter's dog. She slept next to his bed. She went to his games when he played Little League."

Whenever Hunter was in treatment at Upstate University Hospital, Betsy would bring the dog to the hospital, so Hunter could wave to Smudge from his window. Sometimes, when Hunter was under the sway of potent drugs, he would call out for his dog from his dreams.

As for Betsy, she readily admits that she was not always strong. She remembers attending one of Mariah's dance recitals. A woman behind her wouldn't stop complaining. The woman kept saying she wanted more time to herself, that she was sick of taking her kids to soccer practice every day.

Betsy turned around. "I wish I could take my son to soccer," she said.

Instead her son, when he was hurting, always looked for Smudge.

Hunter would sign up for agility competitions—in which handlers lead their dogs through an obstacle course—even when it looked as if the boy would be too ill to compete. Once, as they hurried straight from the hospital to a competition in Cato, Betsy had to stop every 20 minutes or so to allow Hunter to be sick along the road.

"I never gave him any limits," Betsy said. In whatever time Hunter had, she'd let him live his life. When Smudge had a litter, Betsy encouraged Hunter to train one of the puppies for formal dog shows. He named the pup Kodak Moment, and Hunter turned the dog into a champion.

Kodak Moment, in the weeks after Hunter's death, qualified for the famous Westminster Kennel Club Dog Show in New York City. It was an emotional day. Reaching that show had been one of Hunter's goals.

"But Smudge was still the dog of his heart," Betsy said.

Last January, Hunter learned his cancer had returned. In his final weeks, the boy sprawled on his recliner or the couch, drifting in and out of consciousness. On a July day, Hunter asked for a chance to tape a message. Betsy videotaped him. He was unable to speak in much more than a whisper, a 13-year-old offering a summary of life.

He spent part of the time telling his dog goodbye.

"I'm sorry, Smudge," Hunter says on the tape, as the panting, anxious dog licks at his face. "I wish I could go out there and run and help with you . . . out in the woods and fields, and just (be) with you, and (show) you at dog shows."

At that point, the boy looks directly at the camera. "Smudge," he says, "is a blessing from God to me."

Hunter died a few days later. Betsy keeps his sneakers where he left them, near the door. Smudge retreated to the basement, to stay near the boy's recliner. Betsy tries not to impose human thoughts on dogs, but she has an idea of what is going on. Australian shepherds, beyond all else, are born to do a job.

Mom and dog both struggle to believe this job is done.

Smudge lived another three and a half years without her boy, although Betsy Atkinson said the dog "never got over him not being there. She became much quieter, much less joyful." Smudge died at 10.

As for Betsy, thirteen years after losing Hunter, she said she always hangs onto a great lesson: "Every day, someone asks about him or remembers him. He touched so many people, and this is what I learned: I used to wonder why dogs can seem so important. It's because of the relationships, the lasting relationships, they build between people. Hunter is still teaching me that."

Coach Never Forgets
This Equipment Manager
Monday, February 20, 2006

This afternoon, a few hours before West Virginia plays Syracuse in a critical Big East Conference men's basketball game at the Carrier Dome, the Mountaineer team bus will come to a stop in front of the Kiddle home on Nelson Avenue in DeWitt.

West Virginia coach John Beilein will climb out to begin a familiar ritual: He will go to the door and ask Teddy Kiddle if he's ready to go. Then Beilein will shake hands with Shirley Kiddle, Teddy's mother, and with anyone else in the family who happens to be around, before Teddy and the coach get on the bus and leave for the Dome.

Once the game begins, a seat on the West Virginia bench will be reserved for Teddy, the assistant equipment manager at Le Moyne College.

It extends a friendship that began when Beilein coached at Le Moyne. He would pick up Teddy before every home game and drop him off once it was over. That continued until Beilein left Le Moyne in 1992 to coach at Canisius, before the coach moved on to Richmond, and now to West Virginia.

Every time Beilein's returned to Syracuse with any of those teams, Teddy has had a seat on the bus and a spot on Beilein's bench.

"This just speaks volumes about this man," said Le Moyne athletic director Dick Rockwell. "He's coaching on that elite level, and he's got to come here and play Syracuse in a hostile environment, and he still takes the time to do something like this."

The benefits, in Beilein's view, come to him. "He's a good friend, a great friend, who's been with us through thick and thin," the coach said of Teddy. "Every day, he really shows you what's important in life."

Teddy, 55, has worked at Le Moyne for 33 years. He was brought in by Tom Niland, Beilein's uncle and the school's athletic director at the time. Shirley Kiddle remembers how a teacher from East Syracuse-Minoa, where Teddy had taken special-education courses, went to Niland and told him about Teddy.

"He had some limitations," Shirley said. "But he could do a job."

Niland, who died in 2004, hired Teddy to work in maintenance in Le Moyne's Henninger Athletic Center. Yet Teddy was never really happy with his job until Rockwell asked if he would shift into a position as an assistant equipment manager under John "Doc" Joiner.

Every morning, Teddy takes a cab to work. At 7 a.m., he unlocks the athletic center's doors. Then he gets busy with tasks that include washing Le Moyne's team uniforms. It often falls to Teddy to make sure each uniform is in the appropriate locker before a varsity game.

"There isn't an athlete who comes through Le Moyne who doesn't know Teddy Kiddle," said Rockwell, pointing to a wall covered with cards and notes from student ballplayers, thanking Joiner and Teddy.

Through his job, Teddy became friends with retired boxing champion Carmen Basilio, a former Le Moyne physical education teacher who'd drive Teddy to celebrity sports banquets. Teddy also spent years helping out at East Syracuse-Minoa High School football games. He was the guy who toweled off the ball on muddy nights, a duty that earned him an award of thanks from ES-M for 25 years of service.

No bond was as enduring as the one he forged with Beilein, who asked Teddy to distribute water from the bench. "I'd give him a ride to every game, and he'd always wait patiently for me to give him a ride home," Beilein said.

He particularly appreciates how Teddy had the grace to provide the coach with space after painful losses, space many people around a team don't understand. Teddy, for his part, said the courtesy went both ways.

"He's always been good to me," Teddy said. "He's a really, really, really good coach. He's proved it in the NCAAs with Canisius and Richmond and with West Virginia."

Tonight, Teddy will receive the privileges of anyone associated with West Virginia, a major college basketball team. He'll have open access to the locker room in the Dome, and he'll sit on the floor with the team beneath the crowd, where he'll help—as always—with getting the players water.

Beilein sometimes jokes with Teddy about his secret loyalties. He asks him not to share Mountaineer strategies with Syracuse University coach Jim Boeheim. Beilein wonders out loud if Teddy, at heart, is a fan of the Orange.

That kidding brings an earnest reaction from Teddy. To him, Beilein is the guy who always sends him Christmas cards, the guy who brought the West Virginia bus to pick him up during a snowstorm, the guy who mentioned Teddy's name in an interview in the *New York Times*.

Teddy is a Central New York loyalist who likes Syracuse just fine, but on the day of any West Virginia game he goes into an office at Le Moyne, where he asks the staff to fax Beilein the same message:

"Good luck," he tells his friend. "I hope you win."

Teddy Kiddle retired and moved to Hamilton, Ohio, where he lives with his sister, Peggy Sander. Yet Teddy remains in close touch with John Beilein, who now coaches at the University of Michigan. In 2013, Beilein made sure that Teddy and his family had choice seats for an important game between Michigan and Ohio State, and Teddy also made an uncanny prediction about the Final Four. He said Michigan and Syracuse University would both get there, and that Michigan would defeat SU. He was right, although the good luck ended in the championship game, where Louisville beat Michigan for the title.

Forgotten Truth

Clean Lake as Fitting Tribute to Six Nations
Wednesday, September 20, 2006

Onondaga Lake, its waters gray and restless Tuesday in a September drizzle, spread out in front of Tom Porter as he told a story. Porter is a Mohawk Indian, and he was explaining what he knows about the Mohawk hairstyle to a crowd that included Jane Goodall, the renowned scientist.

Many young Americans use that style to express rebellious individuality. But the real meaning, Porter said, more closely involves despair. He said an old man told him the tale when Porter was a child at Akwesasne, the Mohawk territory to the north.

Porter recalled how the old man said Iroquois men and women always believed their hair was a spiritual message given at birth as "a stamp from the Creator." The longer you wore your hair, the old man said, the closer you were to the divine.

But the Creator also rejected killing and bloodshed, which meant there was no blessing for going into war. The old man said that Mohawk men, when they prepared for battle, would shave off all their hair except one stripe in the middle. In that fashion, Porter said, "they could not take the creator with them" as they committed acts to violate their reverence for life.

For that reason, Porter said, he does not like to see young people— Iroquois or not—wearing their hair in that style today. It was a story that offered a new way of seeing the familiar, the quiet theme for much of what happened Tuesday at the lake.

The gathering, held near the Salt Museum at Onondaga Lake Park, was called "The Roots of Peacemaking." The many sponsors included

27. Jane Goodall with Onondaga Faithkeeper Oren Lyons. (John Berry/*Post-Standard*)

Syracuse University and the State University College of Environmental Science and Forestry. It came together for a simple reason: Philip Arnold, an associate professor in SU's department of religion, learned Goodall was coming to Syracuse to offer an academic lecture.

He called and asked if the famed primatologist and peace activist, who did groundbreaking studies on communities of wild chimpanzees, would also participate in a ceremony on the lakefront with the Onondagas. Goodall didn't just agree. She changed her entire schedule to stay in Syracuse for an extra day.

She stayed because she appreciates basic truths that are often forgotten, close to home. The Onondagas are one of the last Indian nations to use their original form of government. They live on a piece of land that has never left their hands.

The Onondaga Lake shoreline is the birthplace of both their long-house beliefs and the Iroquois Confederacy—the place, they believe, where the Iroquois Peacemaker gathered five warring nations and had them bury their weapons beneath a tree of peace.

Around Syracuse, the lake hardly retains such reverence. The combination of industrial poisons and human waste has turned it into one of the most polluted bodies of water in the world. The fact that it is "sacred yet filthy," Goodall said, "is so symbolic of things today in the world."

So Goodall, a 72-year-old woman with a remarkably young face, kissed a leaf on a maple tree planted by the Onondagas to commemorate the day. She stood behind the dais and offered a hooting greeting to the delighted crowd in the way of a wild chimpanzee, just before the wind swept a paper holding her notes into the air—and Goodall, quick as a cat, reached out and caught it.

In her speech, she closely reflected the thinking of many Onondaga leaders. She spoke of a material culture that has grown out of control. She talked about the cruelties inflicted on livestock in factory farms. She spoke of a greater human mission that is "not just about making money; it's about reaching out to those who have less than you do."

And she showed an understanding for the meaning of Onondaga Lake.

While the birth of the confederacy is often forgotten in Syracuse, it is easily the most historically significant event associated with our region. Considering that, it would seem as if there ought to be some beautiful and striking memorial to signify that meaning.

Goodall realized only one tribute could do the job: "This lake—this filthy, dirty, still-polluted lake—can be cleaned," she said.

That same point was made by Goodall's old friend, Onondaga faithkeeper Oren Lyons. It was also made by Porter, and by Onondaga faithkeeper Wendy Gonyea, and by the Onondaga children who threw handfuls of dirt into the hole during the planting of the tree.

In the end, the collective message was both practical, and a prophecy: This community will never rise to what it was until we finally make peace with our lake.

In the late 2000s, to the wonder of the Six Nations and the greater Syracuse community, bald eagles—sometimes in the dozens—began wintering along the Onondaga Lake shoreline, in the city. The Onondagas revere the great birds as messengers of the Creator. While many observers saw the development as proof that a remedial plan for the lake is working, Mohawk scientist Henry Lickers told the Post-Standard *that an eagle also serves another purpose, underlining Six Nations concerns about the cleanup of the lake: "He is the one who will call out when something is amiss."*

Even Death Couldn't Part Them

Wednesday, March 7, 2007

His real name was Gerald Austin, but since he was a boy everyone knew him as "Austie." Sunday, from his bed at the Van Duyn Home & Hospital, Austie looked toward his wife, Kate Austin, asleep in another bed in the same room.

Austie wanted to take a nap, but he feared no one would watch over his wife if he did. Sensing that anxiety, his youngest daughter, Colleen Costello, and her husband, Jeff, assured him they'd be around if Kate woke up.

"It's good you're here," Austie said, and he allowed himself to fall into the last sleep of his life. He died at 2:24 a.m. It was a few weeks after his 88th birthday. He and his wife, dozing across the room, had learned only last year that they were both suffering from lung cancer.

They understood the realities. They chose to leave their longtime home on Whittier Avenue in Syracuse. They moved into Van Duyn, on the provision they could stay in the same room.

Austie seemed a little stronger than Kate. The couple's five surviving children—Mary Ellen Muir, Tom and Bob Austin, Kathy Flemming, and Colleen Costello—did not believe they would lose him first. Early Sunday, after he died, they bent down and quietly told their mother he was gone. From beyond the drugs and the pain, she made a sound that was almost like a sigh.

Kate, 85, would take her last breath at 2:24 p.m., the children said, which they believe was 12 hours to the minute after their father died. To them, it was both fitting and reassuring that their parents died with that kind of symmetry, on the same day.

"What always amazed me was their resilience," said Mary Ellen, the oldest sister. "Despite what they went through, it never killed their spirit. They were able to look around and remember that there were still blessings in their lives."

Mary Ellen was speaking of how she lost her brothers, Jim and Jerry. Both suffered from mental illness. Both committed suicide in separate incidents as young men. Kathy, another sister, said her parents always believed they would see their boys again, and in that confidence they never seemed terrified of death.

To Mary Ellen, Kathy, and Colleen, the most powerful element of their parents' lives was the way they fell into grief and somehow emerged whole.

"They taught me that life is a gift and a blessing," Kathy said, "and that when it gets hard, if you stick together, you'll make it to the other side."

The sisters see that as a message, a condolence, to other families struggling with similar loss and heartbreak.

"Mental illness is biological or physiological," Mary Ellen said. "It's not something you bring upon yourself."

Colleen said her parents made it through their trials because of what she simply called "their graces." The Austins were devout Catholics. Every day, Kate prayed for a list of names she kept written down on paper, a list that always began with her lost boys.

The daughters remember how their dad finally came to a point, after that pain, where he again could tell a joke. He often tried to share his newest ones at family parties, but long before the punchline he would dissolve in helpless laughter. The next time the family gathered, he would try again, with the same inevitable result—until the telling grew funnier than the joke itself.

Kate was raised within a warm Irish family on Tipperary Hill. Austie met his wife on a blind date more than 70 years ago, and his children say he never really dated anyone else. Austie's father died when he was young, and his childhood was spent in Depression-era poverty in the Syracuse neighborhood known as "Skunk City."

What that meant, Kathy said, was that her dad never stopped appreciating the smallest gifts of family life. His children have rich and simple memories: their father worked for the railroad, and their mother worked for the phone company, but their parents were always around when it mattered.

When the kids came home from school for lunch, even if their mom was working, they'd find sandwiches awaiting them on the kitchen counter. They often went for long family rides in the country, or for picnics at Burnet Park, or for excursions to a little camp at Oneida Lake.

Kate used an old and trusty jigsaw to cut apart walls, fix wiring and do other jobs around the house. Austie was a storyteller who cheerfully shared tales about their courtship: about buying nickel beers, or going to movies at grand downtown theaters, or ice skating arm in arm on winter nights.

Their crisis came in pain beyond the ken, when two of their sons took their own lives. That would be enough, in countless cases, to destroy a marriage.

Not this one.

"Some relationships get stronger," said Mary Ellen, "when you reach places you can't go without going through those trials."

That was her parents. Their loyalty was rewarded with a gentle retirement. They'd get up in the morning and walk in the mall for exercise, before sitting down for coffee at Burger King. Austie, until a year ago, would still get out to golf. He and his wife were pleased with the choices their children made in marriage, and they got a chance to watch their grandchildren grow up, and beyond all else they stayed at each other's side.

All that was left was one reunion that could never happen here, the one remaining journey that might somehow mend their grief.

When it was time, as in all else, they went together.

Every St. Patrick's Day, in honor of Kate and Austie, the extended Austin clan gathers for Mass, followed by a family meal—where the siblings express appreciation for what they believe is the quiet and continuing presence of their parents, in their lives.

Remembering the Block

City Man Recalls Tough Times Growing Up in Armory Square

Monday, February 1, 2010

The nickname has stayed with Donald Caldwell for roughly 80 years. All his closest friends refer to him as Peewee, which was coined for him by Emanuel Henderson Sr., best known as Emo.

When Peewee and Emo were boys, they lived in a massive apartment building called "the Block." It dominated Franklin Street between Jefferson and Walton streets, on the site that is now home to Center Armory—a new Armory Square landmark with a Starbucks on the corner.

During the 1930s, the Block held about 150 residents, Peewee said. All were African American. He offers that reflection as Black History Month begins in Syracuse, a month that often involves tales of the old 15th Ward, on the near east side of Syracuse. It was the center of black culture in the city, until the area was leveled to make way for Interstate 81.

The Block was a much smaller black community, on the west side of downtown. It is almost entirely forgotten, maybe because conditions were too grim for wistful nostalgia.

"There was no heat, not unless you could afford a stove," said Emo, 90, who spent his teen years in the building. As a boy in Fairmount, and then at the Block, he ate so many boiled potatoes that he hates to even look at one today. He remembers bitter nights when it would get so cold in the Block that he would sleep in a booth at a nearby nightclub, where the owner was a friend. The only toilets in the Block were in the hallways. If you wanted to take a bath, you heated water on a stove—if you could find one.

209

28. Donald "Peewee" Caldwell in Armory Square in downtown Syracuse, once the site of "the Block." (Michael Greenlar/*Post-Standard*)

As for Peewee, his father worked as a waiter for the New York Central Railroad, and often traveled. Peewee lived with his mother, his older brother, Danny, and their extended family in the Block. One uncle, Homer Hasbrouck, figured out how to attach a wire to a street lamp near the corner. In that way, for years, they had electricity in their rooms at night.

Emo, who was eight years older than Peewee, would often see the Caldwell brothers as they played outside the building. Emo got a laugh out of Danny's tiny sidekick. That caused Emo to come up with a nickname that would stick.

A skilled journalist, Emo went on to write a column for the old *Progressive-Herald*, a newspaper in the black community. He and Peewee, a retired postal worker, now find themselves in a dwindling handful of men and women who can remember Syracuse in the days of the Block.

To help convey what that means, they tell this story:

Ellsworth Hasbrouck, another of Peewee's uncles, grew up in the same building. He was an ambitious student who went to Syracuse University at a time when few blacks were being admitted. Once he graduated, he wanted to attend medical school in Syracuse.

He was turned down. Peewee and his family didn't have much doubt about the reason.

Ellsworth left town to earn his medical degree at Howard University, before opening his own practice in Chicago. By then, Emo and his wife, Muriel, had started a family in the 15th Ward. In 1941, their second child, Bryce, was born premature. The infant was ill. Bryce struggled to hold down food. The doctors said his internal organs were out of place, and that he would not survive past early childhood.

During a visit home, Ellsworth learned of the child's condition from Peewee. He met with the Hendersons, and asked them to travel to Chicago.

Ellsworth examined Bryce. He said he could operate, but there was only a 50-50 chance the boy might survive. To Emo and Muriel, that offered better odds than awaiting the inevitable. They told Ellsworth to go ahead. The operation was successful. Bryce Henderson would never be free of troubles with his health, but he lived for almost 40 years—far beyond the best chance given to him by doctors in Syracuse.

Peewee and Emo aren't the kind of guys who go for easy sentiment, and they share this tale in a matter-of-fact way. As youths, they lived in what essentially was a downtown tenement without electricity or hot water, and they were glad when they finally got out of the Block.

Yet something precious survived those years, a quality they both hope outlasts them in the city.

Call it black history, if you like. The simpler word is love.

Syracuse lost two of its great community historians in 2010, when Peewee and Emo died within months of one another. Yet if you stand outside Starbucks in Armory Square and look up—from the middle of one of the trendiest, most upscale city neighborhoods in Syracuse—you can still see the window where Peewee's mother, as she worked as a seamstress in an industrial sweatshop, would look down and keep watch as her little boys played.

Dad's Home!

Christmas Wasn't Christmas until Father Returned from Steam Station
Thursday, December 23, 2010

Every Christmas, I go back to it. I can still feel my mother's hand on my shoulder, gently shaking me awake, and I can see the gray murk of a December dawn as clouds rolled in from Lake Erie. Each year, those moments pass through my mind while my own children come downstairs to open presents, although I rarely stop to share a tale from a world I can't expect them to understand.

Even so, to me, it still defines Christmas.

My father worked on the coal pile at a Niagara Mohawk steam station in Dunkirk. He had grown up in an orphanage, and sometimes he would tell us stories about what that meant, how you were happy to get an orange in your stocking. So he loved Christmas with a deep passion, as did my mom, whose mother was dead and whose dad had left by the time she was three. To my parents, Christmas was a beacon, a reminder of what they achieved and what they lost.

I think, by the way they lived it, that's what they tried to teach.

Maybe it was because I was a little kid, but the simplest moments of the season always seemed most beautiful. My mother had her rituals: she would bring the decorations down from the attic on December 15, those magical boxes containing talismans of the holiday, like the plaster Santa Claus my parents bought just after World War II. My father would put up the outdoor lights, those big 1960s bulbs, and then on December 20—as a family—we would get the tree.

As Christmas approached, the one thing we knew—the reality we accepted—was that electricity is something that gets made around the clock. The steam station never shut down. During the winter, my dad would get called in for long shifts in which we'd hardly see him for days. The coal, sprayed by mist from the lake, would freeze together like cement. He worked with a crew that was responsible for breaking it apart. He'd be out there, in the snow and wind, for many hours: frostbite had left scars on his face, even though he wore a cap and hood, three pairs of socks, heavy leather mittens.

Even now, as communion, I shovel snow in the lined work suit—tattered and frayed—that he used on the coal pile.

My father loved heavy equipment and he loved what he did, but one downside was the need to do it on Christmas. The workers would divvy up their shifts so that no one had to stay longer than five hours. Sometimes my father would luck out and get it off, but often he'd be there from 7 a.m. to noon, and for us that became a part of Christmas.

My older brothers would go to midnight Mass, and then sleep in. I would go to bed on Christmas Eve and struggle to sleep, until suddenly it would be 5 a.m., and I'd feel my mother's hand on my shoulder. She would wake up my sister and then come and get me, and I received a life lesson in her soft voice in the half-light of Christmas morning, how she'd praise us as "troopers" for rolling out of bed, how she'd tell us that success in life often went to those with the guts to get up early.

We'd climb into the car and go to 6 a.m. Mass, a small and quiet service mainly for waitresses, nurses, and factory workers. My father would drive us home and then leave for work, and we'd walk into a living room where Santa had already eaten his cookies and left behind a note—his handwriting detailed and passionate, almost like my mother's—not far from the presents stacked in piles near the tree . . .

And we'd wait, seated on the couch, staring at the presents. We'd wait as my mother made some breakfast, as the family who lived in the other side of our duplex rumbled up and down the stairs, as my brothers finally climbed out of bed. We'd watch episodes of *Davey and Goliath* on the black-and-white TV, and we'd each get to open one small present, but basically the morning took forever as we waited . . .

And in that wait, somehow, was Christmas.

Because it was not fast. It was not all at once. It was not about what we wanted. It was about our father, and the understanding that this day meant as much to him as it did to us, and that he wanted to be there as we opened our gifts. It was about the truth that my parents hammered home by sheer example, that what is good almost always demands some kind of sacrifice, and that Christmas could not be Christmas without our father.

So we'd be at the front window, waiting, when the clock struck noon. Fifteen minutes or so later, he'd pull into the driveway. I see it now as I will see it on Christmas morning: I remember how we'd all spill out the door, sprinting toward the car, crowding around it as my dad emerged—lunch bucket in hand—and he'd be laughing, cigarette dangling from his lip, as we pushed and pulled him toward the house . . .

I remember it all, the sound of his laugh, the smell of oil on his clothes. What's ceased to matter, what I can't recall, is opening the gifts.

My mother died of lung cancer at 65, in 1987; my father, who never really recovered from the loss, died the following year. I still wear his old work suit from the steam station when I shovel snow. And on Christmas mornings, as real as the scent of coffee and dawn light on hardwood floors, I can still feel my parents in our house.

For Sale

A House? No, So Much More
Wednesday, May 23, 2012

By last week, the rooms were empty in the little house on Wadsworth Street in Syracuse. Nick DeMartino donated much of the furniture and decorations to the Winds of Agape, a charitable organization, although he kept a small pile of things for himself: His Little League trophies. An electric football game, familiar to many of us who grew up in the 1960s, still in the battered box it arrived in on some distant Christmas morning.

Nick also set aside a tubular green vase. When he found it in the basement, it made him catch his breath.

He is 54, a lawyer in Syracuse. About 45 years ago, Nick wanted to buy a Mother's Day gift for his mother, Ida. The child spent weeks saving up his change. He took the bus downtown, where he came upon the green vase in the old Dey Brothers Department Store. He brought it to a clerk and poured his money on the counter.

"I don't think I had enough," Nick said. The clerk, sensing the little boy's intent, sold it to him anyway. Nick gave the vase to his mom, and the years disappeared like one of those flickering calendars in an old movie. Nick left for Brockport State, went on to law school, then returned to become a Syracuse judge and prosecutor. He didn't live far from his parents, who stayed in the house on Wadsworth that Nick's dad, George DeMartino, built just after surviving World War II.

George was one of those Depression-era guys who never went to college, but seemed to master every skill. He died, at 92, just over a year ago. His wife, without George, was too ill to be alone. Ida moved to Clare Bridge, an

215

29. Nick DeMartino on the day his family sold his childhood home. (David Lassman/*Post-Standard*)

assisted living community in Fayetteville. "It wasn't until my father died," Nick said, "that we realized just how much he did to protect her."

Nick's brothers, George and Mike, left long ago for other states. It was up to Nick to sell their parents' house. Through a realtor, he found a buyer who loves the place. Last Saturday, they closed on the deal.

Friday, Nick walked for one last time through the rooms where he grew up.

He dawdled in a small bedroom he once shared with his brother Mike. Nick peeked into the crack of a sliding closet door. Somewhere in there was a poster of Boston Red Sox pitcher Jim Lonborg. Nick put it up in the 1960s. It didn't quite fit when he would close the door. Finally, the poster got jammed inside the crack.

On closing day, 2012, it was still there.

Two doors away was a room once used by his other brother, George. Every Christmas, at 3 a.m., George would crawl out of bed for a whispered conference with his little brothers. They'd decide upon the earliest plausible moment to start hollering for their parents to get up.

Nick told the story, then stepped into a big and empty kitchen, centerpiece for his memories.

"This is where it all happened," he said.

When his dad built the house, he made the kitchen the largest room. That's where the extended family—all the aunts and uncles and cousins—would gather for holidays, birthdays, or any good excuse. Nick recalled all the jokes, stories and passionate arguments that would shift between noisy English and Italian.

That generation, for the most part, is gone. On December mornings, Nick would roll out of bed to the aroma of his mom baking holiday ribbon cookies. His father, a maintenance supervisor at General Electric, always stopped in at noon on Fridays, bringing his paycheck so his wife could do the shopping. In the spring, he'd be in the kitchen with his Postum, a drink he preferred to traditional coffee, when Nick walked home for lunch from the nearby Le Moyne Elementary School. Father and son would make plans to go and hit some baseballs.

The game, to Nick, still equates to growing up. He kept his baseball glove in a cabinet by the garage door. He'd race home from school, say hello to his mother and then run outside, making a one-handed grab for the glove. He'd meet his buddies for endless games on a neighborhood diamond. On weekends, Nick's dad would bring out a box of baseballs. The father knew an empty spot at Woodlawn Cemetery where he could pitch to his boy and they'd be in no one's way.

Nick would hit the ball, and his dog Bandit would go and find it in the weeds. He and his dad performed that ritual so often the dog's teeth wore holes into the balls. For Nick, those moments were as good as life could get.

Four decades later, those memories flooded back—vivid and immediate—when Nick poked his head into a small room in the basement and found the tattered balls, still in the box.

His dad had not been able to throw them away, a realization that almost brought Nick to his knees. For an instant, he ached for one last impossible chance to see his father. But Nick gathered himself. He thought about why he was there.

"You can't take everything," he said. "That's the problem."

Even so, the green vase and the box of well-chewed balls went home with him, while the rest of his childhood was given to the Winds of Agape.

Ida DeMartino, Nick's mother, died in February 2015 at the age of 90. According to her obituary, "She was known for her cooking and baking, which included her famous Christmas cookies, Saturday pizza and her spaghetti sauce."

PART SEVEN

Loyalty

For a Teammate of Unitas, a Memory Goes Deep

Saturday, February 27, 1993

Johnny Unitas was swept up in the pocket. The VIP lounge at the Onondaga County Oncenter in Syracuse was filled with men and women who met that status, most of them in expensive black clothing, all of them wanting to shake the same hand that changed football history.

Unitas excused himself to go out and see Blix.

Blix is Jim Donley, a balding, 62-year-old director of an Auburn center for the developmentally disabled. Blix was also a senior fullback in 1948 for a tiny Pittsburgh high school called St. Justin's, which had a skinny, bucktoothed freshman quarterback.

"Blix," said Johnny Unitas, as he rushed out of the VIP lounge. "Where's your hair?" Then he held out that right hand, on which every digit was bent into a peculiar shape, undoubtedly from being broken numerous times.

"You've done great for yourself," Blix told Unitas.

They hadn't seen each other in 44 years. They put a hand on each other's shoulder and went into an intimate discussion of high school friends no one else could possibly know, while nervous schedule-makers stood just behind Unitas, glancing down at their watches.

Unitas was here for the annual AT&T Sports Dinner. Blix, a nickname acquired because of some obscure baseball player named Blix Donley, couldn't stay for long. He plays poker every Friday with the boys back in Auburn, and the whole point of the trip was to prove to them that his story was for real, that he didn't buy his old program at some celebrity card show.

That program survives from St. Justin's 1948 season. Perhaps 50 kids are in the team picture, representing about one-fifth of St. Justin's total enrollment. Blix was a good-looking guy, with a full head of hair. In the back row, a tall, skinny kid is wedged between wider teammates.

Unitas wore No. 18 at St. Justin's, one number lower than when he played with the Colts and helped turn pro football into America's favorite televised sport.

Blix went from St. Justin's into college at St. Francis, Pennsylvania, where he played some linebacker. He joined the Marines, got out, and spent five years studying for the priesthood, then changed his mind and went into human services, which eventually carried him to Auburn.

He never forgot that he was in the backfield on the first day John Unitas took an official snap.

At St. Justin's, the football field was about five miles from the school. The players had no choice but to hitchhike to practice. Unitas had never played organized football. On his first day in pads, he warmed up at midfield.

"We stopped practice to watch this skinny little guy with buck teeth and round shoulders, who was winging that thing 60, 65 yards with little or no effort," Blix recalled.

Forty-four years later, Blix showed up with no ticket and no guarantees. For all he knew, Unitas would not remember, or would not care.

Fat chance. They talked for a long time, out in the corridor. Unitas called over his son and business manager, John Unitas Jr., and introduced him to Blix. Finally, reluctantly, Unitas allowed himself to be dragged off to the dinner.

Blix sat for a while, alone on a bench. He started to cry. "I'm sorry," Blix said. "But he's the greatest quarterback in all the world, and he came out here to talk to me."

Jim Donley and John Unitas revived a friendship that would endure until Unitas died in 2002. After Donley lost a daughter, Seanna, in a 1996 automobile accident, Unitas became an annual contributor to a charitable fund in Seanna's honor.

Donley died in 2015, at 84, in his native Pittsburgh. He had moved there to be near another daughter, Mary Swindal, and to relish the proximity to four grandchildren.

His Angel, His Loss

*Ray Seals Takes the Memory of
His Cousin to the Super Bowl*

Monday, January 22, 1996

Just like that, one day last fall, Ray Seals lost all electric power. There had been a billing foul-up, and the lights went out in Ray's Pittsburgh apartment. So he called Jonny Gammage, his cousin and his full-time business partner.

When Ray got home from practice with the Pittsburgh Steelers, the answering machine carried Jonny's deep, familiar voice. The problem was solved. As usual, when it mattered, Jonny had Ray covered.

That is why Ray Seals, one week away from playing in the biggest football game of all, made time this weekend to fly back to Syracuse to honor his angel.

"Over the last six or seven games, things have happened to us that I can't really explain," Ray said. "I think it's Jonny. I think he's still with us."

On a frigid Sunday morning, Ray drove with the Gammage family to Oakwood Cemetery. He stood off a little as his aunt and uncle huddled with their children above the grave. It was the first time Jonny's mother, Narves Gammage, had returned to that place. Jonny Sr. spoke to the earth in a quiet voice:

"You made it, son. Finally going to the Super Bowl. You made it there."

The Gammages placed a few silk lilies in a mound of snow, and Seals for a while stood alone by the grave. "It makes no sense," he said. "People die in accidents, and people get sick. But he's down there now, and for what? For nothing."

30. Ray Seals at the Oakwood Cemetery grave of his friend and cousin, Jonny Gammage. (Dennis Nett/*Post-Standard*)

He shrugged, and he turned toward his dad, Tommy Seals, who already had the car engine running. There were still four hours before Ray's plane left for Pittsburgh. It gave father and son time to do what they do when Ray comes home, which is simply to go driving on the streets of this city.

Ray stared out the window and spoke about Jonny.

Seals is a 300-pound defensive end for the Steelers, the champions of the American Football Conference, who on Sunday meet the Dallas Cowboys in the 30th Super Bowl in Tempe, Arizona. Seals was second on the Steelers in sacking the quarterback. This game will be the zenith of his childhood dreams. He never went to college. Few people believed he could make the NFL.

Now, he is a key player in football's showcase, and he said he is going because Gammage is his angel.

"After I lost him," Seals said, "everything (in football) turned for the better."

The Steelers got hot. They roared into the playoffs. Ray insists Gammage knocked the ball loose on the final play of the conference championship game against the Indianapolis Colts, when Colt receiver Aaron Bailey said he couldn't quite grasp a last pass.

"That was our angel," Ray said, holding out his big arms as if someone had them pinned.

Barely three months ago, on an everyday morning, Seals walked into the Steelers locker room to hear a low buzz of nervous conversation. The television stations were reporting on a high-speed chase in the suburbs, and how a man driving a Jaguar had died in custody. The Jaguar, police said, was owned by a Pittsburgh Steeler.

Seals felt a little jolt, because he knew Jonny had been driving his Jag. But his cousin had never had problems with police. Besides, the two of them had plans to fly home that night to Syracuse, where Ray's grandfather—a legendary minister—was critically ill.

Then a Steelers public relations man called Ray aside and said, "Look. It was your car." The guy calmed Ray down, told him the Jag had probably been stolen, and they sat at a desk and started making calls. That is how Ray, an African American, found out his cousin died by the hands of six white policemen. The coroner soon determined Jonny Gammage was beaten to death.

"A college-educated man," Ray said Sunday. "A man with no reason to fear the police." Ray said that while seated next to his father, a veteran officer on the Syracuse Police Department.

When he learned of Jonny's death, Ray asked for a chance to identify the body. They wouldn't let him. They showed him a photograph. He began pushing for an investigation, and a routine traffic stop raised huge questions about race and the law. Manslaughter charges have now been filed against three of the officers, which Ray feels is hardly the full measure of justice.

"I respect the police," he said. "You need to have cops. But there are good cops, and there are bad cops, and a bad cop is in a position to do a lot of damage. I want the FBI to get involved. I want this to become a federal civil rights case."

For the last three months, he has tried to make that argument on a national level, even as he's had his best season on the field. Head coach Bill Cowher called Seals in, quietly told him the Steelers would play their games for Jonny. Many of the players, such as Yancey Thigpen and Leon Searcy, told Ray they'd be there if he needed any help.

Ray was interviewed on *Geraldo* and *Good Morning America* and other national shows, and always his comments were measured and calm. He never used hateful words, or urged an eye for an eye. Instead, he spoke of the need for both justice and the truth.

"I grew up in the church, and that's the way I am," Seals said. "I have to get through this. Football is my profession, and Jonny was my personal life. I can't show any signs of weakness. People who didn't know Jonny but who knew that I'm his cousin, they're looking now at me to see what kind of person he was."

Still, his greatest joy has also become his greatest hurt. He is going to the Super Bowl without his best friend. They grew up together on the playgrounds of the South Side, and their distinct goals in life became clear very early. Ray was going to be an athlete, and Jonny was going to be a businessman. They dreamed out loud about where that would get them.

Jonny went off to college. Ray got out of Henninger High School to attempt the impossible, to make it to the NFL without any college. When it happened, when Ray succeeded in Tampa Bay and then signed a big contract in Pittsburgh, Jonny joined up with him as a partner-manager.

They did autograph shows and promotions. They started a line of successful Pittsburgh T-shirts and caps based on the theme of "the 60-Minute Men." And they did a lot of charitable work, because both of them remembered exactly where they came from.

On Sunday, Ray and his dad drove through the neighborhoods where Ray and Jonny used to play. They drove to Kirk Park, where Ray had a young tree planted in Jonny's memory.

"It looks good," said Tommy Seals. "I think it's going to make it."

For the past two months, when the National Anthem was performed before each Steelers game, Ray found himself thinking of his cousin. They always talked of what would happen if Ray made the Super Bowl, how his rags-to-riches story would get big-time exposure. Next Sunday, when Vanessa Williams sings the anthem for the whole sports world, you know who Ray Seals will be remembering.

"The Super Bowl is what me and him were all about," he said.

Ray will be there, and he insists that his angel is going there, too. That is why he flew home this weekend, to visit the grave and to walk the old streets, to make sure his focus remains clear in Tempe. He is about to play the biggest game of his whole life, and he assumes—just like always—that Jonny has him covered.

While the Steelers lost the Super Bowl to the Cowboys, 27–17, Ray Seals was credited with a sack of Dallas quarterback Troy Aikman. As for Jonny Gammage, Ray never forgets the way he lost his cousin; in 2014, amid calls for justice from the Black Lives Matter movement, Seals did several interviews recalling a traffic stop in greater Pittsburgh—always emphasizing that Jonny ought to be alive today.

Syracuse Homecoming Bittersweet for Biden

Friday, May 31, 2002

The young man was a student at the Syracuse University College of Law. He and his wife lived on Stinard Avenue in Syracuse, neighbors to Joanne Del Vecchio and her parents. The young man, a newlywed, took notice when Joanne's German shepherd gave birth to some puppies.

This was 35 years ago, in 1967. One day, the young man knocked on Joanne's door. He explained how his wife, a teacher at the old Bellevue Junior High, loved to watch the puppies play. He wanted to buy one. He wanted to surprise his wife when she got home from work.

Del Vecchio, now a Spanish teacher at Fowler High School, sold a puppy to the law student, whose name was Joseph Biden. He and his wife named the dog Senator, which makes them seem almost prophetic.

Biden's political career took off after three years in Syracuse. He was married to the former Neilia Hunter, an Auburn native and an SU homecoming queen. Biden speaks of that time as "magical," even if he pays for those memories with pain.

He was in Washington, D.C., on December 18, 1972, only weeks after his election to the U.S. Senate, when Neilia's station wagon was broadsided by a tractor-trailer as she drove home with a family Christmas tree. The accident happened in Delaware, where the Bidens moved after Joe graduated from law school. Biden's wife and their one-year-old daughter, Naomi, died. His two young sons survived, despite serious injuries.

"Sometimes it just overwhelms me," Biden said last week, a few days after he gave the commencement address at the SU College of Law. "When you get (to Syracuse), it's almost impossible not to feel it."

For many years, Biden rarely mentioned Neilia's death in public. He married again, and his second wife, Jill, raised his two boys as her own. Few beyond Biden's immediate staff understood why he never worked on December 18.

Yet he has spoken of Neilia and Naomi—nicknamed Amy—several times since September 11, mainly to demonstrate empathy for thousands of Americans still grieving over the terrorist attacks. "You get tested in ways that you never expect to get tested," Biden said.

His link to Syracuse began in 1964. Biden, a student at the University of Delaware, scraped together enough money to join some friends on spring break in the Bahamas. He introduced himself to Neilia, whose good looks stopped him cold in a hotel lobby.

"I never met anyone who didn't like Neilia," Biden said.

He described her as an "incredible person," a striking woman whose kindness matched her physical beauty.

Biden fell in love. He intended to enroll in the Cornell Law School, at least until the day he drove to Syracuse after a visit to Cornell, planning to meet Neilia when she got out of work. She left a note for him, stuck to her car in the Bellevue parking lot. She was running late. She suggested that Biden kill some time by looking at SU's college of law.

He did. He liked it. He applied and was accepted.

Joe and Neilia, married in 1966, settled on Stinard Avenue. They were completely broke, Biden recalls, and completely happy. As a wedding gift, Biden's father—a car dealer—traded in their used cars and replaced them with a brand-new Corvette. Biden remembers how he and Neilia would sit in their kitchen, eating cereal for dinner, laughing about this exotic car just outside their door.

Biden walked the dog at the Woodland Reservoir. He played football in the street with neighborhood children. Neilia lived close enough to Bellevue for an easy walk to work.

The link to Syracuse was reinforced, years after Neilia's death, by Biden's political crisis of 1987. His presidential campaign was damaged by allegations that Biden stole passages for some of his speeches. Someone then leaked an old school paper from SU, in which Biden failed to footnote sections taken directly from an article. A rising presidential hopeful became the butt of jokes.

Amid the uproar, SU invited Biden for a visit. Biden said he won't forget that show of loyalty. Many of his old professors showed up to shake his hand. Biden's son Beau came along for that trip. Father and son took a walk on campus, winding up at the Kappa Alpha Theta sorority house on Walnut Avenue, the sorority to which Neilia Biden once belonged.

Beau discovered a photograph of his mother, as homecoming queen, hanging on a wall. Biden watched as his boy reached out and touched the photo. Then Beau said out loud, "I'm going to law school here." In 1994, Biden was commencement speaker when Beau earned his degree.

Biden describes Syracuse as a city where he often surprises himself with the places he spontaneously visits, or the things he freely says. Joanne Del Vecchio can offer an example:

One afternoon in the 1970s, long after Biden became a senator, Joanne's mother was startled to find Biden standing at her door. He happened to be in Syracuse, he said. He decided to make a side trip to Stinard Avenue, hoping to find at least one familiar face.

Or maybe, more precisely, to hang onto one.

Beau Biden, as attorney general of Delaware, returned to Syracuse in 2011 to deliver the commencement address for the Syracuse University College of Law. Despite his family's tragic past in the community, he told the Post-Standard *that Syracuse always reminds him of love and resilience: "Families can get torn apart and never recover or they grow even closer. My dad set about rebuilding his family."*

Four years later, when Beau died from brain cancer, his father—as vice president—was forced to take on that task again.

The Party Isn't Over for Dennis Riley

Friday, April 6, 2007

Dennis Riley has been missing.

He has not been shouldering his way to the front of political rallies or news conferences. He has not been showing up for concerts and recitals at Syracuse University's Crouse College or Hendricks Chapel, where he appears with such regularity that SU students have taken to calling him "Crouse Man."

To them, and to countless others in this community, Riley is the guy who rides downtown streets on his bike, the guy with the big beard and wide headband, the guy with the sunglasses and clanking set of keys who is front and center at every community gathering in Syracuse.

Riley offers no particular reason for why he shows up everywhere, except for a quick reflection that maybe someday he'll be famous. He is more interested in talking about the way he gets to his beloved "events," rather than the why.

The simple truth is that for years, in the snow and heat of Syracuse, he has used his bicycle to reach the biggest political bashes and the smallest ribbon-cutting.

Once there, if he can do it, he goes straight to the front.

That is why this week feels so strange.

Not long ago, those closest to Riley grew worried about the dark circles around his eyes. "He looked yellow," said Dr. Michael Klein, a friend and a retired physician. "He looked like a banana."

Last weekend, Riley was admitted to St. Joseph's Hospital Health Center. Colleen Deacon, press officer for Syracuse Mayor Matt Driscoll, said Riley's absence was noticed this week around city hall. Deacon was

31. Dennis Riley at Clinton Square. (Katye Martens/*Post-Standard*)

relieved when he finally called to say he was in the hospital. Riley, nervous that some event might slip his notice, didn't stop with one call.

At the downtown YMCA, where he is a regular, he will often ask Scott Sears or other staff members to call around for a list of concerts and events. Many professionals who work out at the Y are accustomed to Riley's long conversational riffs. That's how Klein came to know Riley.

Until he became ill, Riley would get around on his bicycle or by taking the bus. Yet Riley, who at 63 rarely seems short on energy, admits his sickness made him feel "down in the dumps."

Finally, during a recent stop at the Samaritan Center, a couple of friends lobbied him to go up to St. Joe's. For a while, he resisted. The last time he was in a hospital, he said, was to get his tonsils out, and he remembers "ether and a needle and (how) they almost killed me."

But his stomach was swollen and he was feeling sick, and he didn't want to stay in what he calls "denial world." So he was admitted to St. Joe's for some tests.

Thursday night, Klein made sure Riley had a grasp of the results. The retired doctor, half-smiling, had to squeeze in the message between Riley's nonstop questions: "I'm going to have a good life? I can get back at it?"

The answer, Klein said, was a qualified yes. There was no cancer, but Riley does have inflammation of the pancreas, which means at the least that he ought to take it easy.

Riley doesn't know how.

"I want to get out of here so bad," he said. "If there's something at city hall, I don't want to miss it."

He recalled how one of Driscoll's staff members recently pulled him aside. The aide asked Riley to give the mayor some room, a discussion held after Riley cut in front of Driscoll and other officials during a photo event in the days before the St. Patrick's Parade. Riley, a little grudgingly, agreed. His instincts are to push to the front, but he described the mayor as "my best friend! He's like family! I like him!"

Riley feels a similar affection for "Senator John," as in DeFrancisco, and "Mr. Pirro," the county executive, and all Syracuse firefighters and city police.

Come to think of it, he doesn't say a bad word about anyone. He lives in Fairmount. His parents are dead. Their absence is the saddest theme in his take on life:

"Good times!" he said. "When my parents were alive, the times were good. Now my parents are gone, I miss them and times are tough."

That leads into a line he often says out of the blue: "Once they tell you there's no Santa Claus, the party's over."

Or is it? Riley is an informal Central New York celebrity who talks nonstop, barely pausing to breathe, to the amazement of his nurses and bemusement of his friends. Barb Cimildoro, facilities coordinator for SU's Setnor School of Music at Crouse College, said his absence created a kind of void this week. He routinely shows up for student recitals, events usually attended only by relatives, faculty, and friends.

"We did have to talk to him a few times," Cimildoro said. "Once he tried to leave early, and we told him, 'You can't come in late or leave early.' Once he dropped his hairbrush and it made a big clunk."

Riley learned and adapted, to the point where Sue Martini, scheduling secretary at SU's Hendricks Chapel, said the man in the big beard, sunglasses, and fatigues has a devotee's understanding of the correct moments to applaud during classical music.

While Riley did not offer many reflections Thursday on his child-hood, he said he grew up in Solvay, and that he worked for a while at a bowling alley. Mary Beth Roach of the city parks department, another longtime recipient of Riley's calls, said he began showing up at events not quite 20 years ago, during the first term of Mayor Roy Bernardi.

He now has one of the most recognizable faces in Syracuse. His speech is an astounding pinball game of consciousness, rolling from how his mother "made real sauce, not that Ragu stuff," into how he might someday wear a pompadour, into how he decided many years ago to give up alcohol, after he drank too much one night and thought he saw live snakes.

What he wants, above all else, is to leave the hospital. There is an Easter egg hunt Saturday at Onondaga Park, and a dawn Mass on Easter at Burnet Park. At both events, look for Dennis to be in the front row.

As treatment continued, doctors learned that Dennis Riley's symptoms were the result of cancer. He died in July 2007, and his absence is still felt at any gathering in the heart of Syracuse. His friends know he would have been front and center in recent years as the city's downtown experienced a signifi-cant revival, as the big crowds and big events that Dennis loved became even more commonplace.

Vice President (to Be) Left Mark in Syracuse

Friday, November 7, 2008

Kevin Coyne stuttered as a child. Other children were not kind. Once, as he played in his yard on Stinard Avenue in Syracuse, several older boys taunted him relentlessly. Kevin tried to brush it off. This was nothing new.

Out of nowhere, a college student who rented a place next door vaulted a fence and told Kevin's tormentors to knock it off. The young man was beside himself with fury. He warned them to never tease Kevin about his stuttering again.

The older boys were stunned. They admired this guy. He drove a Corvette. He had a beautiful wife. He often invited the boys to play touch football in the street.

As he got older, Kevin outgrew his speech impediment. He'd eventually become a project manager for Raulli & Sons Ironworks, although he never forgot that childhood incident. Tuesday, as the results of the presidential election became clear, he was among the few Americans more interested in the second spot on the winning ticket.

Joe Biden, who as a young man helped a little boy in Syracuse, will soon be vice president of the United States.

"He really stood up for me," said Kevin, 54. "That's just the kind of guy he was."

In 1968, Joe graduated from the Syracuse University College of Law. For much of his time in Syracuse, he and his wife, Neilia, rented a flat at 608 Stinard Avenue. Dennis Connors, curator of history at the Onondaga Historical Association, said Biden is the first vice president to have lived in

236

the city. No president has; while Grover Cleveland's boyhood home was in Fayetteville, he never resided in Syracuse.

For a young couple without any neighborhood roots, the Bidens left an unusually strong impression. Neilia often walked to her job as an eighth-grade teacher at Bellevue Junior High, a city school. As for Joe, he'd sometimes take neighborhood kids for rides in his sports car, a gift from his father, who worked as a car dealer.

Joe also played driveway basketball at a nearby house on South Geddes Street. That was the home of City Court Judge James Fahey, father of Joe Fahey, now an Onondaga County Court judge. The young men shot baskets or shot the breeze about politics. Joe Fahey's younger sister Jane, then a student at Most Holy Rosary school, was closer to Neilia.

"She was just a lovely, lovely woman, a schoolteacher who was very cognizant of children's needs," said Jane Fahey Suddaby, a BOCES administrator in Oswego County.

Neilia, raised in Auburn, had been a homecoming queen at Syracuse University. She met Joe while they were on spring break in the Bahamas. They settled on Stinard Avenue until Joe finished law school, and then returned to Joe's home state of Delaware.

In 1972, only weeks after Joe was elected to the U.S. Senate, his old neighbors in Syracuse were shocked to learn that Neilia's station wagon had been crushed by a tractor trailer. Neilia and Naomi, the Bidens's one-year-old daughter, were killed. Joe and Neilia's sons, Beau and Hunter, were badly injured but survived.

"I remember sobbing as I looked at the picture of the car in the paper," said Pat Cowin Wojenski, 54, who had Neilia as an eighth-grade teacher at Bellevue.

Pat, at that time, was in a hard place: her parents had divorced, and her mother was struggling with cancer.

"Neilia must have known that about me, and she was there for me when I needed an extra word of encouragement or kindness," Pat recalled.

She said Neilia spent many hours with students who seemed to need particular nurturing and attention. Those girls, Pat said, were in awe of the Bidens, a stunningly good-looking couple.

And, of course, they had that Corvette.

"Joe used to come and stick notes on it while Neilia was in school," Pat said.

Dick Carroll, a biotech researcher in Syracuse, was a student at Le Moyne College at the time. His family lived across the street from the Bidens. Dick said that Joe and Neilia forged a lasting relationship with his mother, Dorothy Carroll, and with Mary Coyne, Dorothy's close friend and Kevin's mom.

Before they left for Delaware, the Bidens threw a goodbye cookout for the entire neighborhood. Years later, when Dorothy and Mary traveled to Washington, D.C., Joe went out of his way to see them in his office.

The Stinard Avenue children of that era have grown into adults, who still mourn for Neilia and speak fondly of Joe. Pat Wojenski works as a community assistant at Bellevue, where she developed a mentoring program inspired by her eighth-grade teacher. She is involved in conversations at the school about planting a tree or creating a memorial in Neilia's honor.

As for Kevin Coyne, he always followed the career of this national politician who had shown such concern for the lonely kid next door. Kevin was elated Tuesday, when Joe—the guy who once raced to his defense— earned a place in the White House as vice president for Barack Obama.

It made Kevin remember a little fact he learned years ago, long after the Bidens left the neighborhood:

Joe, as a boy, had his own stuttering problem. The kid next door could have been him. That's why he jumped the fence.

During a May 2009 visit to Syracuse, Vice President Joseph Biden met with schoolchildren at Bellevue Elementary School—on the site of the building where his first wife once taught—then walked through the neighborhood to stand in the yard of the house where he and Neilia rented an apartment. Among those greeting him were Kevin Coyne and Jane Fahey Suddaby, who wept as she embraced Biden and introduced him to her son Ryan. It was Mother's Day, and Suddaby—who would die of melanoma in 2013—was thinking about Neilia.

Mountain of a Promise

Pledge over Body of a Fallen Soldier
Kept 65 Years Later
Wednesday, November 11, 2009

During World War II, Thelma Guenther's brother Paul was hospitalized for malaria in Sicily. From Syracuse, she began writing letters to Paul and to a young soldier he met in the hospital. After the war, that soldier paid a visit to the Guenthers and never left, mainly because Thelma made a fast decision.

"I can tell what I need to know about someone in five minutes," said Thelma, who would soon marry Joe Bonzek. "And I knew, right away, that he had integrity."

Joe had a tough childhood in Massachusetts. He left home as a teen to work on a farm. Once he met Thelma, he saw her as the best luck he'd ever had. Husband and wife kept few secrets, but the one thing Joe rarely spoke about was the war.

They raised their children—Michael, Terry, and Christopher—in a house Joe built on Reed Avenue in Syracuse. About 20 years ago, after they retired, Thelma was going through a few boxes. She came upon some photos from Joe's time in the Rangers, a legendary unit that endured relentless fighting. One image showed a smiling young man outside a tent.

"Who's this good-looking guy?" Thelma asked, expecting only a few quick words of response.

Joe took the photo. He struggled for composure.

The man's name was Jesus Gallardo, although everyone called him "Jesse." He was Mexican-American, a native of Texas who became Joe's

32. Joe Bonzek at home. (David Lassman/*Post-Standard*)

best friend in the Rangers. Joe said they shared a certain perspective. Joe's parents were Polish, and their son did not speak English until he went to school. As for Jesse, he was raised in an America that often was suspicious and hostile toward Latinos.

"He was a quiet kid," Joe said, "and I don't know if he had any other friends besides myself."

In September 1944, they went up a French mountain of stark terrain. "It was not a stable front," Joe said. "We were on one side and the Germans were on the other, and they attacked us with mortar and artillery."

When it was over, Jesse did not return. His body was found among the rocks. Joe heard the news from other Rangers.

He lifted Jesse. He carried his body down the mountain.

Joe had always prayed that he would not die in Europe, that he would not be buried far from everyone he knew. Instead, it is Jesse who lies beneath a white cross in France. From then until now, Joe still wonders why it happened to his friend, and not to him. After the war, Joe brought home a quiet mission: He would tell Jesse's relatives about the mountain. He would explain just how much Jesse meant to him.

But it was the 1940s, and there was no Internet, no easy way to find that family. Jesse was often on Joe's mind as the Bonzeks raised their children, as decades seemed to flash by overnight. Finally, the day came when Thelma found the box, and Joe—for first time—told her about his promise.

The couple renewed the vow to find Jesse's survivors.

The Bonzeks checked available records, without luck, and Joe began attending reunions of his outfit. Their children and grandchildren offered to help. "My grandfather is my hero, the kind of man whose life you want to emulate," said Kraig Bonzek, a grandson who settled in Texas. "My grandmother is just very passionate, a very strong fighter for the underdog and the underprivileged. Growing up, being around her, that's something you picked up."

On a business trip to Europe, Kraig went looking for Jesse's grave and brought home photos of the white cross. In Syracuse, the Bonzeks read about a World War II oral history project for Latino families at the University of Texas. During a visit to the Austin home of their daughter, Terry, the Bonzeks got in touch with Maggie Rivas-Rodriguez, director of the program. The quest came to the attention of the *San Antonio Express-News*, a newspaper that did a front-page piece in May on Joe and Jesse.

That story made its way to Juan and George Gallardo, two brothers whose father, Francis Gallardo, had been a career soldier in the army. Like Joe Bonzek, their dad rarely spoke of the war. But Juan and George knew they had an older brother who died as an infant. He was called Jesse, and their mother once told them why:

He was named after an uncle, a brother of Francis, who was killed in the war.

Joe Bonzek is now 88. Francis Gallardo is in an Ohio nursing home. A few weeks ago, George went to see his father and hooked up a telephone speaker, so they both could listen. From Syracuse, Joe told the two Gallardos about what happened on the mountain. Francis, Jesse's brother, had "an emotional reaction," said George, who expressed wonder at the way Joe kept the faith.

Thelma was thrilled, but hardly surprised. Her husband hasn't changed from the day she met him, when they spoke for five minutes and she knew who he was.

His friends, she will tell you, are most often the same way.

His quest completed, Joe Bonzek died of cancer in 2012. Thelma, his widow, said his dignity at the end reflected the reason she'd loved him from day one, the first instinct she felt at the moment she met him: "He had integrity," she said.

Passage of a Way of Life, a Way of Thinking

Monday, June 21, 2010

Often, while holding a conversation in English, Dorothy Webster would pause to hunt for the right words. At the Onondaga Nation, she grew up speaking the ancient language of her people, which Dorothy described as "thinking Indian." She said there were concepts, entire ways of thought, that simply did not translate from one tongue to another.

At 81, Dorothy died Friday from lung cancer. Until her final weeks, her willingness to speak her mind made her a formidable leader at Onondaga. For decades, she was also an annual mainstay at the Indian Village at the New York State Fair, where she sold corn-husk dolls she made by hand. She was renowned for her skill as a baker, especially for her legendary molasses cookies.

Her daughters—Debby and Karen Webster, and Mary Cook—say those skills meshed with what it means to be a clan mother, a position that combines political, ceremonial, and family importance.

"She was a strong woman," Debby said.

The sisters paused for a moment Saturday at the Onondaga cookhouse, where visitors from throughout the Six Nations kept stopping in to pay respects at Dorothy's wake. She was a monumental figure, master of a native language she worked fiercely to preserve. At the wake, Debby, Karen, and Mary passed around a sheet of paper, which they used for jotting down reflections about their mom.

"She believed you led by example," Mary wrote. "She respected those who embraced the Haudenosaunee tradition. Her spirit was lifted when younger persons learned a new traditional song or a ceremonial speech."

243

33. Dorothy Webster at the Onondaga Nation. (Tim Reese/*Post-Standard*)

Dorothy also was a living bridge to an epic and heartbreaking saga. She was a direct descendant of Ephraim Webster, often described as the first white settler in Central New York. In the late 18th century, Webster married an Onondaga woman and had a son. The Onondagas gave Webster a significant piece of their territory, and he was the translator for the talks in which the Onondagas lost most of their land to state negotiators, transactions the Onondagas still maintain were fraudulent.

Ephraim Webster would later walk away from his Onondaga wife and child. The son, Harry Webster, remained with his people. He would grow up to serve as Tadodaho, the spiritual leader of the Six Nations.

The story, like so much of Dorothy's knowledge, came down through the generations. She married William Webster, an Oneida who shared Ephraim as a distant ancestor, and the couple settled at Onondaga. William died in 1994.

Their daughters and grandchildren grew accustomed to Dorothy's prowess as a clan mother, a longhouse position she held for more than 60 years. One day, Dorothy might be serving as a Brownie leader. The next, she would be helping with some landmark cultural victory.

She was part of a Six Nations contingent that sought the return of ceremonial wampum, or native belts made of shells that held profound significance. In Albany, state officials told Dorothy and her companions to put on gloves before touching the wampum—an order that Dorothy found especially appalling, since the belts held a sacred link to her Onondaga ancestors.

"To her, it was all common sense," Debby said. "She told (historical curators), 'Would you like to see your grandmother's things hanging in a museum?'"

Amid great joy, the wampum finally came home.

Saturday, at the cookhouse, Dorothy's friends spoke of her cultural wisdom, how a woman who never graduated from high school became a trusted source for researchers and historians. She was known for her dry humor, for her joy in simple things. Money, travel, or possessions meant little to her; she loved to watch the change of seasons from the door of her small house.

Certainly, she felt her share of frustration. She had a special passion for Onondaga Lake, a body of water held sacred by the Onondaga, and she maintained the state and federal governments weren't moving fast enough to make it clean. But she also had a patient faith that ran against a mainstream culture in which everything, as her daughter Karen said, is "now, now, now."

"She believed (good) things would happen," Debby said. "Maybe not in her time, maybe not even in our time, but they would happen."

By "thinking Indian," Dorothy found words for that belief. Few have them now.

Two years to the month after Dorothy Webster's passing, the Onondaga Historical Association took the rare step of voluntarily handing over human remains and sacred artifacts to leaders of the Onondaga Nation. During the ceremony, Gregg Tripoli—executive director of the OHA—said the process really began in the late 2000s, when Dorothy approached him at a crafts fair. He remembered how she told him, "You have something that belongs to us." Tripoli, still new to the job, was startled when he learned what his museum had kept in boxes on back shelves; Dorothy's force of conscience helped right that old wrong, even after her death.

Our NBA Legend Believed in Our City

Monday, July 12, 2010

Dolph Schayes doesn't remember the date of the conversation. What he remembers is that he was on a train with Eddie Gottlieb, a team owner from Philadelphia who helped to found the National Basketball Association. They were approached by a mutual acquaintance who asked Schayes where he was living at the time.

The man was startled to learn that Schayes had remained in Syracuse. Gottlieb, smiling, stuck in a friendly needle:

"Dolph doesn't know any better," he said.

To this day, Schayes thinks he knew just fine. He was a New York City kid who became the focus of a bidding war. Schayes turned down the powerful New York Knicks when they couldn't match an offer from Danny Biasone, an Eastwood bowling alley operator whose Syracuse Nationals played in the Coliseum at the state fairgrounds.

That was in 1949. Schayes would go on to score more than 18,000 points. He was the most prolific scorer in the NBA until Wilt Chamberlain shattered all the records. A few years ago, the NBA listed Schayes among its 50 greatest players of all time, confirming his place in the same Valhalla as Michael Jordan and Bill Russell and Oscar Robertson.

At 82, Schayes and his wife, Naomi, remain in Syracuse. They are such a gracious and cheerful part of the civic tapestry that it is easy to take them for granted.

"I liked it here and felt comfortable here, and it was just a wonderful fit," Schayes said.

That commitment takes on magnified importance when set against the furor of the last few days. LeBron James is leaving Cleveland for Miami. There is no getting around the economic blow to Cleveland—James was the rare star of enough sheer magnetism to energize a downtown by himself—but the most painful damage was inflicted upon the civic psyche.

It is easy to understand in Syracuse, or Buffalo, or any big industrial town that's been hurting for decades. Those of us who stay always tell ourselves there is much to love about our cities. Every now and then, we dare to hope that some beloved figure with a chance to leave will reaffirm our loyalties by choosing to stick around.

When Schayes speaks of Syracuse, he uses the words that all of Cleveland hoped to hear.

"From my point of view, this was just a wonderful place, and everyone on the street would pat you on the back and say hello, and we had an owner who preached teamwork and loyalty," he said. Schayes has often said the Nats were built in the image of their upstate audience: they were a fierce, dogged, and emotional group, much like the spectators who turned out for their games.

In that way—because Schayes came to feel that he was playing for Syracuse, rather than simply in it—he believes James is making a mistake.

Schayes fully understands the desperate hunger to claim a championship. In 1950 and 1954, his Syracuse teams made it to the NBA finals before getting knocked out. At the time, it was easy for Schayes to believe he'd never win an NBA title. Yet the missing ingredient fell into place when Johnny Kerr joined the squad and gave it a real center.

In 1955, for the first and only time, the Nats reigned as NBA champions. Schayes knows how that felt in his belly, and he believes a title with the Cavaliers—even if it meant waiting a while longer—could have provided sweet fulfillment for James.

"I think if he had stayed, and won it in Cleveland, it would have been a more satisfying thing with him as the go-to guy," Schayes said. In the same way as Jordan's Bulls or Kobe Bryant's Lakers, history would have recorded that James took his team, and his city, to the heights.

The deeper issue, to Schayes, involves the rare communion between a player and a region. He remembers hearing rumors in the mid-1950s that the Knicks again wanted him in Madison Square Garden. While there was no free agency in those days, a star eager to get out of town could find ways to make life miserable for a team owner.

Schayes wouldn't do it. He had grown to love Syracuse. During the summer, he'd play softball with many of his teammates. Their families routinely got together for picnics. Years later, when the Nats moved to Philadelphia, Schayes held onto his house in Onondaga County, knowing he would eventually return.

As James grows older, Schayes wonders if he will come to gradually appreciate a quieter set of career incentives.

"Family and Central New York," Schayes said. "It's like that."

In 2015, in an emotional ceremony at the Onondaga County War Memorial, Dolph Schayes, Jim Tucker, and Billy Kenville—the last surviving members of the title-winning Syracuse Nationals of 1955—were finally awarded the championship rings their team had never received 60 years earlier, a gift courtesy of the Syracuse Crunch hockey team. Eight months later to the day, Dolph Schayes finally said goodbye to his adopted city: he died of cancer, at 87, in Syracuse.

As for LeBron James, he lived out Schayes's prediction: James returned to the Cavaliers and wept on the court in 2016, when he helped to finally win a championship for Cleveland.

Tale of Friendship, Perfect Ending

Eric Carle's Quest for "Girl in the White Dress"

Sunday, February 15, 2015

Flo Trovato paused, not far from the front door. Palm trees swayed last Sunday in the Florida breeze, a different world and more than 80 years away from a hill where she'd often visit her immigrant grandparents on the North Side of Syracuse.

She gathered herself, buoyed by her son Charles and daughter Angela, who punched a button to announce their arrival.

Bobbie Carle hurried out to greet them, wrapping them in hugs, and then they all made their way to the main door . . .

Where Eric Carle, Bobbie's husband and a legendary children's author and illustrator, embraced Flo as they'd embraced some 82 years ago when they posed for the childhood photograph that led to this reunion.

"You haven't changed at all!" Eric shouted, before they held each other for a long time.

Flo brought a bottle of champagne and a loaf of bread, which to Eric carried powerful symmetry: Flo's grandparents were landlords to Eric's family on John Street. When Eric was six, and the Carles returned to Germany—a sad departure—Leila Barresi, Flo's grandmother, gave the child a loaf of warm, fresh bread to take on the trip.

Almost 83 years later, another loaf became a symbol of reunion.

The meeting was the climactic step in what Bobbie Carle, Eric's wife, calls "the Easter Miracle."

In 2014, Eric released a children's book he titled *FRIENDS*. He built the tale around a black-and-white photo taken in Syracuse during his early

250

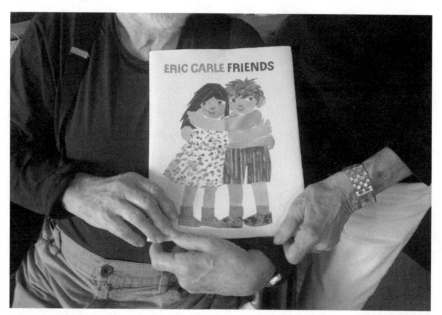

34. Eric Carle and Florence Trovato hold a copy of Eric's book *FRIENDS*. (Sean Kirst/*Post-Standard*)

childhood, a photo that showed him—as the three-year-old son of German immigrants—hugging a small girl in a white dress.

In Syracuse, his family often moved from apartment to apartment. When a longtime colleague, Motoko Inoue, asked him about that photo in a family scrapbook, Eric couldn't remember the street where the photo was taken or the name of the girl. All he recalled was that she was from a family of Italian immigrants, and that—almost certainly—she was his first true friend.

FRIENDS involved an imaginary quest for the girl in the white dress. At the end of the book, Eric included the actual photo and a note for readers:

"I often think about my long-ago friend," he wrote, "and I wonder what happened to her."

That little girl, now 86, walked through his door last Sunday.

Flo, a retired New Jersey school secretary, also lives in Florida. Like Eric, 85, she has vivid memories of John Street. "Such a pleasant part of my life," Flo said.

Still, the idea that an internationally renowned author was moved by her long-ago friendship was both touching and almost overwhelming, for Flo. She had no idea what to expect when she met Eric.

Sunday, he took her by the hand. He showed her around his waterfront home on the Straits of Florida. He sat with her and paged through a book that includes memories of his Syracuse childhood.

"So sweet and soft-spoken," said Flo, any jitters quickly draining away.

"I immediately liked her," Eric said, "as if nothing had changed in 82 years."

Even after everyone settled in for a meal, Eric would occasionally smile and shake his head in disbelief. In 1932, two little children from immigrant families embraced for a quick photo on a Syracuse street. Eric believes his mother had the camera; Flo thinks it might have been her aunt.

They would both soon leave our city. Flo's parents took her to Brooklyn two or three years before Eric's family went to Germany. The odds of them finding each other again seemed beyond imagination.

But this was Eric Carle, creator of *The Very Hungry Caterpillar* and other children's classics. The beauty and struggles of his boyhood, he said, provide "the deep springs" of his work.

In his 80s, through the new book, he publicly announced this long-shot dream of finding his long-ago friend. At the *Post-Standard*, we decided—without much hope—we'd try to find the answer.

We cast a wide net, starting with old records at the Onondaga Historical Association. Dead end after dead end led to what can only be called a digital Hail Mary pass, an Internet search that brought us to Angela Trovato, in New Jersey.

She'd been looking for family history linked to her great-grandparents, the Barresis, of John Street in Syracuse. After hearing the story, Angela told us there was a chance the girl in the white dress was her mother, Florence Ciani Trovato, a Syracuse native. We contacted Flo, who was intrigued; she remembered how her relatives said she played with a "German boy" in the 1930s on John Street.

Angela found a way to prove it, beyond all doubt:

On Easter Sunday, she discovered her family not only had a copy of the original image showing Eric and Flo together, they had a photo of the two children, arms around each other, that Eric had never seen.

That day, when Eric heard the news, his voice rose to a shout, from sheer elation.

"In those two pictures, we look so easy together, so compatible," Eric said.

You can tell, by seeing the images, the little children were good friends.

Eric's book describes the girl moving away, an accurate memory: Flo's parents took her to Brooklyn before she started kindergarten. Her dad was a barber, and her family endured harsh years in the Great Depression. She went to work shortly after high school, and she met and married Charlie Trovato, with whom she'd raise three children.

Charlie died in 2007, a year away from their 60th anniversary. Flo, after a lifetime of hard work, had enough left in savings to retire to Florida.

A year ago, out of nowhere, she learned through a journalist that Eric was trying to reach her. On Easter, by phone, they had their first conversation in 82 years. They spoke of meeting in September, but that reunion fell apart.

Eric became gravely ill. For more than a month, he said, his condition was "near death." Those closest to Eric braced themselves for losing him.

Then he rallied, a turnaround described by Ann Beneduce, his editor and close friend, as "near miraculous." While he's still recovering and sometimes uses a wheelchair, Eric's strength is coming back.

In December, after a long break in correspondence, he contacted Flo to wish her a happy birthday.

They made plans to meet in February, at Eric and Bobbie's Florida home.

This time, nothing got in the way.

Over dinner, they looked back on their long lives after John Street: the people they've loved, the children they've raised. Flo was thrilled to learn

Eric is finishing another book. The best way to stay well, she told him, is to always find a purpose.

Before Flo and her children had to leave, Eric led them on a tour of his studio. They noticed a copy of the photo showing Eric with Flo still hanging above his desk, kept there for emotional reference while he worked on *FRIENDS*.

For Eric, the image recalls warm and peaceful years in Syracuse, just before traumatic change. Eric's mother had grown homesick for her homeland. The family left Syracuse in the 1930s to return to Germany, where the Nazis had ascended into power.

Eric's memories of that period are intertwined with war, horrific violence, bombing raids. His father, drafted into the German army, was "physically and psychologically broken" as a Russian prisoner of war.

Once the war ended, Eric said, the decision was easy. He was still an American citizen. He left for New York City, where he eventually became a celebrated author and illustrator.

He didn't know Flo was building her own life in the same place.

Eric never discarded the photo of the girl in the white dress, a symbol of a warm and secure time in his childhood. Sunday, he marveled out loud at how Trovato means "found" in Italian. He wondered how different both their lives might have been if their parents had decided to settle in Syracuse.

"Clearly, I loved her the way a three-year-old can love," he said, "and she must have felt the same way about me."

He based that on what he sees in two snapshots, these two brief instants, on the North Side of Syracuse.

Two little children were then separated by the quiet and relentless forces that rule everyday lives, until they came together again—after almost 83 years—for an impossible reunion.

Very quickly, they felt comfort in each other's company. Before Flo left, she invited Eric and Bobbie to someday come to her home for dinner.

The meeting, in itself, was a miracle. What they learned, after lives long apart:

They still are friends.

Eric Carle had a difficult year in 2015—he lost his wife, Bobbie, to breast cancer, even as he recovered from his illness. He takes strength from the many people who care about him, and doubts he will write another book. As for Flo, she and Eric remain in contact; they had lunch together not long ago in Florida, and both still marvel at the unlikely events that reopened their friendship after 82 years.

PART EIGHT

Love

A Couple Walks Side by Side to the Last Step
Saturday, July 2, 1994

Every day throughout his two-week stay in the hospital, despite all the tubes and the pain, 80-year-old Leonard Mancini kept asking his three kids about his wife.

Rose Mancini had cancer, and she was failing. He wanted to know who was with her, who was taking care of her. "We're watching her, Dad," they'd tell him, and they'd go home knowing he took comfort in that.

At the house, where her own condition got worse by the day, Rose asked the kids to help her buy a new recliner for Leonard. She figured he'd need it once he got home.

The whole thing left the three middle-aged "children"—Margaret Sykes, Carol Brostek, and their father's namesake, Leonard—sick with worry. Their parents had been married 55 years, all but two of them spent in the same Hawley Avenue house. There seemed no way either one could go on without the other.

Leonard was a particular concern. He was a former steel worker and professional painter, a loud and passionate man who always confronted trouble head-on. Yet during his wife's long battle with cancer, he refused to accept that her terminal lymphoma would eventually claim her life.

He had a bad heart, but he hung the laundry, did the dishes, drove Rose around town, as if convinced the raw effort could make the cancer go away.

Two weeks ago, the heart attack put him in the hospital at the same time Rose was starting to go. It left a chance Leonard would return to an empty house. "It would have killed my father," Margaret Sykes said.

259

The two sisters and their brother were thinking of calling a social worker, trying to find some way to prepare their dad for the worst. They could not bear the thought of telling him. They never had to do it. Call it coincidence, if you want. The Mancini "children" prefer to see it as part of the big plan.

On Saturday, the same day Rose dropped into a final coma, Leonard lay in the hospital and never asked how she was doing. It was strange, the way he simply dropped the question he'd been asking all the time, almost as if he already knew. Instead, he asked only about the garden at the house.

Leonard and Rose loved the garden, where they'd grown their own flowers and vegetables for as long as anyone remembered. Leonard broke the ground every year with a hoe and his two hands, chasing off any suggestion that he use a rotary tiller.

He told his son Saturday to make sure someone hurried to get up the scallions. A few hours later, Leonard's heart gave out. Rose, in her coma, never learned he was gone. She died the following Tuesday.

"I can't tell you how much I'll miss them," Margaret said. But she knows it is the way her parents wanted it to be.

"They couldn't have gone on without each other," said Betty Genninger, a Hawley Avenue neighbor of 32 years.

You may have known Leonard and Rose, even if you never met them. The Mancinis never bought a dryer, always choosing to hang their wash on the line. Each year, they dug and tended the garden. They would take from it little gifts for the neighbors on their street, bright roses or tomatoes or pieces of garlic.

And they took care of each other, in small and gentle ways. Leonard was not one for sweets. When Rose baked a cake, she always left him one unfrosted corner. She could sense in advance his hard days at work, the kind of days when it was best for the three kids to give him peace.

Since Rose didn't drive, Leonard would take her to the public market or the store or out to eat at Dominick's. He was loud, a storyteller who loved to laugh and yell and argue with his brothers. They never had much money, but every Friday was allowance day for Leonard's children, no matter how tight things got. Rose enjoyed him, took delight in him, but also ran the house during the day with a quiet strength.

Rose inherited that house from her own mother, a native of Italy who mastered English in Syracuse. The children remember how older immigrants in the neighborhood would stop by to get help reading their letters from home. It became a kind of haven in a difficult New World.

When Rose's mother died, those visitors looked for the same help from Rose. It is a childhood memory that stays with the three Mancini children, a house filled with gentle strangers who spoke in the old tongue.

Leonard worked in a steel mill and later as a professional painter, and in retirement he and Rose made the most of their time. They went on long bus tours, to Canada and even to Disney World. Three months ago, the whole family celebrated Leonard's 80th birthday.

Retirement had given him time to do a lot of fishing with Jim Genninger, cementing their friendship of 32 years. In 1962, when the Genningers were new to the street and just a little bit unsure, Rose and Leonard walked over and gave them a warm welcome.

The "new neighbors" became regulars at Mancini family parties, or the New Year's Eve get-togethers where Leonard's booming voice took center stage. The Genningers were still kids, a young couple, when they landed on Hawley Avenue. The Mancinis became almost their surrogate parents. Jim and Betty always wished they had a way to tell them thanks.

Last winter, during the big snows, the Genninger grandchildren volunteered to go over and shovel Rose and Leonard out. The kids waved off Leonard's noisy attempts to pay them for the work, which is the way a real neighborhood rewards acts of kindness.

"All they ever wanted to do was take care of us," Margaret Sykes said. "This week, we found out they had everything ready for whenever this happened. They even had their obituary written out. They were very loving people, who did everything for us."

Something about the timing of their deaths, about the photograph that ran with the notice in the papers, has touched a chord. Complete strangers, clerks and workers in banks and stores, have offered spontaneous regrets to the family.

Friday would have been Rose and Leonard's 55th anniversary. The funeral is this morning, at St. Vincent de Paul Church. The Mancini children will watch as their parents take one last trip together, although the "kids" already paid their highest form of respect. This week they were on their knees in the garden, making sure to get up the last of the scallions.

More than 20 years after the passing of their parents, the long, hot days of August still trigger memories of Leonard and Rose for the Mancini children. It is a point in the year that still serves as a lesson: work hard enough, and a time comes when you harvest the garden.

Memories of Brotherly Love Yet Undimmed
Thursday, March 9, 1995

He sits in his recliner in the nice house in Camillus, looking far too frail even to speak. Edward Cronauer wears a bathrobe above his thin limbs, and he leans back in the recliner with his eyes rolled out of sight.

Your first impression is that he is incapable, infirm.

But that is a colossal mistake. He is going to be 100 on March 23. He is legally blind, and he struggles to hear. But he still sits up late, listening to Syracuse University games on the radio, while 69-year-old Edward Jr. yells out the play-by-play.

The old man finds nothing surprising in his deep interest in the team. He was at SU not long after the program got started. He was a top reserve on the 1917-18 Orange basketball team that won the national championship, a season that ended with one of the greatest games in school history.

Penn came to Syracuse. The game was supposed to decide Eastern supremacy, which in those days pretty much equated to the best team in the country. Twenty-five hundred fans jammed into the old Archbold Gym. Cronauer had left to join the U.S. Army just the week before. But his younger brother, John, was a rising star for SU, the team's second-leading scorer with 129 points.

It was a rough, intense game. Penn won, 17-16, although the Quakers scored only twice from the floor. The rest of their points came on free throws by Mike Sweeney, who took the shots after every foul called against the Orangemen.

The game would touch off an assault on that rule. Even the *New York Times* argued that the man who got fouled should take his own shots. The dispute may explain why the Helms Foundation, a private institution in California, picked the Orange as its national champion.

But the loss would carry greater meaning for Edward Cronauer.

It was the last time his little brother took the court for Syracuse. The two of them learned to play the game together. They would go to an ice house in Cooperstown, one of those wooden buildings where communities stored blocks of ice throughout the year, before easy access to refrigeration. The boys would scatter sawdust on the slick floor, fill an old sack with leaves, and then hang the rim of a barrel from the wall.

For hours, they'd shoot the sack through the hoop.

You can trust those details because Edward Cronauer remembers.

When the brothers parted, it was Edward who seemed ready to put himself at risk, joining the military during the Great War. He was stationed that summer in Oregon. John worked as a Fuller Brush salesman over summer break. Syracuse All-American Joe Schwarzer had graduated. John Cronauer was expected to carry the team.

He went home one weekend in September, started to scribble a postcard to Edward, and fell dead in his mother's arms. He was 20 years old. The doctors said he died from "athlete's heart."

The news came to Edward in a letter. Even now he finds it hard to accept. John was about to start his junior year. Edward made another soldier read the letter to him again, only then trusting the message as real. His parents gave him the half-written postcard his brother had started, the handwriting feathery, then fading out.

Seventy-seven years later, Edward keeps it pasted in his scrapbook.

The older brother did a lot more at SU than play basketball. He was a law student. He was a football cheerleader. He was a member of the 1916 lacrosse team, the first one in Syracuse history. The following season, he was elected team captain. He remembers playing in the stadium against a native team from the Onondaga Nation; one of the Onondagas, he recalls, wore purple spikes on the field.

The loss to Penn in basketball still riles him. Syracuse had already beaten the Quakers on the road. The undefeated Orangemen had won 16 straight games. The defeat was a bitter way to end the season. "We challenged them to one more game at Madison Square Garden," Cronauer said. "They wouldn't play us."

Stretched out in his chair, hands folded on his lap, he fretted out loud about being interviewed. He worried he'd be wrong on some detail or date. Instead, he was remarkably accurate. An article in the *Post-Standard* of 1918 noted that Penn did indeed turn down a rematch, arguing its team had disbanded for the season.

There are times in conversation when you think the old man has gone to sleep. You shout a question in his ear, and for a while there is silence, convincing you Cronauer hasn't heard a thing. But his memory works like a strong pump, hidden and powerful. Abruptly he will answer, voice strong and precise.

Sometimes, if you struggle to understand a particular word or phrase, his son will interpret. Edward Jr. brought his father to live with him almost 30 years ago. That was right after the death of the old man's wife, Mary. Later, the son would mourn for his own wife, Marcella. The two men are now a couple of seasoned widowers, comfortable and content in each other's company. The elder Edward can't see or hear very much. But his memory and good sense have proved much more durable.

He grew up on a farm. There was no electricity. He saw his first automobile while driving a buggy on a dirt road. He was taking the family milk to a creamery. The car rounded a corner, kicking up a cloud of dust. Cronauer's horse reared. The driver of the car had to leap out and quiet both the animal and the startled boy.

After college, Edward wound up running a general store in Skaneateles Falls. He was a police court justice and a clerk to the school board. He will abruptly ask, in the middle of a conversation, how much a teacher now earns in salary. He will shake his head upon hearing the answer. In his day, he'll remind you, a teacher was lucky to make a few hundred a year.

The conversation always returned to basketball, and basketball always reminds him of his brother. "A good soul," Edward said of John Cronauer. This is his example. In the final game before Penn, Syracuse played Dartmouth. It was Edward's last chance to suit up. He was a top substitute, but his skills did not match John's.

So for one night John Cronauer gave up his position to his brother. He sat out the entire game and let Edward take his place. It is hard to imagine such a thing today. SU beat Dartmouth. Edward scored. The two of them parted on that high note. Ed would raise a family, build a business, outlive a generation.

But he still very much remains a big brother.

"I never got over it," Edward Cronauer said.

Edward Cronauer Sr. died in 1995, five months shy of his 101st birthday. Years later, Syracuse University archivists visited his son to make copies of family images and photographs, including what amounts to a sacred artifact: the postcard John Cronauer was writing to his brother, at the instant of his death.

Alone, He Still Follows Yellow Brick Road

Wednesday, June 3, 1998

When Marie Raabe first met her husband, Meinhardt, she did not even know what a munchkin was.

That was 1941. Marie was working as a "cigarette girl" at the Mayflower Hotel in Akron, Ohio. She had no idea that Meinhardt played a famous role in what would become a classic movie. Besides, Marie already rubbed elbows with celebrities. Many popular bands played at the hotel. She was a friend of Glenn Miller's. Frank Sinatra knew her name.

"If she was impressed by me, she didn't show it," Meinhardt said this week.

Instead, he recalled how their immediate bond was based on being "little people," a bond that blossomed into a wedding in 1946. The marriage lasted almost 52 years, until the couple climbed into a car last fall for a routine drive near their home in Florida. They slammed into a car stopped in traffic. At the time, they were both 82.

Meinhardt survived. Marie didn't make it.

"I never really had a chance to say goodbye," Meinhardt said.

He played a familiar role in an American pop epic. Marie helped him market his own small piece of fame. Fifty-nine years ago, Meinhardt was the munchkin coroner in *The Wizard of Oz*. He was the guy who declared the witch dead when Dorothy's farmhouse fell on Oz. Meinhardt then went to work promoting Oscar Mayer, which is how he crossed Marie's path in the Akron hotel.

Meeting a Munchkin meant nothing to her. Marie had worked in vaudeville as a teenager. She already knew many of Meinhardt's friends in show business. Their deeper connection came through the insights of

35. Meinhardt Raabe, the actor who played the munchkin coroner in *The Wizard of Oz*, with his wife, Marie, at a garden dedicated in Meinhardt's honor behind the Chittenango Village Hall. (Nicholas Lisi/*Post-Standard*)

being little people, or "midgets," as they were all too typically called. It is a word Meinhardt heard too often, a word he's glad is finally going out of use.

Neither he nor his wife, he said, stood taller than four-foot-eight—which hardly stopped Marie from attaining extraordinary stature in life.

"She was a very exceptional person, a real Christian," said Louise Jerome, whose family played host to the Raabes during Chittenango's OzFest for the last eight years. "She took care of Meinhardt. She made all the arrangements for their travel. She wrote the letters. She remembered the holidays. She took care of the luggage and made sure he had his costume."

Just last year, Louise said, Marie quietly remarked how she hoped—for her husband's sake—she would not die first.

This weekend's OzFest is dedicated to Marie. Ten years ago, Meinhardt Raabe called Beverly Brickner, one of the festival founders, after

Meinhardt spotted a small magazine article about a celebration in the childhood home of L. Frank Baum, author of the *Oz* books. Meinhardt asked if the fledgling OzFest might have room for the munchkin coroner. The call was beyond the best hopes in Chittenango.

Meinhardt's presence gave the festival national authenticity and led to an annual Central New York reunion of the surviving munchkins. Meinhardt is expected to fly into Syracuse today for his 10th festival, although Louise cannot imagine the coroner without his wife.

The OzFest people all have stories about Marie. She grew to appreciate the magic of Oz, and children were drawn to her just as they remain drawn to her husband. She wore her hair in a waist-long ponytail. Every morning, she would sit and brush it out. Because of her size, she often wore children's clothing. One of her favorite parts of OzFest was visiting area thrift stores. Those stores often sold "older," more dignified styles of kids' clothes. Brickner particularly remembers a long blue dress Marie loved, a dress she found in Chittenango.

As for Meinhardt, he still struggles to talk about his wife. He recalls little of the accident, except for the impact when they hit the car in front of them. Meinhardt broke his ankle and was covered with bruises and cuts. It took him several months to recover. The couple was never able to have children. Meinhardt returned to a home that to him was without its soul.

"Life can be very, very lonesome," he said.

He deals with his loss by trying to stay busy. He has always been "a performer, a public person." His best memories with Marie involve the Oz reunions, the way she chatted with fans as she stood at his shoulder, the way she always kept a firm hand on their receipts.

Without her, Meinhardt continues to tend their flowers, including the gardenias Marie loved so much. On Earth Day, in her memory, their friends in Florida held a butterfly release.

Marie had no official link to *The Wizard of Oz*. You can watch the film 100 times and you will never see her face. That hardly mattered. In Chittenango this weekend, when children run to the famous coroner for hugs and signatures, they'll wonder why he came this time without his munchkin wife.

Meinhardt Raabe remained a regular visitor to the Oz festival in Chittenango until his death in 2010; he was among the last of the actors who played munchkins in the classic film to make the annual journey to Central New York.

It's Waves, Waggles Some 50 Years Later

Monday, October 18, 1999

Mary and Paul Ryfun, as the guests of honor, stood up Sunday to eat first. They walked toward the buffet at Barbagallo's Restaurant in East Syracuse, while their guests laughed and waved napkins in the air, waving them in furious circles until Mary looked their way.

"I was going to eat," she said, through an interpreter, "but I see that you want me to stop and kiss." She turned around and gave her husband a big smooch, a little present to help celebrate 50 years of marriage. Friends and family dropped the napkins and raised their hands high in the air, waggling their fingers, a sign-language version of applause inside the hall.

The Ryfuns are deaf. They were married October 22, 1949, at Our Lady of Pompei Church in Syracuse. Back then, no one waved napkins at deaf weddings to urge newlyweds to kiss. Hearing people could clink glasses. For their deaf counterparts, a subtle revolution was not yet quite underway.

What the Ryfuns always had was each other. Their only child, also named Paul, was born in 1953. His father worked at the General Super Plating Co., and his mother was one of many deaf women who sewed purses at a Syracuse pocketbook factory. The Minoa couple's refuge, every night, was the shelter of their marriage.

"She's always happy," Paul Ryfun said about his wife. "When I get down, she always brings me up."

Sunday's party was a big deal in the deaf community. Bea Murphy, an interpreter, said only a few hundred deaf residents live in greater Syracuse. With those small numbers, a 50th anniversary for a deaf couple remains extraordinary. "It goes so fast!" said Frances Harmon, a close friend of the Ryfuns.

271

At their wedding, the priest knew a smidgen of sign language. Fifty years later, when the couple renewed their vows at St. Lucy's Church, interpreter Marion Baratta made sure they understood every word.

Younger deaf couples—such as Jeff and Devon Sterly, married 10 years—said the Ryfuns and their contemporaries were pioneers.

"They had no phones, no relays, no closed captions, nothing," said Jeff Sterly, 40, a state transportation engineer. "In those days, they had to go and ask a neighbor for help if they wanted to make a phone call. I can't imagine how they did it."

The marriage endured, the Ryfuns said, because they had each other. Their son was born with hearing, and he grew up knowing both sign language and English. He is married now, with two teenage daughters who have a love for music.

"They taught me to look at life in a wonderful and honest way," the son said of his parents. "In the deaf community, they always deal with people straight. There's not much phoniness."

His mother and father, both deaf since infancy, lack that nostalgia about their own childhoods. The elder Paul Ryfun was introduced to sign language at 12, when he entered the Rome School for the Deaf. Before that, he said, he had no way to speak. As a boy he stayed at home, saying little, living in a world of silence.

Mary attended a school for deaf people in Rochester. She met her future husband in 1948, when they were introduced in a Syracuse bowling alley.

Many white-haired friends from that era attended Sunday's celebration. They recalled the 1950s as a difficult time. A strong marriage, they agreed, became a kind of haven.

"It was very frustrating," said Caroline Moore, who has been married to her husband, Robert, for 48 years. "I had to ask my children to make my phone calls. The TV would be on, and I would have to ask my kids what they were saying. I couldn't go into the school and speak to my children's teachers. It really bothered me."

She broke off to watch as the Ryfuns left their table. Dozens of hands rose up, poised and waiting, as the guests of honor cut their anniversary cake, and then the fingers waggled in happy and silent applause. Old friends stood in groups, exchanging hugs, speaking in sign. Dinner was over. It was time to celebrate.

"It's quiet in here," Baratta said, "but it's very loud."

The Ryfuns celebrated their 60th anniversary in 2009; Mary died about five months later, in a world where the Internet is shattering so many of the old constraints about communicating. Paul died in 2015, at 91.

Shunned by Family, Mourned by Many

Monday, December 10, 2001

Dick Reed died at 1 a.m. Saturday. He lived through Pearl Harbor Day and just into December 8. It was one final gift for his wife, Hatsu.

She was Japanese and a practicing Buddhist. Dick, who died at 71, was a nonbeliever. Yet they kept a small Buddhist shrine in their North Syracuse house. For years, when Hatsu worshipped there, Dick would kneel with her. He always hid his lack of faith. He worshipped as a Buddhist just to make her happy.

"She did so much for me," Dick once said. "I thought this was one small thing I could do for her."

December 8 is Rohatsu, the day when believers recall how Buddha truly saw the morning star and became enlightened—the moment when Buddhism was born.

For Dick, who lived for Hatsu, it was a fitting day to die.

He spent his last three years without her. She was killed in September 1998, a victim of the Labor Day storm. Dick and Hatsu were in the backyard of their home, trying to chop apart a 100-foot tree brought down by the high winds.

Dick cut off a limb. It fell on top of him. He crawled out, bleeding, and found Hatsu doubled over. The limb had struck her in the head. She insisted she was all right.

She went to bed that night and never woke up.

It was impossible for Dick, an Air Force retiree, to imagine life alone. He met Hatsu in the early 1970s, when Dick was stationed in Japan. He called her "Hatsi," but her family didn't like him at all. The cultural wounds remained fresh from World War II. Dick eventually won over his in-laws, mainly by learning to speak some Japanese.

He and Hatsu were married. She left her family to move to Syracuse, where Dick was stationed at Hancock Field. They didn't plan to stay. Dick wanted to return to his childhood home in Pennsylvania. Before they visited his family for the first time, Hatsu made two elaborate Japanese dolls and mailed them to Dick's mother.

Once they got there, Dick's mother and brothers turned their backs on Hatsu. Dick found the dolls, hidden away in the attic. Hatsu, upset, ran from the house. "What'd I do wrong?" she asked. "Nothing," Dick said. He told her to pack her bags.

They returned to North Syracuse. They never heard from Dick's mother, or the rest of his family, again.

Considering all that, Pearl Harbor Day would have also been an appropriate day for Dick to die.

He and Hatsu tried unsuccessfully to have children. Their focus was each other. "He was a very likable guy, a guy who'd give you the shirt off his back," said Tom Cregg, an Air Force retiree who knew Dick in Japan and later moved to Syracuse—and whose wife, Yoshiko, is also Japanese.

In Japan, Dick and Cregg were close friends. In Syracuse, the two men rarely saw each other. Hatsu was not one for going out. She planted a few Japanese shrubs in their yard on Homeland Road, and she hung some Japanese paintings on the wall. Her favorite color was green. In the days after Hatsu was struck in the head, when Reed believed she'd come home from the hospital, he painted the porches green as a surprise.

She never saw them.

Aside from the Creggs, few attended Hatsu's calling hours. Dick buried her alone. He vowed, at the time, that he would find ways to go on. He sold his house and used the money to visit Hatsu's family in Tokyo. He moved to an apartment in East Syracuse. He'd often visit Fred Fergerson, director of the North Syracuse funeral home that buried Hatsu.

Dick would talk about a rash on his leg, or a problem with his car. Not quite two years ago, the visits abruptly stopped. The last that Fergerson heard of Dick, he was taking drives and then forgetting where he was.

He died, at 1 a.m. Saturday, in the Rosewood Heights Health Center.

Dick left behind no money or belongings. He left no next of kin or list of friends for his lawyer.

"He died of a broken heart," Fergerson said.

In the end, Dick was simply finishing a great love story. "When we married (our wives), there was still quite a bit of prejudice, just as some of the Arab people are feeling right now," Cregg said. Dick made a choice, paid a price, and never regretted it.

His burial will be Wednesday from Fergerson's, on Route 11 in North Syracuse, following a public calling hour from noon to 1 p.m.

Fergerson expects the calling hour to be as deserted as Hatsu's— unless, of course, a few strangers stop by.

Almost 200 readers showed up at Dick Reed's wake, paying homage to a great Syracuse love story. "A few of us talked about it at the North Medical offices," said Kathy Wilson, a registered nurse who told the Post-Standard *she came to the funeral home on her day off. "We wanted to be his friend, even if we're strangers."*

Sarah Leaves a Sadness "Beyond Tears"
Sunday, August 8, 2004

Sarah Webster grew up with the Internet. She was part of a generation that's made an art form of the away message and user profile, the little biography left for anyone who might be trying to reach you.

Paul and Joanne Webster, Sarah's parents, are glad she had that skill. When someone needs a description of their daughter, they hand over a printout of the way she described herself online:

"My name is Sarah. I spell my name with an 'h' because the name just looks naked without it. I enjoy listening to Yanni and vacuuming my car on a regular basis. Occasionally I procrastinate by playing with my numerous desk gadgets, especially Willy the WeeWee. I love 90 degree weather and driving my friend Stephanie's standard car, even though I've only done it once. Occasionally I sip on Jack Daniels when I have writer's block.

"I look exactly like my Mom but have the personality of my Dad. I go to a school where it snows nine months out of the year, but that's OK because we have wonderful Canadian neighbors. I have incredible friends and an awesome dog. One of my sisters tells me I don't take life seriously and the other (one) is too intelligent to put up with me. My brother is awesome because he has no problem answering the front door of our house wearing sudsy dish gloves.

I also enjoy the color purple."

Now you pretty much know Sarah Webster, native of the Valley neighborhood in Syracuse, graduate of Corcoran High School and St. Lawrence University. You should also know that she was 22 when she wrote this message, and that her parents would sing "You Are My Sunshine" to soothe their first child when she was tiny, and that she loved purple even more than she lets on in that message.

She lived to travel. She had scaled the Pyramid of the Moon in Mexico and walked through the Palace of Versailles in France. She had two younger sisters, Stephanie and Caroline, and a younger brother, Tom, who put up with her musical tastes—which included Beethoven, Eminem, and a habit of listening to Christmas carols in the summer.

Sarah also had a boyfriend, the first great love of her life, and she had even dropped a hint or two about getting married.

She was the first child of a classic Syracuse marriage: her dad is a descendant of Ephraim Webster, an early Upstate pioneer, while her mom was raised by Italian immigrants in Liverpool. For one last summer, Sarah had moved back in with her family, one last summer after college before she jumped into the world.

"As long as she wanted to be here, she was welcome to be here," said Joanne, a teacher at Roberts School in Syracuse. "Basically, it was selfish because we didn't want to let her go."

Not quite two weeks ago, on a Monday morning, Paul Webster went to his job at Purcell's Wallpaper & Paint. Joanne drove Caroline to a driver education class, and then stopped at Roberts to do some work in her classroom. She returned to the house just before noon. She was surprised to see a car in the driveway. Sarah was supposed to be at work.

Joanne went upstairs. Her daughter was dead in bed.

There would be a wake, with thousands of mourners, in which friends waited up to three hours to pay respects. There would be a funeral at the Cathedral of the Immaculate Conception, one of the few churches big enough to hold the crowd. There would be so many flowers of condolence that they spill from the Websters' house and onto the back deck.

There would not, however, be any answers. Tests have yet to determine why Sarah, a seemingly healthy young woman who worked as a transportation analyst, went to bed and died in her sleep.

"This sadness is beyond tears," Joanne said. "Tears, when they come, are a relief. This sadness is so profound I can't even touch it."

She and Paul are glad for some things. They are glad their daughter died in her own bed, in her own house. They are especially glad for the first month of this summer, including the sounds that can drive a parent nuts: three daughters bickering about car keys and which flip-flops belong to whom, Sarah telling her younger brother he should really do more around the house.

"It was music," Joanne said, just her kids being her kids, a song that ended on the morning when she found Sarah in bed.

The only consolation for the Websters is to look into their pain: Their daughter had packed "so much living" into 22 years. She had been interviewed by National Public Radio as part of a college research project. She had been to Mexico, the Caribbean, Ireland. She'd seen the redwoods in California and gone to Paris, this year, with one of her sisters and her dad.

And she was dating a young man, Jon Putney, described by her parents simply as "the one."

This was the biggest surprise of them all. Sarah, a serious student, had always told her folks she was "too busy for a boy." Then she introduced them to Jon, and she brought him home to play Monopoly, even if she kept saying she wasn't ready to get married.

On that last Sunday, Sarah was at the computer just before she went to bed. She was reading about Nik and the Nice Guys, the renowned Upstate musicians. To her surprise, she learned they first played together at St. Lawrence.

"Now I've got a band," Sarah said, a clear reference to a wedding reception, which her parents think might be the last thing they heard her say.

That was it. No parting drama, no big good-byes. They found her in bed and thousands came to mourn for her. Her dad and mom went home and braced for life without their daughter, for what Joanne predicts will be "long talks with God" about why she isn't there.

Yet they've discovered they still feel her in the house. "There's a spark of her," Paul said, "in the other three." And a few things have happened they don't try to explain—events they see as bound to the mystery of Sarah's death.

A couple of days ago, Joanne was walking through the house when she heard the far-off tinkle of an ice cream truck, the kind of truck that usually plays some old recording of "The Sting." This time the truck was playing a different tune, and Joanne froze, listening hard.

It was "You Are My Sunshine," Sarah's baby song. Joanne thought that maybe she'd lost her mind, and she ran onto the deck, calling for her husband. Paul, with his back to her, was hanging some wet clothes. He turned and looked up, already in tears, father and mother thinking the same thing:

An away message. Paul climbed the stairs and hugged his wife.

Joanne Webster is retired from teaching in the Syracuse city schools. She and her husband do their best, she said, not to dwell on the "why" about losing their daughter: "For Paul, his driving force is to find her goodness in other people. For me, I try to honor her life in all I do."

Pat Ahern Would "Love You until You Loved Yourself"

Sunday, May 4, 2014

Ricky's life changed as a passenger in a big tan Buick. He doesn't recall exactly why the conversation began, only that he was at a point in his life that seemed about as bleak as it gets. He was drinking so hard he'd embarrass himself at night, then feel sick and "broken" in the morning.

This was years ago. Pat Ahern was driving. They'd met through mutual friends who had faith Pat would understand. In the car, Pat brought no judgment. He simply told Ricky his story.

Ricky, in recent days, has been thinking of the moment. Last month, Pat died of complications from a stroke, just before his 69th birthday. His brother John, a Catholic priest, gave the sermon during the funeral at Holy Cross Church in DeWitt. The brothers grew up in a crowded house on the Near West Side, and the service was rich with the Irish culture they revered.

The pews were filled with those who knew Pat from the Ancient Order of Hibernians or from such events as the Syracuse St. Patrick's Parade, where Pat—a decade ago—served as grand marshal on what he called one of the great days of his life.

At the service, a niece held an iPhone to a microphone and offered a recording of Pat, on tin whistle, playing "Come by the Hills," a beautiful Irish melody. Once it ended, there was a collective gasp of laughter, sorrow, and longing when everyone heard Pat's familiar voice, captured on tape.

As always, he offered his thanks. The sentiment was familiar to so many in the pews, men and women linked by clear eyes and an understanding:

281

36. Pat Ahern (right) and his brother, the Reverend John Ahern. (Frank Ordonez/ *Post-Standard*)

They were like Ricky, among those Pat once helped.

Several spoke with me, on one condition: Their names could not appear. They agreed to anonymity when they embraced the 12-step program that transformed their lives. Honoring the friend who helped them cross that bridge also meant adhering to the code.

They are recovering alcoholics, as was Pat. One guy—George is as good a name as any—chose Pat as a sponsor, the guide who'd introduce him to sobriety. George realized quickly that Pat sponsored so many women and men he'd sometimes lose track of their names. Pat would see one of them on the street or in a coffee shop and he'd welcome them with arms wide, calling out, "Me darling!"

He loved them. They knew it. That was enough.

"What I remember about Pat is how we would laugh and laugh," George said. "I had thought the world without alcohol would be a very humorless place, and he taught me the exact opposite. I had been a very cynical guy when I was drinking, and I never laughed as long or hard as I did with Pat Ahern."

The same went for Ricky, once beaten so savagely while he was drunk that he ended up hospitalized, his life at risk. He was thrown out of college. He was all too familiar with the police. His relationship with his family—as his drinking spiraled downward—turned to ash.

"I was just a hollowed shell of a dude," he said. "I was destined to be a punk kid from Syracuse, leading a mediocre life, if I didn't get sober. I drank to connect, and I drank because I wanted intimacy, and I drank because I wanted to be interesting, and instead it took it all away."

Through friends he met Pat, a retired Syracuse police officer who'd walk into a room and take it over without trying. What Pat became, by being sober, is what Ricky had tried to achieve by getting drunk.

"He was going to love you," Ricky said, "until you loved yourself."

Another guy—call him Marty—said he was introduced to Pat "when I'd been really beaten up by booze." In the early days of recovery, when Marty was broke, Pat would hire him to do odd jobs. For two years, Marty made it without a drink, but he couldn't overcome his own growing despair. Alone, sometimes, he'd contemplate suicide.

One day, over a sandwich, Pat said:

"You're not looking so good."

Marty poured out the truth: He'd assumed quitting drinking would resolve his problems, but there was something else, this utter darkness. The moment, he says now, was his "second surrender." He was clinically depressed. Pat got him to a doctor, got him the right help.

"A rogue, a gent, the John F. Kennedy of Syracuse," Marty said. "Everyone he touched, it was a ripple effect."

As for Ricky, that night in the Buick was a pivot. Plenty of adults had tried to tell him what to do, but no one had ever talked to him like this: Pat spoke of a day when his own drinking brought him to such a place of shame and grief that he pulled over in his patrol car—physically nauseous, emotionally spent—and took his police revolver from its holster, ready to kill himself.

When Pat told the tale, he'd demonstrate exactly how high he'd lifted the gun when his hand stopped.

He thought of his wife Carol, of his children, and he dropped his hand.

"The grace of God," Pat always said.

That was more than 30 years ago. He made his way to "the program," where he said he became a better husband, a better father—and the Irishman he wanted to be. To Ricky, it was as if Pat always remained amazed at his own sobriety, at his good fortune.

He'd found joy. He didn't keep it to himself.

Ricky is now a company executive in Chicago. Marty has a job he loves, and a wonderful family, in Central New York. George is a successful realtor, in New England.

Take their stories, they say, and multiply them by the hundreds. Multiply them again by all the children who now wake up to sober, clear-eyed parents. Think of the thousands in coming generations who won't even know they were saved from escalating damage by this retired cop who helped a grandparent or great-grandparent turn away from drink.

Think of that, and you'll understand why so many wept - even as they laughed - for Patrick Daniel Ahern.

"He was a guy," Ricky said, "who always had that light."

For a few months after the passing of Pat Ahern, there was such grief at the Syracuse Open House—a longtime meeting place for those recovering from addiction—that someone painted a shamrock on Pat's chair and it remained empty, in his honor. That didn't last. Newcomers are always arriving at the Open House, which is the entire goal, the highest purpose. Before long, others new to recovery were walking the same rooms and sitting in the same chair Pat once used. His children know that that was his dream. It's exactly what he would have wanted.

Yet Pat retains a warm presence at the Open House. His framed photograph is in a prominent place, and his wife, Carol, donated a bench in his honor. There is a plaque on it that reads: "God bless all in this house," the words Pat used whenever he addressed men and women embracing the 12 steps, the men and women he saw as his salvation—and as part of his family.

Susie and Matt

Indomitable Daughter, Retired Trooper,
the Meaning of Thanksgiving
Thursday, November 27, 2014

Back in the 1960s, Matt Kerwin was a state trooper, an army veteran who'd started out on a loading dock at the old E. W. Edwards department store. It took a lot to faze him. At the time, they'd still make a father pace a waiting room while his wife delivered a baby, which is what Matt did one day at St. Joseph's Hospital Health Center, until the nurse came out and said:

It's a girl.

A typical moment for that era, but this birth would not be typical. Later, after Matt went home, his wife, Barbara, learned from a doctor that their daughter—their second child—had been born with Down syndrome, a condition that would affect the infant's physical and mental development.

The Kerwins named the infant Susan, although she'd soon and for-ever become Susie. In those first days, Matt put up a good front about the news. But in his moments alone, he felt utterly stunned, with "no idea of what was going to happen."

It was 1969, still in the early stages of the great civil rights movement that changed the landscape for those living with disabilities. A social worker went to Barbara's hospital room while Matt wasn't there and tried to frame her message in the most delicate way:

If they wanted, the Kerwins could send their baby to a state institution.

Wife and husband reacted in the same fashion: This was their daughter. Whatever was coming, the three of them would face it together.

37. Retired state trooper Matt Kerwin and his daughter, Susan. (Gary Walts/ *Post-Standard*)

Even so, Matt didn't know what to expect. In the way these things go, word spread quickly through his neighborhood. Before long, he was stopped by a guy on his street who'd been in the same situation. He offered a thought that Matt sees today as a prophecy:

"Now you're privileged," the guy said. "You've got one of God's angels."

Forty-five years later, on the Monday of this Thanksgiving week, Matt sat at a table in his Syracuse home with Linda, his second wife. His oldest daughter, Lisa Anne, teaches in Switzerland, but Matt and Linda were joined by Susie and her younger brother Matt, 43, a Syracuse lawyer who's not a junior because his middle name is different from his father's.

That hospital waiting room, to "Matt the older"—as he calls himself— seems a long time ago.

Susie is a high school graduate who now has her own apartment, with the help of Transitional Living Services of Onondaga County. The center of her life, the way she copes, is through her digital watch. She gets up every day at 6:30 a.m., on the nose. She turns on the news—for Susie, it's got be Channel 5—and before long, she's out the door to catch her bus to a McDonald's restaurant, at Shop City.

She's worked there for about 23 years. She takes care of the dining room, cleaning tables and making life easier for customers, many of whom know her by name. Every Christmas, she comes home with a bunch of cards, from the regulars. She is puzzled by why people do such nice things for her, although her dad, stepmother, and brother think they know why, exactly.

A clue: ask Susie for the meaning of this week's holiday.

"I'm thankful for everything," she said.

Her brother said that attitude explains why he and his wife, Delisa, consider Susie a role model for their two older children, Noah and Erin; as for Allison, their youngest, Susie is her godmother.

"She taught me not to judge," the younger Matt said of his sister. Possessions, wealth, or status make no difference to her; from early childhood, Matt's watched as Susie greets any new person in her life with the same gentle respect she offers every customer at McDonald's.

Susie, said her brother, builds her life around schedules, around patterns of regularity, a discipline she brings to her favorite pastime: playing Uno. The card game dominates the younger Matt's recollections of his sister, who'd play game after game with Matt in their living room.

Their father, the elder Matt, underlined those points. He remembers how Susie, as a child, endured two open-heart surgeries. She would go on to graduate from Corcoran High School, and her father is fiercely proud of her independence, the way she has her own place and handles every routine of daily life—including calling in her own prescriptions to the pharmacy.

"She teaches me and teaches other people every day," he said. "She teaches us to remember how everyone is important."

That long-ago neighbor, in speaking of Susie's birth, was correct, Matt says now: the Kerwins are privileged, fortunate, to have her in the family. Just how much became clear to Matt a decade ago, at the low point of his life, when Susie's quiet faith helped to bring him back.

Matt and Barbara were married in 1966. Thirty-nine years later, after Matt retired, they were living in Radisson, when Barbara—for no apparent reason—abruptly fell and hit her head. They went to a hospital for some routine tests, and they listened as a doctor once again offered news that shook their lives:

Barbara had a rare and fast-moving cancer, in her brain.

She was a nurse. She understood the finality of her illness. Barbara chose not to go through radiation. She chose to maximize the quality of living, of being with her family, in the brief time she had left.

"All dignity," said Matt, 74, who remains stunned by her grace.

She died seven weeks later. Matt had known her since kindergarten. It seemed unthinkable to go on without her.

"To me, the world had ended," he said.

Yet honoring Barbara demanded remembering what she cared about the most. He thought back to his own parents, to their everyday example of how your family always comes above yourself. He thought of how his wife had been the one to quietly support Susie with her day-to-day appointments, her schedule, her obligations.

"She was the driving force," Matt said of Barbara. "I found out fast just how much she did."

He stepped into that role. He knew Susie missed her mother terribly—on Barbara's birthday, every year, Susie still buys her a card—but he needed his daughter as much as she needed him. He and Barbara had always taken an annual trip to Florida with Susie, and he remembers how he and Susie did it by themselves, not long after his wife died.

They found comfort in each other. On that trip, Matt said, he and Susie "must have played 300 games of freaking Uno."

Back in Syracuse, they did their best to resume their daily lives. Every now and then, with plenty of time around the house to worry, Matt would stand it as long as he could, and then go downtown to the bus station. He'd watch from a distance, unseen to Susie, as his daughter caught her bus—just to make sure she was all right, that no one bothered her.

No one did. Susie handled herself just fine, which only amplified her father's admiration. But Matt's concern was a way of channeling his grief. It helped him heal.

During that time, what Susie meant to their father—and what her presence did for him—"is something I don't think you can quite put into words," said the younger Matt.

A few years went by. The older Matt established a routine, including a part-time job at the pro shop at the Green Lakes golf course. One day, a woman bought a set of clubs. Matt found himself thoroughly enjoying the conversation.

When she left, she forgot to take a club the family now calls "the golden putter."

Matt delivered it to her home, in Radisson. It turned out that Linda Bjorn, too, had lost a spouse to cancer, and that she also had a daughter named Lisa Anne. That provided conversational traction. They talked for a long time. Matt left. He figured he should call her again.

He did. From that point, it all kept rolling.

Matt and Linda were married. Afterward, Susie offered what's become a legendary family toast:

"To the best stepmom I've ever had," she said.

Everyone loved it, just as the way they loved it when Susie—in the years when she swam in the Special Olympics—would somehow manage to wave to the crowd in the middle of each stroke. It was part of the way she finds comfort in repetition, security in patterns.

She still listens to cassette tapes from many years ago—Donny and Marie Osmond are particular favorites—and she makes a point of calling her father every night, at exactly the same time.

Susie tells him she just wants to be sure that he's OK, because her life is built around sure things.

The surest one of all: how much her old man loves her.

There it is. That's her Thanksgiving. But to her father?

It's all her.

Two years after this column was published, for father and daughter, life remains beautifully, reassuringly the same.

PART NINE

Triumph

"This Is the Best Story There Is"

Monday, March 31, 2003

Tyrone Albright was the second Syracuse Orangeman to climb the ladder. Kueth Duany went up first and snipped a few cords from the net, and then it was Albright's turn to do the same thing.

He stood there Sunday, with his head near the rim in the Pepsi Arena, in Albany. He paused just long enough to find his wife, his daughter, and his best friend in the crowd. He needed to lock eyes with some folks who understood:

Tyrone Albright, near the top step, going to the Final Four.

You can sing wonderful songs about the freshman trio of Carmelo Anthony, Gerry McNamara, and Billy Edelin. You can admire the heroics of Duany and Hakim Warrick. You can talk about the role-playing of Jeremy McNeil, Josh Pace, and Craig Forth.

Yet Albright, 26, a guard who has officially played only 20 minutes this season, may have traveled the most unlikely road of all. "I spent all my life wondering what this feeling would be, to be up on that ladder," he said.

Albright is a married guy, the father of three. He didn't start playing the game until he was a teenager in Syracuse. He learned his skills on playground courts at Onondaga Park and Sunnycrest. He dreamed of playing varsity basketball at Corcoran High School.

As a senior, he went out for the team, and got cut.

He and Keturah Cochren, his wife, had a baby barely a year after they got out of Corcoran. After high school, Albright didn't go to college. He held several jobs to support his growing family, including a position with the Boys & Girls Club. In 1996, the last time SU went to the Final Four,

293

38. Tyrone Albright celebrates with Syracuse University fans at Manley Field House, after his team returned from earning a visit to college basketball's Final Four. (Michelle Gabel/*Post-Standard*)

Albright sat with a group of children at the club and watched the Orange-men lose to Kentucky in the championship game.

He could not imagine that he would someday play for Jim Boeheim. He could not imagine that he would sink a three-pointer in the Carrier Dome while playing against an AAU team that included SU legend Lawrence Moten. He could not imagine that he'd be going to New Orleans, for the Final Four.

"For me, this is the best story there is," Albright said.

It started when he enrolled at Onondaga Community College. He was 24. He went out for basketball, made the team, and became a star. "That was because of my wife," Albright said. "She always believed I could do more than I ever thought that I could do."

He also credits Tremaine Crawford, a friend so close that Albright describes him as "my brother." They learned to play basketball together, on city playgrounds. Crawford was in Albany, watching as Albright snipped the net.

Crawford understood. He knew that Albright didn't go to SU dreaming of basketball. Albright wanted a diploma and better computer skills. But Dave Pasiak, Albright's junior college coach, quietly called Boeheim. Pasiak suggested that Albright would be a terrific walk-on player. Boeheim listened. Albright became an Orangeman.

Even though his name rarely shows up in box scores, Albright is integral to this young team.

In the chaos after Sunday's win over Oklahoma, McNamara hunted Albright down on the court. He credited Albright with helping him to make it through the season. McNamara and his fellow freshmen sometimes called Albright "grampa," or "old man," but they listened to him, like an older brother.

Now, Albright wants to cherish these last days before the Final Four. Much has been made of Edelin's harsh suspension by the NCAA, but Albright is paying an even higher price. He is a junior who lost his eligibility for his senior year. The NCAA penalized him for playing in a three-on-three tournament five years ago.

"That really hurts to finally get to this level, and then to have a year taken away from me," said Albright, whose goal was some real playing time with next year's Orangemen. "So this is it, my only year, and the rest of these guys have really made it worth my while."

For many residents of Syracuse, Albright is the personal connection to this team. His oldest daughter, Patricia, seven, is a pupil at the Central New York Charter School. His daughter Quiarra, five, attends Dr. Weeks Elementary. And Albright is a legend for the children at the Boys & Girls Club on Shonnard Street, who see him as proof of why they shouldn't quit.

Albright doesn't take that lightly. He remembers just how far it can seem from city streets up to the dome. He remembers how much it hurt to get cut from his high school team. He remembers loudmouths on the playgrounds who would taunt him as "sorry," and then tell him to go home.

Instead, with all our hopes, he's going to the Final Four.

Thirteen years after he stood on the ladder to cut the nets, Tyrone Albright works as an IT technical security analyst with Excellus, in Syracuse. His family is his priority, but he said many Central New Yorkers still remember his role on the 2003 SU team, which won the national championship. Albright hopes that might provide inspiration for young people who—in any fashion—face what seem to be insurmountable odds.

Finally, We Know We Don't Deserve to Lose

Wednesday, April 9, 2003

Nothing really changed. The weather is still crummy. We still need to go to work, and the kids still need to go to school.

Nothing changed, except for everything.

The Syracuse University Orangemen are NCAA basketball champions. They defeated Kansas Monday 81–78, not that you need a reminder. An awful lot of us allowed our kids to stay up and watch this one, and the kids were thrilled and happy to cheer for a champion, and we have reason to be even happier for the kids.

At the instant SU won, the children were freed from ever being us. They will not go through life wondering if they'll live to see their team win it all, and wondering in some secret way if they deserve to lose.

Today, our kids know how it feels to win a championship. It is there for them, if they live to be 100. And you can bet that somehow they sense just how much it means to us.

This whole thing was mystic, beyond mere basketball. In the past, it almost seemed as if the Orangemen absorbed some anxiety from us, as if they knew some regional phantom was working against them. Not this time. These teenage "Orange babies" weren't rattled by anything.

After the Texas game in the NCAA semifinals—when Syracuse could have lost and the whole season still would have felt just fine—people around Syracuse somehow knew the Orangemen were going to pull it off, in the same way they had known so many other times that Syracuse would lose.

Even so, until it happened, they were terrified to say it.

Now, in these days after, every minute feels brand new. There is no second-guessing, no wondering, no need for the "what-ifs." There is no

297

sick feeling in the solitude as we drive our cars, no replaying one jump shot countless times in our minds, no wondering how things might have changed if one more free throw had gone through.

None of that matters. The Orangemen are champions.

The weather is no different. The air is cold, the sky stone gray. New and bigger worries are rolling into town. Carrier Corp. executives are making ominous sounds about "significant challenges" at their DeWitt plant, a bedrock industry that employs 2,700 men and women.

We're at war. The state is broke. The Middle East is nitroglycerin. The plan for Destiny USA nears its third birthday, with no construction underway.

Despite all that, people walking alone on downtown sidewalks wore smiles on a chill Tuesday morning, still caught up in a feeling they've never had before.

Syracuse did it. We all want to be the best at something big, and college basketball is about as big as it gets. The sport has become the true national pastime. Millions upon millions of boys and girls grow up playing ball in cities, suburbs, and small towns, with the best going on to Division I, and the very best of them going to the Final Four.

Where the Orangemen became national champions.

Monday's game ended and nothing changed, except this feeling in the gut. It is akin to the relief of finishing a job put off too long, except that SU basketball is out of our control—in the same way, really, as the fortunes of our city.

Whether the Orangemen win or lose falls on the shoulders of some young men and their coach, which should hardly reflect on how we feel about ourselves. But it does. By season's end, for many of us, they are somehow who we are. And if some phantom always conspired to wreck their finest hour, the same phantom who guided Keith Smart's jumper through the hole, then it also seemed to be conspiring against us.

The phantom went along to New Orleans, and it tiptoed just past the 3-point arc with Michael Lee, a Jayhawk who took the ball with the seconds winding down and squared off for the jumper that would once more crush our hopes.

Hakim Warrick, wearing orange, rose up and knocked it out of bounds. Nothing changed, except for everything. The phantom is at rest.

If you want a statement of how much this game meant to an entire region, consider this: in the days and weeks after the victory over Kansas, many Central New Yorkers went to cemeteries and left mementoes of the championship at the tombstones of loved ones—true believers who never got the chance to see it happen.

A Career Cued on a Championship

Monday, November 8, 2004

Babe Cranfield wanted his billiards cue. In the last days of his life at Crouse Hospital, Babe kept telling his wife, Ruth, he knew exactly where it was. He said the cue was locked inside the poolroom at the Brunswick Holiday Bowl, where Babe spent countless hours practicing his game.

Ruth saw no reason to tell him that the Holiday Bowl had been knocked down years ago. Instead, she'd lean forward and gently offer him the truth: "Babe, don't worry. I've got your cue."

"You're sure," he'd reply. "You're sure that you've got it?"

She was sure. She remains in possession of what's now a precious artifact. On Halloween, Arthur "Babe" Cranfield died at 89. While Ruth doesn't know the official cause of death, she said Babe was weakened years ago by a stroke. Last month he took a bad fall in his bathroom, and at the hospital the doctors discovered cancer in his colon.

Babe died after surgery. Ruth decided against a funeral or calling hours. They'd lived on Livingston Avenue in Syracuse for almost 60 years, and she figured she'd be in contact with the people who always stayed in touch with Babe.

For those of you who've never heard his name, Babe was one of the great pool players in American history. As a child, he learned to shoot left-handed in his father's billiards hall in New York City—where he got his nickname by following around a regular named Babe Ruth—and the boy kept shooting when his dad opened a hall in Syracuse.

"We were never rich," Ruth Cranfield said. A few old trophies dominate the mantel in her living room. At 15, her husband won the national junior billiards championship. In 1938, he captured the first of three consecutive national amateur titles, which turned him into a young Central New York celebrity.

It would be a long time before the addition of the most important trophy. Babe served in the Army Air Force during World War II, where he became pool champion of the American armed forces. He returned home to resume a successful pro career, and at one point in the late 1940s he finished second in the world.

Still, he could not quite achieve the status he'd held before the war. In 1951, Babe retired. He dedicated his time to Ruth and his two children. He became an executive in the Muzak Company, and he put his pool cue in the attic, the cue that Babe told reporters was given to him by a friend, the great Willie Mosconi.

Sunday, Ruth gently placed that cue atop a pile of scrapbooks on her table.

Pick it up, and it has the feel of a relic. The polish is almost entirely gone from the wood. It still carries a Band-Aid that Babe used to keep the wrap from coming off the handle.

In 1963, bothered by the idea that he'd never won the world championship—and needing some extra money to help get his boys through college—Babe retrieved the cue from the attic.

He began a comeback that earned him a shot for the world's title in 1964 against Luther "Wimpy" Lassiter, one of the dominant players of the era. The match was held in the Palm Room of the Commodore Hotel in Manhattan. Lassiter was the big favorite. LeRoy Neiman, the famous sports artist, showed up and did a painting. It shows Babe, in black tie, taking a shot as spectators watch from behind velvet ropes.

At one point, Babe made 147 consecutive shots, described by a pool historian as "the greatest pressure run" in the annals of the sport.

That night, Babe and Ruth drank champagne from a silver cup that's now set out on the mantel, the cup awarded to pool's world champion.

"He was a gentleman," Ruth said, and she started to cry, the only time she cried as she spoke about her husband. They met on a blind date in the late 1930s. When she graduated from Central High School, he sent her a dozen roses. Years later, after their marriage, she'd travel along when he went on tour, sometimes waiting for hours in the car if Babe had to play in an especially rough hall.

Her husband was superstitious, Ruth said. He wouldn't change his tie if he was playing well. He'd always make sure that he walked in the same door, and he always set his chalk on the same diamond on the table.

"Once he'd broken the balls," Ruth said, "he knew every ball he was going to play."

That is one trait of the great ones: They all think in the future. Another is the balance between confidence and utter humility. Six years ago, in an article in *Esquire* magazine, writer J. D. Dolan described how he and Babe once walked into Cap's Cue Club on Teall Avenue, where a man was showing off by making the same difficult shot again and again.

Babe, in a voice loud enough to be heard around the hall, used a profanity to describe the man's game.

"If you want to be a champion," he told Dolan, "practice your weaknesses."

The New York Times, *in covering Babe Cranfield's upset victory over Lassiter in 1964 for the world championship, noted that Babe would walk all the way around the table or fiddle with the chalk or take a long, long time lining up a shot—a strategy intended to frustrate and derail Lassiter, who played in fast-moving, brilliant bursts. As for Cap's Cue Club, it closed a few years ago. Regulars still mourn its passing on a Facebook page, where they often recall routine visits from one of the greatest pool players who ever lived.*

Founder of St. Pat's Parade
Never Paraded Her Ego

Friday, December 29, 2006

Richie Walsh, a Syracuse police captain, is a longtime member of the Ancient Order of Hibernians. He first heard of the idea for a local St. Patrick's parade in 1982, during the old Irish Festival at the New York State Fairgrounds.

Nancy Duffy, he recalls, was one of many people standing in a circle beneath an outdoor tent. She said it was time for the Irish to throw a parade for everyone in Syracuse.

Immediately, Walsh said, others tried shooting holes in the idea: It wouldn't work. It would be too hard to put together. They'd never reach agreement on the right place or the right date.

Duffy refused to budge. "She didn't want to hear any opinions to the contrary," Walsh said. Duffy said the parade would need to be downtown on a Saturday, because the mission would be involving the larger community.

"She already had it in her head how it was going to be," Walsh said.

Duffy was buried Thursday. She died Dec. 22, after a long illness. She will be remembered, certainly, as a passionate journalist for WSYR-TV (Channel 9).

The parade is her civic monument. It offers a blueprint for getting things done in Syracuse, where the success of the parade is a vivid contrast to the maddening Upstate tendency to smother fine ideas before they get a chance to work.

"She understood that a lot of good can be done if you're willing to give someone else the credit," said Joe O'Hara, executive director of P.E.A.C.E.

Inc. and an early parade volunteer. In the mid-1990s, Duffy persuaded O'Hara to do that job for a while. O'Hara said he was reluctant, but Duffy made an offer that was hard to refuse:

"She told me she'd do all the work," O'Hara said. All she needed was someone else to be the public face of the parade.

If you moved to Syracuse in the last 10 or 15 years, you probably can't imagine this town without the St. Patrick's Parade. The event has become a green and festive civic holiday. In the snowiest big city on average in the United States, it provides symbolic passage from winter into the hope of spring.

Yet it did not exist until 1983. In the early 1980s, the food and beverage director at the Hotel Syracuse was John Farrell, a native of Ireland and an early ally of Duffy's. He remembers sitting with her at a table in the hotel while she poured out a vision for the parade as it still operates today.

"In the beginning, a lot of people said, 'Nahhh!'" recalled Farrell, who put contemptuous emphasis on that final sound.

His memory of Duffy matches that of Walsh: She never wavered in understanding what the parade should be. She knew that it had to be on South Salina Street, and she knew it had to climax at the grand hotel.

Beyond all else, Duffy's friends recall her shrewd, self-effacing way of handling potential opposition. "There are a lot of divisions among the Irish in Syracuse," O'Hara said. Plenty of people thought any St. Patrick's parade ought to be based on Tipperary Hill.

"Sure, that's where they wanted it originally, but Nancy knew it had to be for the entire city of Syracuse, not just one neighborhood," said Van Sterio, then-director of catering at the Hotel Syracuse. "It had to be downtown."

Duffy smoothed out most conflicts before they had a chance to happen. As a gesture of respect to the Irish community, many parade meetings were held on Tipp Hill. Still, the carping didn't stop about who should participate and how much the organizers could afford to spend.

"At that point, when there were too many opinions, she stopped holding committee meetings," recalled Sheila Shattuck, a close friend of Duffy's and another parade founder. "Then it became, 'We're going to do this by fiat.'"

Even so, Shattuck said, Duffy remained careful to give committee members the public credit.

The result was a parade that succeeded as if it had been around for a century. "My God," Sterio said. "A 3 1/2-hour parade? In Syracuse? Are you kidding?"

As it grew, as it became one of the biggest attractions in the region, Duffy intentionally avoided the spotlight.

"She didn't do it for herself," said Kathleen Kelly, director of Project Children, which brings boys and girls from Northern Ireland to Syracuse, for a summer respite. With the late Tom Higgins, former chairman of Merchants National Bank and Trust Co., Kelly was one of the parade's first grand marshals. She soon realized that Duffy's interest was in results, not personal attention.

Duffy was willing to sacrifice credit to soothe larger and needier egos. She understood that you inevitably face pockets of resistance to visionary change. But she respected the history and traditions of Syracuse, and she was adept at the kind of sure-handed juggling that could ease multiple fears and still create a fine result.

More than anything, say Duffy's friends, she was always moving forward. Not long ago, Kelly spoke with her old friend for the last time. Duffy was clearly failing, in need of constant care, but the conversation swerved away from Duffy's illness.

Instead, Kelly said, they talked about the next parade.

The route of the wildly successful St. Patrick's in downtown Syracuse now has its own set of signs: in green and white, each one proclaims, "Nancy Duffy Lane."

The Company of Legends

Karen DeCrow Takes Her Place
in Women's Hall of Fame
Monday, October 12, 2009

Karen DeCrow, striking gray hair parted in the middle, strode into the National Women's Hall of Fame in Seneca Falls. It was barely an hour since she had given her speech at Sunday's enshrinement ceremony at the New York Chiropractic College, a speech that led to a standing ovation from most of the packed house.

DeCrow, who has a law practice in Syracuse, did not expect her own plaque to be ready. But there it was, leaning against a display that will showcase the 10 new inductees. "Look at this," she said to Meg O'Connor, a New York City lawyer who once clerked for DeCrow. The two women stepped back to study the inscription, while O'Connor recalled the influence of her old friend.

"She taught me to take my job seriously, but never to forget how to laugh," said O'Connor, who drove in from New York. "She taught me to never give up my integrity, to (never) get so lost in a case you forget who it's about. And she taught me to kill your enemies with kindness, because that way they never know how smart you are."

Hearing that, in this hall of honor, DeCrow began to laugh.

She is a prolific writer, a civil rights lawyer, a former president of the National Organization for Women. In Syracuse, she is to feminism what Dolph Schayes is to basketball—so familiar, and so well-known, that we sometimes forget her national significance.

306

39. Karen DeCrow on her first visit as an inductee to the National Women's Hall of Fame, Seneca Falls. (Michelle Gabel/*Post-Standard*)

No one forgot it Sunday in Seneca Falls. Donna Jennings Carter, a law student from Atlanta, was one of the reverent spectators who stood in line at DeCrow's table for handshakes or autographs. DeCrow was inducted along with such luminaries as Emma Lazarus, whose memorable poem about the Statue of Liberty—"The New Colossus"—was read out loud by a descendant.

As for DeCrow, she winged it with her speech. She was funny, appreciative, warm. She spoke with appreciation of the 19th-century founders of the feminist movement. She expressed awe at the growth of opportunities for American women in her lifetime, but she also offered a challenge:

"We have an enormous task in front of us," she said, as the place erupted in applause. "We have to change the roles of boys and men."

True equality can't happen, she said afterward, until more men willingly embrace the hard work at home with children. At the hall, to underline that point, she made her way to the plaque of Charlotte Perkins Gilman, who in the early 20th century rejected the notion that women are intrinsically drawn to the playroom or the kitchen.

Gilman wanted economic equality for women. Like DeCrow, she did not buy into the belief that boys and girls naturally drift toward distinct roles, based on gender. "I don't think men and women are any different," said DeCrow, who began moving from plaque to plaque at the hall.

Many depicted women with whom DeCrow, 71, was personally familiar—feminist Betty Friedan, former Supreme Court Justice Sandra Day O'Connor, Secretary of State Hillary Rodham Clinton. Yet DeCrow offered some of her warmest tributes for those who are not quite as well-known, such as Margaret Sanger, who campaigned for birth control almost a century ago, or Martha Griffiths, a congresswoman who made sure that gender rights were part of the Civil Rights act of 1964.

The act gave a foothold to a movement that was already gaining strength. When DeCrow was a young woman, most American careers were all but closed to women. They rarely became engineers, doctors, or lawyers. A little girl could aspire to be a teacher, nurse, or clerk, but not much else.

In her lifetime, DeCrow helped to make those walls crumble and fall.

"The young females today, they seem to think they can do anything," said DeCrow, sounding quietly amazed. She kept returning to that thought as she wandered through the hall, giving reverent credit to the giants on the wall, these women who had served as heroes throughout her life.

As of Sunday, in Seneca Falls, they are her peers.

Karen DeCrow died of cancer in 2014. On the day of her passing, in a situation the younger DeCrow could hardly have imagined, the two most powerful elected officials in the region were women: Syracuse Mayor Stephanie Miner and Onondaga County Executive Joanie Mahoney. As for DeCrow, those closest to her say she took satisfaction in the wave of change she helped to bring about, and that she died without fear or regrets.

Seeger on Libba

Genius Cast in Bronze

Wednesday, September 19, 2012

Pete Seeger is 93, living in Dutchess County, but the groundbreaking American folk singer tells the tale as if it happened yesterday: How his stepmother, Ruth Crawford Seeger, went shopping in the 1940s in a Washington, D.C., department store. How her young daughter, Peggy Seeger, wandered away. How Ruth was searching frantically when "this tall and stately black woman . . . stepped up with little Peggy."

While the store employee went by the name of Elizabeth Cotten, the Seeger children were soon calling her "Libba."

The friendship unleashed a lifetime of public creativity that will be honored October 2 in Syracuse, where a bronze casting of Cotten will be dedicated at State and Castle Streets, in a park that already carries her name.

"She'd be very proud," said Johnine Rankin, a granddaughter, "and I can just see her telling everyone, 'Love one another.'"

Cotten settled in Syracuse to join others in her family. Such luminaries as members of the Grateful Dead would sometimes make the pilgrimage to see her. They knew the legend: a left-hander, Cotten created an extraordinary sound by turning a right-handed guitar upside-down.

She died in 1987, four years after the dedication of the Libba Cotten Grove. As for the sculpture, Otis Jennings—city parks commissioner until 2002—spent years putting together enough support to make it happen. Syracuse University, with the backing of Chancellor Nancy Cantor, kicked in about $13,000. State Senator John DeFrancisco, of Syracuse, came up with a similar amount from the state. The Central New York Community Foundation added $4,500.

Jennings praised many contributors for their efforts, including Francis Parks and members of the Libba Cotten Committee, Jesse Dowdell of the Southwest Community Center, and current city parks commissioner Baye Muhammad.

"It's such a thrill to see it up: it's done and it's beautiful," said Jennings, speaking of the way sculptor Sharon BuMann depicted Cotten with a guitar. "You need a living monument like this to give people in the community a connection, to give children that connection, so they can dream about the possibilities out there."

Cotten's fame certainly underlines the nature of a dream. Dan Ward, curator of the Erie Canal Museum and a friend of Cotten's, said she taught herself to play as a child in North Carolina by secretly practicing on a string instrument her brother made by hand; because she was left-handed, Ward said, her family had forbidden her to touch it. Cotten wrote "Freight Train" as a girl, and the song is now recognized as an American classic. Still, her music might never have found a larger audience if she had missed that chance meeting with Ruth Crawford Seeger.

Pete said his stepmother was in a bind: she had a chance to make some money as a teacher, but she had no one to look after her young children. Cotten, needing extra work, took the job. The story goes that Peggy and her brother Mike—"He was the best musician in our family," Pete said—listened, deeply moved, when Cotten began to play guitar. Before long, Pete said, the children were begging Cotten to let them do the dishes so they could hear her do another song.

Mike Seeger, who died in 2009, "helped develop her genius," Pete said. Once Mike's musical career got underway, he'd often give Libba a chance to play, until her star burned so brightly that he told her: "You don't need me."

Cotten's unique style made her an emissary for folk music in its purest form, and also gave her a compelling stage presence. "The way she played 'Freight Train' was a very clear example of the African way of playing the guitar," Pete said.

The guitar was primarily an upper-class instrument until Americans began 19th-century incursions into Mexico, he said. Guitars started finding their way into the hands of working people, including men and women held as slaves.

"They invented an African way of playing it," Pete said, "with a steady beat with the bass strings, and a syncopated melody with notes on the top strings, and this style was picked up by white people . . . they called it 'Travis picking,' because Merle Travis was very good at it . . . and once you graduate from 'wham, wham, wham,' playing chords, you know you're Travis picking."

Pete doesn't travel that much anymore, and he doubts he will be here for the dedication. But he vividly remembers the first few times he saw Cotten perform, and how she surprised him with an unexpected ritual. Once she finished her set, "she would step off the little stage, or wherever she was playing, and she'd walk down the aisle and as people started to stand up, she'd embrace them . . . 20, 30, even 40 people."

In his long career, Seeger had never seen anything like it. It was sincere. It was communal.

It was folk, in purest form.

The Libba Cotten sculpture was dedicated on October 2, 2012. Dana Klipp, who often performed with Cotten, offered a version of "Freight Train," ignoring the gray skies. Otis Jennings, former Syracuse parks commissioner and a champion of the sculpture, told the Post-Standard: *"To suffer all she suffered, and to still be successful, that is the one message we want to convey to every child in the neighborhood: 'You can do it. Don't give up.'"*

A Return to St. Pat's, 50 Years after "Adios"

Tuesday, October 15, 2013

For many in the Tipperary Hill neighborhood of Syracuse, the conversion of the empty St. Patrick's School into apartments offered a signal of community revival.

Mike Quinn, certainly, shared in that feeling.

Yet excuse him if he also thought:

Adios.

That was just about the last word Quinn heard 50 years ago at the old St. Pat's school, a primarily Irish-American institution closed in 2006 by the Diocese of Syracuse. Quinn, now 67, did most of his schooling there. He started as a kindergartener in the 1950s, when St. Pat's went all the way through high school.

Quinn was supposed to graduate in 1964. He didn't quite make it.

He and a buddy, Chris "Smoky" Davis, got together last week to recall what happened. It is worth noting that "Smoky" is a classic Tipp Hill nickname: there was a fire at Davis' house when he was a child, and a firefighter carried the boy to his anxious family. Someone shouted, "Is he all right?"

The firefighter replied: "He's just a little smoky."

At St. Pat's, Davis and Quinn shared a similar fate. The two young men—like so many others—ran afoul of Monsignor Thomas Driscoll, a legendary pastor.

Driscoll ruled the school "with an iron fist," Quinn said. He was a big man without much hair, which led the boys—from a safe distance—to label him "the Cueball." He kept a close and intimidating eye on classroom behavior, and he'd dispense old-school justice in front of full assemblies.

Students who misbehaved were liable to get paddled in Driscoll's office, Quinn said. Disrespect him to his face? Davis, who does a dead-on imitation of the old priest's growling brogue, recalls how he once talked back and got slapped so hard that Davis swears the monsignor's palm hit him in the cheek while Driscoll's fingers stretched around to catch the far side of Davis' head.

As for Quinn, Driscoll told him that if St. Pat's had classes in clowning, then Quinn might have earned at least one "A." The two young men were part of a group of friends nicknamed "the Mafia." They had a wooden shack they used as a clubhouse, by the railroad tracks.

The other name for the group was "the 5 O'Clock Club," because the monsignor would routinely keep the boys after school until 5 p.m., sweeping floors as punishment. Quinn and Davis, looking back on it, said members of the Mafia would occasionally retaliate with one-liners—although they often paid a high price.

They recall the time when Driscoll ordered one of their teenage friends to spend a week in kindergarten, because the monsignor said that's where he belonged. The boys would walk by the classroom and see their pal, long legs jammed behind a tiny desk. At an assembly, Driscoll singled out the young man for a question:

Being that he was in kindergarten, could he say what you get if you add two plus two?

The boy replied he wasn't sure: he and his classmates, he said, were more worried about tying their shoes.

His friends choked back laughter. Driscoll didn't laugh. He kicked him out of school.

Quinn and Davis came to the same hard end. At the beginning of senior year, Quinn showed up for an assembly where students were typically assigned to a new homeroom. Driscoll summoned Quinn to the stage, in front of everyone, and gave him a brief one-word message:

"Adios."

Quinn was finished. He hadn't passed Regents exams in geometry or world history, requirements of the time at St. Pat's. Quinn stood there, stunned, until Driscoll repeated the command.

"You're gone!" Driscoll hollered. "Adios! Pronto, Tonto!"

Quinn went outside. On the sidewalk, he joined many guys in the same boat. They pretended to celebrate, although they dreaded going home to face their parents. They scattered to other high schools: Westhill, Most Holy Rosary, Central Tech. Quinn's parents sent him to Sacred Heart, a heavily Polish-American parish, where his schoolmates took to calling him "Quinnkowski."

Life for Michael Quinn turned out just fine. He spent a career with the telephone company. He married the former Beatrice Carr, and they raised a family in their Camillus home. Twelve years ago, Quinn retired. A few years later, after 39 years of marriage, Beatrice died. Their house, to Quinn, suddenly seemed very empty.

That gave him plenty of time to reflect. He bore Monsignor Driscoll no ill will; he'd even showed up, in 1970, at the old priest's funeral. Looking back on it, he figures he needed a boyhood lesson, and the monsignor they called "the Cueball" was ready to provide it.

"I respect him to the highest," Quinn said.

Even so, you'd love to hear what Driscoll might say about where Quinn hangs his hat today.

Not long ago, Quinn learned the Hayner Hoyt Corp. was converting St. Pat's into apartments. He stopped by the old school, where Kevin Valente of Sutton Real Estate showed him a nice unit in what used to be classroom 10B.

When the place opened in July, Quinn was the first tenant—the absolute first—to settle down in the school from which he'd once been expelled. The move made sense. The space is right. He is close to his old neighborhood and to his favorite pubs, and he insists he had no larger motive.

Still, the 5 O'Clock Club remains in close touch. His new residence is already a matter of legend, real life turned into one classic Tipp Hill tale. Not long ago, some of his old friends stopped by Quinn's place for a visit. As they left, many turned and offered a farewell, a punch line, a benediction:

Adios.

As of this autumn, Mike Quinn, now 70, will have spent three years living in the old St. Patrick's—tying him for the number of years he spent there, in high school.

I Paid My Way

Longest-Lived Woman from
Ireland Reflects on Epic Past
Monday, March 17, 2014

Kathleen Hayes Rollins Snavely knew that I was coming. Some longtime friends—David Liddell and his daughter, Laurie Black—stopped to visit her today at the Centers at St. Camillus in Geddes, where Kathleen lives. They carried a proclamation signed by Syracuse Mayor Stephanie Miner and Onondaga County Executive Joanie Mahoney.

St. Patrick's Day, it turns out, was also Kathleen Snavely Day in the city and county.

Even before David and Laurie dropped off that proclamation, they'd asked Kathleen if it would be all right if they brought along this journalist who'd written a couple of columns about her.

Yes, she said. That would be fine.

Provided that I agreed to a few conditions.

Kathleen is 112. She was born in 1902 in County Clare, Ireland. Genealogists say she is the longest-lived person born in the history of the Republic of Ireland, and the second longest-lived ever recorded from the Irish isle. Only Annie Scott, who died 113 years after her birth in Northern Ireland, has lived a longer life.

To Kathleen, who turned 112 in February, the attention is overblown. David Liddell told me Kathleen doesn't like being identified only by her age, when she is—as she established Monday—a sharp, funny, and occasionally formidable human being, in full.

315

40. Kathleen Snavely at 112. (Sean Kirst/*Post-Standard*)

Before she'd do an interview, she told me there were some things she wanted cleared up in the paper. Chief among them: I'd mentioned in one column that when Kathleen sailed from Ireland, the ship's manifest listed her as "a domestic."

The manifest was wrong.

"A domestic, I never was," said Kathleen, with some fire. "I'd heard about all the rich people on James Street, and about all the immigrants who worked in those houses, but I wasn't here to change sheets or wash clothes."

She was 19 when she arrived, in 1921. She remembers seeing the Statue of Liberty from the ship—she held up her arms, her eyes wide, mimicking the reaction of the passengers—and she settled in Syracuse, where she lived on the third floor of an uncle's house.

For a time she worked at what was called the state school, for those with developmental disabilities, before she took a job at the E. W. Edwards department store. Her mother had a friend in Syracuse, a widow, with a couple of daughters. The two young women befriended Kathleen. They had boyfriends. They wanted her to have one, too.

"I didn't want to dance the American dances," Kathleen said. She kept rejecting young men her friends brought to her, until they introduced her to this guy whose job was flipping pancakes:

Roxie Rollins.

"It was a Godsend," she said. "We were very much in love. It was the secret of our success."

In the early days, they'd meet downtown and go to movies at the grand theaters of the 1920s. Afterward, Roxie would attempt to buy her dinner. She'd refuse. He was baffled. He confided to a mutual friend that he wondered why she kept rejecting him.

It wasn't rejection. She already loved him. She just thought that he was broke and she didn't want him spending money on her.

"I paid my way," said Kathleen, who soon agreed to marry Roxie. It was the best decision of her life: she was alone here, she said, and he "was the greatest guy."

They never had children. Kathleen joined Roxie in building the old Seneca Dairy in Syracuse into a prosperous business. A young immigrant who hadn't gone to college was soon working in the office and helping to manage the books.

Years later, after she was twice widowed, she made significant donations to both the University of Findlay in Ohio and to Syracuse University, where she provided some of the seed money for the Whitman School of Management.

She liked the idea of young men and women, from lives of struggle, receiving an education.

"Not a penny was given to me," Kathleen said. "I'm giving them what I didn't get."

Her voice still carries the lilt, the music of Ireland. For St. Patrick's Day, she wore a green sweater, green slacks, a shawl with green highlights. Around her neck: a shamrock charm, a rosary, a necklace of green beads.

I sat by her side, taking notes. If she told some personal story she didn't want published, she'd reach down, grab my wrist and say:

"Don't write this."

She wasn't kidding. You won't find those stories here.

I mentioned how a reader, Judie Thelen, told me she credits Kathleen with saving her aunt's life.

Kathleen was surprised anyone remembered the story.

It was true.

She and Judie's aunt, Harriette Shaw, both lived at the Regency Tower in Syracuse. They remained close friends after Harriette moved to a little house near Le Moyne College. Harriette and Kathleen spoke by phone every day.

Until, one day, they didn't.

"I didn't hear from her and I said to myself, 'Something's happened,'" said Kathleen, who asked a friend to give her a ride to Harriette's. "We drive up and we go to the door and it's unlocked, and her little dog—I don't remember the name—came up to us."

They went in. They found Harriette unconscious on the floor. They called for help and emergency crews arrived.

Harriette recovered. She lived until 2005.

"I like people," Kathleen said. "I really like people."

She enjoys St. Camillus, where old friends often visit, where she'll often go to Mass or a rosary service. She always appreciates the seasons. In the warm weather, she watches birds at a feeder through a big window in her room.

Her memory is astounding, even if she claims that it's not: "I've forgotten a lot of history," she said. "I've been living my whole life. I didn't think I'd need to remember these things."

Throughout a long conversation, she was always in good-natured control. She gracefully deflected questions about her sheer longevity, choosing to joke about where she'll end up once she's gone. As for St. Patrick's Day, "it wasn't as much of a fuss" in her childhood as it is in Syracuse, she said.

Yet she loved Ireland. Her family didn't have much money. She came to the United States for a shot at a better life. Once she established herself, she sent what she could to her family in County Clare.

On the day she left her homeland, as a girl of 19, she rolled from bed just after midnight. Some neighbors were ready to take her to her ship.

Bags packed, she lined up her two younger brothers. The grief of that moment returned to her face at St. Camillus, more than 90 years later:

"I gave them a lecture about growing up," she said. "Work hard and you be careful about drinking and grow up to be someone to be proud of."

They did. So did Kathleen. Tale told, she leaned back, looked at my notebook and said:

"Is that enough?"

In 2015, Kathleen Hayes Rollins Snavely officially became the longest-lived person ever born on the Irish isle. She died in July, at 113. David Liddell, her longtime friend, offered this succinct thought: "We were fortunate to meet such a person as she."

Heart! Heart! Heart!

Jerry Berrigan on Greatest Moment
in Life of Conscience

Sunday, July 25, 2015

Jerry Berrigan can offer plenty of firsthand stories about giants.

Dorothy Day, one of the founders of the legendary Catholic Worker movement, was a friend. Day believed in "a revolution of the heart," in the idea of hospitality and community for those who have the least.

When Day visited Jerry and his wife Carol in Syracuse, she spent a night at their home in the Valley.

Just over 50 years ago, Jerry traveled to Selma for the great march for voting rights, part of a contingent led by the Rev. Charles Brady of Syracuse. By sheer chance, they had an opportunity to meet Dr. Martin Luther King Jr.

That was three years before King was shot to death by an assassin. Berrigan said his overwhelming reaction—in a place where he witnessed the essence of raw hatred—was a sense of just how willing King was to put himself at ultimate risk, for a higher cause.

Decades earlier, as a young American soldier during World War II, Jerry had served Mass for Padre Pio in Sicily. Pio was revered among Catholics for bearing the stigmata, the wounds of Christ, and he'd later be canonized as a Catholic saint.

At 95, Jerry offers those tales in a voice as soft as a whisper, an English teacher pausing to contemplate the impact of each word, face illuminated by sunlight pouring into the house. Yet when asked about his

41. Jerry and Carol Berrigan. (John Berry/*Post-Standard*)

larger approach to the world—how he found his way to the principles linked to the family name—he does not turn to moments found in history books.

He speaks instead of his father, asking for a glass of water.

Of his mother, telling a stranger to come in. Of the moment when Jerry pushed a doorbell at a back door in East Syracuse, and the gift was the strength that sustains him today.

In those stories, amid times of global grief, he finds his hope.

Jerry and his brother Dan are the last surviving siblings of a Syracuse family renowned for activism. Dan and Phil, another of six brothers, became Catholic priests. In 1963, after witnessing King's "I Have a Dream" speech, they wrote an open letter to the *Post-Standard*, challenging Syracuse to confront rigid borders of segregation.

"Those who help others to freedom," Dan and Phil concluded, "have themselves taken the first step toward becoming free men."

In that way, like Jerry, they lived out a family creed. A few years later, their opposition to the war in Vietnam—including the burning of federal records at a draft board in Maryland—led to arrests that gave Dan and Phil an international profile, and put them on the cover of *Time* magazine.

Phil died in 2002. Dan, in fragile health, lives with other retired Jesuits at Fordham University.

Until their arthritis grew too severe for them to use their pens, he and Jerry would write to each other every week. Even now, when it is difficult for them to speak by telephone, Jerry's grown children serve as intermediaries in sending messages back and forth.

In their 90s, the brothers share an appreciation that became their way of life:

They are among the last witnesses to the quiet mission of their parents, Tom and Frida Berrigan.

Jerry still follows the daily news of the world, the relentless accounts of war, terror, and bloodshed. Asked if his belief in peace remains unshaken, he responded with a smile that seemed to rise from nowhere, and he answered by telling a few stories . . .

His building blocks.

The Berrigans, devout Catholics, often worship at St. Lucy's Church, where Jerry said he defines his faith by the example of his mother:

"It means," he said, "always remaining open."

During the Great Depression, when Jerry was a child, the Berrigans lived near some railroad tracks in Galeville. Wandering strangers, hungry and jobless, often traveled past their house.

A man once came to the door, his body trembling as he asked for food. Frida didn't know him, but she could tell he was ill. She feared for his well-being. She brought him in. He stayed for months, until he rebuilt his strength. To the Berrigan boys, Jerry said, he was simply Mr. Kirby.

Once he left, the Berrigans never heard from him again, but the point—for Tom and Frida's six children—had been made.

"We are not to reject anyone," Jerry said.

His father was a union organizer, an early activist in efforts to confront the ongoing racial divide in Syracuse. Jerry described his dad as "a peaceful man," and one of the son's most vivid memories is a day when Tom

Berrigan came home so exhausted from his shift on a lighting crew that he stepped off a truck and collapsed onto the grass by their house.

Jerry asked what he could do to help. Tom said he'd like a glass of cold water. More than 80 years later, Jerry remembers what the most fundamental of gestures, at that moment, meant to his father:

Everything.

For years, Jerry taught composition, literature, and Shakespeare at Onondaga Community College. He and Carol were close to Reverend Ray McVey, a selfless Catholic priest who embodied the Dorothy Day philosophy. They joined McVey in visiting prisoners in jail. They helped him establish Unity Acres, a place of respite for homeless men.

Jerry was arrested and jailed so often for taking part in peaceful protests that he's lost count, he said, of how many times he wore handcuffs.

From all of it, this treasury of stories, he said the greatest moment in his life occurred in that back yard in East Syracuse. For years, Jerry and Phil studied to join the Josephites, an order of Catholic priests dedicated to the African-American community. Eventually, Jerry decided to step away.

In 1954, he was invited to a gathering at the home of Peg Snyder, who was dean of women at Le Moyne College for seven years and would become a groundbreaking voice at the United Nations for improving the global status of women. Carol Rizzo, one of Peg's friends, came over to share slides of a trip to Italy. When she heard someone at the back door, she answered it.

After 61 years, Carol and Jerry both remember that instant when they first stood face to face. They were married in autumn 1955. They'd raise four children. Jerry speaks of them as the core of all he did. As for Carol, he describes her with three words:

"Heart! Heart! Heart!"

Through her, over the years, he could always find his way to his.

Long ago, he decided against becoming a priest for what he said was the most fundamental of reasons: "I wasn't holy enough."

Carol, upon hearing that, reacted with disbelief. What she sensed when she met him, she said, is what he still demonstrates each day:

Jerry Berrigan, she said, is "the holiest man I've ever known."

Jerry died on the day this column was published. In that last interview, asked to name the greatest achievement in his life, Jerry responded: "It's what I didn't do." He tried to follow what he saw as an ironclad rule of both his church and humanity: even during World War II, he said, "I never killed anyone."

PART TEN

Resilience

Time Stands Still for Biasone

Tuesday, May 19, 1992

Danny Biasone doesn't complain about his illogical absence from the Naismith Memorial Basketball Hall of Fame. The old pioneer has been around too long, and has endured too much, to blow his own horn for some plaque on a wall in Springfield, Mass.

He has other things on his mind. Lately, abruptly, he has been remembering images he had long ago set aside. Biasone was lying on a doctor's table last week, for instance, when he recalled the chaotic day that he met his father.

It was 1920, and Biasone was with his mother and brother on Ellis Island, among a jostling crowd of nervous Italian immigrants. For a week, their boat had anchored in the harbor, while U.S. officials talked about sending them back because of a flu epidemic that was sweeping the nation.

Biasone's mother, Bambina, knew they'd made it when she saw a familiar face in the mob.

"Here comes your father," she said to the boys. Biasone stared hard into the wall of faces.

"Which one?" he asked.

Leo Biasone had come over first, in 1913, to find a home for his family. But World War I exploded in Europe, shutting off casual travel between the continents. By the time the family was reunited, the Biasone boys had no memory of their father.

They settled near some relatives in Syracuse, where Danny grew into a trolley operator, a bowling alley owner—and eventually into a pivotal figure in the history of the National Basketball Association.

He is 83 now, still working among the clattering pins of his Eastwood Sports Center, still ready to talk at length about basketball. Still, the man credited with developing one of the great teams in the early NBA—and with adding the shot clock that defined the game—has never been elected to the Hall of Fame.

He shrugs it off. His supporters aren't so ambivalent.

"Danny Biasone invented the 24-second clock by himself, alone," said Red Auerbach, the longtime executive of the Boston Celtics. "I was at the meeting when he introduced it. He should get all the credit in the world for it."

Yet Biasone isn't in the hall, except for the display case that honors the clock.

To understand the magnitude of that innovation, Hall of Famer Dolph Schayes—whose signing by Biasone helped trigger the merger that led to the modern NBA—points to Michael Jordan, who was a pretty good college player without a shot clock.

In the NBA, he's become a colossus.

Celtics great Bob Cousy was such a skilled ball handler—he could slow down a game by himself—that his skills fueled the drive, out of Syracuse, for the clock. But he is equally adamant about Biasone and the hall.

"Danny belongs in there," Cousy said. "He was one of the pioneers of the NBA, and he may well have saved it."

Biasone was nominated several times in the 1970s. He has received some significant honors, such as the Bunn Award, but never full admission.

As for Biasone himself, still busy running a bowling alley?

He insists the hall is no big deal.

He ignores the lingering pain from a fall last winter that broke one of his hips and left him using a much-hated cane. He rarely speaks of the liver cancer that has ruined his appetite and sends him back every week for chemotherapy.

"A survivor," Schayes says with admiration.

Each day, Biasone sits in his small office, where he drinks his pot or two of black coffee—and remains willing to talk about the shot clock, the historic innovation that Biasone refers to as "the time."

In the heyday of the old Nationals, Biasone surrounded himself with people who knew basketball, from general manager Leo Ferris—he, too, played a key role with the clock—to wily players like Schayes and Paul Seymour. They saw their game being hurt by the slowdown. With no shot clock, a ball-control wizard like Cousy could devour entire blocks of time.

For years, Auerbach recalls, the little guy from Syracuse—in his trademark shirts, buttoned to the larynx—attended owners' meetings in plush New York hotels, pushing for a limit on the time of possession. Finally, in 1954, the rest of the league bought into it.

While Biasone is quiet about his own significance, he remains proud of the shot clock—which later was adopted for international and college competition. "There's no doubt about it," Biasone said. "The time made the game of basketball."

You get the sense, while visiting him, that you are in a uniquely preserved basketball time capsule. He often gestures at specific barroom tables and booths when speaking about events that changed the game's history.

Lester Harrison—the Hall of Fame driving force behind the old Rochester Royals—stopped by in the late 1940s and tried to persuade Biasone to pull Syracuse out of the fledgling National Basketball League.

The Royals, along with other NBL powers, had jumped into the Basketball Association of America. The Nats were left behind, in a league populated by smaller cities such as Anderson, Indiana.

Biasone wouldn't budge. His stubborn defiance helped force a merger. The Nats came into the newly formed National Basketball Association in 1949-50. They tied a league record with 51 victories, and went all the way to the NBA finals before losing, four games to two, to George Mikan and the powerhouse Minneapolis Lakers.

Syracuse remained among the NBA elite, winning a championship in 1954-55. The Nationals survived until 1963—outlasting, by far, Rochester and all the original "small-market" towns.

Then Biasone—lacking an adequate arena—finally let go, and the franchise moved to Philadelphia.

Now, Danny Biasone is an 83-year-old whose thoughts wander far beyond his old team photos. On April 7, Joseph Biasone—the brother who was at Danny's side on the boat ride from Italy—died at the age of 79. Danny, who has no children, grew quiet for a moment after speaking of Joe.

It is a reminder that everything passes . . . even living history.

Last week, the Hall of Fame inducted another batch of members. That won't happen again until the spring of 1993. Bill Himmelman, the NBA historian, says there was much headshaking among retired players at the gathering about the continuing omission of Danny Biasone.

It is an injustice, considering Biasone's condition, that demands immediate correction.

Joe O'Brien, the Hall's director, hesitates to take special steps. He compares the Biasone situation to the status of Magic Johnson, who is suffering from HIV, and worries about decisions "based on emotion."

But emotions, sometimes, are true and noble—and anyone who knows Biasone knows he belongs in the Hall of Fame. The Veterans Committee should be called together, now, to act on Biasone's nomination, which is once again active.

It is time to settle this overdue debt. Before the end of the summer, Danny Biasone should be inducted with full honors into the Hall of Fame—in a ceremony that would be as unique and important as the shot clock itself.

Danny Biasone died on May 25, 1992, six days after this column was published. In 2000, he was finally voted into basketball's Hall of Fame. Five years later, in the presence of such Hall of Famers as Earl Lloyd, Dolph Schayes, Bill Walton, and John Havlicek, civic officials dedicated a shot-clock memorial in downtown Syracuse; it features a working clock that eternally counts down from 24. The plaque recalls how Howard Hobson, a longtime college coach, came up with the original idea for a shot clock—and it credits Biasone, Leo Ferris, and Emil Barboni, a scout and one of the original owners of the Nats, with putting together the version of the clock that saved the NBA.

A Show of Strength

Tuesday, May 23, 1995

Harry Danzey considers himself a preacher. He is eager to offer his theories on world problems, from bringing up children to real peace between the races. But Harry has no church, and no congregation.

His pulpit is a sled and a 60-pound bag of cement.

That has turned him into a man of mystery. Early morning commuters often see him dragging that sled up the hill on West Seneca Turnpike. He carries another 85 pounds of weight on his body. He sometimes runs shirtless on sub-zero days. He will tell you he's in training, although he isn't sure for what.

"I'll know once I get there," Harry says.

What Harry wants is an audience. His son, David, says his dad likes attention. Harry agrees. As a child on an Alabama farm, Harry liked to pick fruit fast, liked to make farmers cringe at paying him by the bushel, liked to put on a show that made people stop and gawk.

Now he is a 62-year-old grandfather, a bus mechanic for the Onondaga Central Schools. He laughs as much as he talks, which is constantly. He chuckles about the foibles in people, and he wants the chance to share his theories with the world. But he feels he needs to earn the attention.

That is why he takes on the hill.

Harry reads the Bible, and he is big on symbols. He was driving to work three or four years ago, watching joggers toil as they pushed up the turnpike. He went home and pulled an old sled from the garage. He threw on a 60-pound bag of cement. He got out some straps he normally used for towing his car, hitched them to the sled, and put them over his shoulders. Then he went for a jog.

42. Harry Danzey working out near Seneca Turnpike. (Frank Ordonez/*Post-Standard*)

Traffic is heavy on the turnpike. At first, a lot of people thought Harry was too much. They frowned or made rude gestures. Harry stayed out there, day after day. He'd pull off his shirt on freezing winter mornings. He'd bulk up in heavy clothes in 80-degree heat. The nasty mood of the commuters changed to disbelief.

Harry sometimes veers from his route to climb a sheer slope along the turnpike, pounding up through loose soil and bushes sharp with thorns, emerging near the Van Duyn Home and Hospital. He will stand there and catch his breath, the Onondaga Valley spread out at his feet, and then he'll descend toward his regular route.

The whole point, he says, is testing his body, which he speaks of as a separate companion. "I know my body," Harry says. "I give it what it wants. If it's got an appetite, I feed it. If it wants to hurt me for something I'm doing, you know I take that into consideration."

Harry was running distance even before he tackled the hill. Once he was able to climb the turnpike dragging the sled, he tried doing it backwards. Then he began wearing ankle weights and the 35-pound backpack.

Many of the same drivers who once snarled at Harry now beep and wave. Harry waves back.

His own wife, Johnnie Mae, is one of the converts. At first, she called her husband an attention-crazy fool. Once, while Harry ran shirtless on an arctic morning, a sheriff's deputy pulled over to make sure Harry had all his marbles. Johnnie Mae was humiliated when Harry came home laughing.

"They should have locked you up," she said then.

Now, she has come to accept it. "It makes him happy," Johnnie Mae says. Her husband is in terrific shape. He can bend his body like a pretzel. Muscle covers his wiry frame. And he has relentless energy around the house.

He rearranges all their furniture every few weeks, because he likes to make each room feel brand new. On garbage day, he'll roam the neighborhood with city trash crews, helping them do their job. "What am I going to do?" asks Nick Smola, a public works foreman. "Tell him no?"

Friends keep telling him it's time to cash in on what he does. They tell him how Levi's and Nike make commercials based on everyday people who do extraordinary things. They tell Harry to call, to try and make a deal.

No, he replies. If some company calls him, fine. But somehow it breaks his rules to go looking.

All he really wants is a forum for his theories. You hear them if you tag along on his jog. He runs, he says, to prove daily toil can be a salvation. His mother, Ossie, is 90 years old, and her identical twin, Ozzie, is also alive and well.

What Harry remembers of his boyhood is how hard they both worked.

As a child, Harry knew his great-grandfather, Gus Danzey, an old man who was born into slavery. Gus told Harry of how he survived in the fields, the secret that became a means of staying free.

"You gotta make work fun," the old man said. "You gotta sing, you gotta talk, you gotta like it while you do it. Do that, and that way, they can never beat you."

To this day, Harry looks for hard jobs and big problems. Twenty years ago, he and Johnnie Mae were among the first African Americans to move onto Barnes Avenue. Most of the neighbors were nice enough, but one morning the couple woke up to find garbage dumped on their front steps. Others might have reacted in rage. Harry remembered the words of his real estate agent.

"Take care of your yard," the guy told him, "and you'll be fine."

Lawn care underlines Harry's theory of race relations. Harry doesn't do anything halfway. He not only made sure to mow his lawn, but he built an elaborate stone terrace in the back yard. Call his neighbors, and they don't mention the way he drags his sled. What they'll talk about is how Harry takes care of his lawn.

That is what prompts Harry to make this offer. If someone would provide him with some gas and a good power mower, he says he'd go up and down Salina Street, cleaning every lot ignored by sloppy landlords. He swears in a few weeks he could transform the whole street.

"It breaks my heart young kids have to grow up around that," Harry says. Change the look, Harry says, and you change the way kids feel. All they need, he insists, are a few adults who care. Even as he runs, he gets upset talking about those children of the city, the odds they fight from the moment they're born, the way so many people write them off.

"It's like this hill," Harry says, and he climbs it every day.

Around greater Syracuse, especially within the local running community, it is still commonplace to hear people say, "Whatever happened to the guy who used to drag the sled up the turnpike?" Harry Danzey's tenacity turned him into an enduring legend; he died at 76, in 2009.

Mind's Eye, Red Lightning, Labor Day, and One Fierce Storm

Monday, September 14, 1998

Labor Day, 1 a.m., half-awake, reading in bed. A lightning flash. Another. The wind growls against the screen. The rain comes, a few big drops, then everything goes nuts. The window sills fill up, becoming indoor waterfalls.

Power dies. You see red lightning. The wind is too strong to slam the window down. Is this a tornado, or are we being silly? Some of us stay put. Others grab the kids and sit on the basement steps. You'll remember, in the dark, a toddler's arms gripping your shoulders.

It ends. All is quiet, except for the worrisome sound of flowing water. You walk around in the pitch black, looking for your glasses. Your bare feet splash on hardwood floors. That is a bad sign. The dog, terrified, has gone under the bed. The cats, who were outside, are scratching madly at the screen.

Can't find your glasses. You knock over a glass vase. After the last storm you bought flashlights, vowed to keep them someplace safe. Within a week, your four-year-old had them in little pieces. The candles and batteries are in the junk drawer. It's bad enough trying to find something in that drawer with the lights on.

From the porch, without your glasses, your street somehow looks strange. Big shapes loom in the darkness. You see a few beams of light. It is the neighbors who were smart enough to keep flashlights and matches handy. Next time, you assure yourself, you'll be just like them.

You lie down to comfort your frightened, tired kids. At dawn, you get the big view: trees uprooted, windows shattered, a crack in your ceiling.

335

Telephone and power lines are jumbled in the street. Neighbors gather to drag away limbs, yard by yard. A pine tree fell across the car. The woman next door, to cheer you up, says she likes that Christmas smell.

What time is it? Who knows? You guess by looking at gray skies. The dog needs to do his business. You hope no hot power lines fell on his favorite tree.

You get batteries in the radio and thank God for WSYR. And you say a quiet prayer when you learn two people died.

Peanut butter on white bread for breakfast. For lunch, we'll use the rye. The neighbor, her arms folded, says NiMo needs at least a week. Driving to work is filled with awe, shock, and detours. There is a park where you took your kids to kick leaves in the fall. The trees, great oaks and maples, are lying on their sides.

A jerk is the driver who won't take his turn at a dark light. Fortunately, nine out of every 10 drivers aren't jerks.

Danny Wegman, we love you and your big-butt generators. Forget food or water. Get me one good cup of coffee.

Someone says Bill Clinton is in trouble. Is that so? Do you have ice?

On storm day, neighbors gather in the middle of the street. They grill chicken and hot dogs before everything goes bad. They drink beer and soda out of Styrofoam coolers. They sit in folding chairs beneath a mountain of dead trees. Kind of nice, actually. One gift from the derecho.

At home, the Popsicles make a puddle in the freezer. We keep the candles burning. The week becomes a siege. A hero is the neighbor cooking pancakes over gas. A jerk is the looter who stole a cockatiel from Phinney's pet store.

The days go on. The kids go nuts. The experts say play indoor games. How about this one: "Let's rip the house to bits!"

If I flick a dead switch one more time, I'll bite off my damned finger. Driving at night, without streetlights, is a downright scary thing. It is a long way to Brewerton to do six trash bags filled with laundry. The place is filled with clean, organized people with their wash in plastic baskets. I stink. I am unshaven. I am a pig.

Down the road, six blocks from your house, your friend got back his power. He watches videos, toasts bagels, and talks about survivor guilt.

Guilt, schmilt. He also watches Mark McGwire, the baseball slugger with 61 home runs. You've waited since you toddled to see someone hit number 62. McGwire hits it. If you're lucky, you hear it on the radio. More likely, you've got your nose three inches from the bathroom sink, trying to remove your contact lenses by candlelight.

You drive to work. On your way, you see the power trucks. Some emergency workers from Quebec yell back and forth in French. Oui, oui! Welcome, allies! Our reward for World War II!

Your basement is flooded. The dirty laundry just gets soaked. You empty the fridge, tossing out even taco sauce and mustard.

The kids sleep downstairs, pioneers on hardwood floors. Maybe you're up late playing cards with teenage kids. Maybe you pay bills with your husband or wife by candlelight. Maybe you sit on the porch and look out at the dark city.

Most often, depressed, you zonk out early in your clothes.

You cut up parts of dead trees and save them for firewood. Your kids want Sega. You just snarl. You're still mad about McGwire. You wonder how much Blockbuster will demand in return for *Wag the Dog*, trapped four long nights inside your VCR.

The kids cheer when the NiMo workers finally hit your street. You come out to greet the troops of liberation. The 5-year-old next door watches hard hats going high in bucket trucks, looks with admiration on their tool belts and big saws.

"When I grow up," the kid says, "I want to be a wire man."

Those old enough to remember the Labor Day storm still see its aftermath on any drive across the city: Many streets once lined with maples are now dotted with small trees. Several parks that once held canopies of leaves and limbs became rolling green lawns. Maybe Syracuse will never see a storm of the same kind, but this one left its mark on all who witnessed it: the wind rose up, the sky exploded, and the world was not the same.

Being Positive Lands Herman
the Autograph He Wants the Most
Wednesday, September 1, 1999

Many years ago, Herman Schatz took some advice in Syracuse from a Secret Service agent. "Herman," the guy said. "Use the slow approach." Herman remembered. He remembers everything. He tried the "slow approach" Monday, when Bill and Hillary Clinton left the Arts and Home Center at the New York State Fair.

The Clintons were with State Comptroller H. Carl McCall. They were protected by a wall of state troopers and Secret Service agents. A crowd was pressed back behind a yellow tape, at least 50 feet away from the president.

Herman didn't flinch. He had one purpose when he rode a Centro bus to the fair: he was going to hug Bill and Hillary. He knew the dates of their birthdays. He planned to tell them of his own, March 3, 1953. Three-three-53, Herman often repeats.

Never mind the wall of somber security. Never mind that no one gets close enough to hug the president.

"I think positive," explained Herman, 46.

He went to the fair. He brought along a pamphlet from the Onondaga County Democratic Committee, which seemed a good thing for the president to sign. Herman wriggled through the crowd until he reached the yellow tape. He saw the Clintons and McCall walking through the parking lot.

Herman ducked under the tape. He walked toward the president. "Bill!" he called out. "President Bill! My friend Bill! Can I have your autograph?"

Six state troopers, fast as lightning, were all over Herman.

Herman was scared, although he has been through worse. He was born with developmental disabilities. He spent most of his life behind the walls of institutions. He remembers, as a little boy, what happened whenever he failed to make it to the bathroom.

"They beat me up," Herman said. That was his childhood.

He also remembers Chet Eisenhooth, an attendant at the Wassaic State School. Chet was kind. He loved politics. He often sat with Herman in the day room of a place called "Building K." Chet taught Herman the tragic lore of the Kennedys. Within his own gray life, Herman mourned for someone else. Teddy Kennedy turned into Herman's hero.

Herman was finally transferred to Syracuse. He spent five years in the developmental center here. In 1977, he was released into a group home. The staff quickly realized that Herman has a certain genius. He can recall the exact birthdays of almost everyone he meets. He can project, into the future, the day of the week when your next birthday will occur.

As a free man, Herman found a lifetime passion. He collects the autographs of famous politicians. Before Monday, the high point of his life was the first time he met Teddy Kennedy. It was the first of many meetings. Larry Sunser, a state counselor who shares his home with Herman, said Kennedy has learned to call Herman by name.

Bill Coughlin was the manager at one of Herman's group homes. Coughlin often joined Herman on trips to Washington, where Herman perfected his "slow approach." Sometimes it worked. He got the autographs of senators Strom Thurmond, Orrin Hatch, Jesse Helms, and Walter Mondale. Sometimes it didn't. At least once, Coughlin said, guards drew their guns on Herman.

Yet Herman's dream remained the chance to meet a sitting president.

Monday, he ducked underneath the yellow tape. The troopers were stunned. They wrapped him up, while the Clintons and McCall watched the whole thing. "Who's that?" asked the president. McCall has known Herman for years. He told Clinton that Herman is a friend. "I felt very protective," McCall said.

Clinton listened, and he said, "Well, bring him over."

The troopers released Herman, who ran straight into the president's embrace. "Were you born August 19?" Herman asked. "I was born March 3!" The president, laughing, took the pamphlet and wrote, "To Herman, nice to meet you!"

Herman turned and hugged Hillary. She also signed the program.

The crowd, pressed up against the tape, cheered wildly.

Herman lives in Fairmount. He walked all the way home. Meeting a president, he said, was the high point of his life.

He expects to meet some more. "I think positive," he said.

At 63, Herman Schatz is still a presence at Syracuse political events. In a conversation shortly before the publication of this book, he said his focus now is on somehow finding his way to another dream autograph: President Barack Obama.

Near the End, Two Brothers "Work Things Out"

Monday, January 14, 2002

It's been almost four weeks since Jack Garvey died. His brother Ed remains grateful for one sentence in their final conversation.

"I'd never heard him say it, not ever, not in all the years that I'd known him," said Ed, 80, a retired maintenance man from Syracuse City Hall. "And I knew him since he was a little guy."

They last saw each other on Veterans Day, when the old House of Providence orphanage in Syracuse held a reunion. Jack, who lived in Florida, didn't call Ed at his North Side home to say that he was coming. Instead, Ed heard about it through their sister, Rosemary Fuller, of Camillus.

The two brothers found each other in the lobby of the former orphanage, now the Catholic Charities headquarters on West Onondaga Street. After a memorial service in the chapel, they went to a room near the cafeteria, where they held what Ed called their first real conversation in "15 or 20 years."

"(Jack) and I were so close, and all of a sudden we just went in different directions," Ed said. "It's stupid. You can always work things out. There's no reason why anyone should go that long without talking without some really paramount reason.

"You know how it goes. Some of the things I did with my kids he didn't agree with, and some of the things he did with his kids I didn't agree with. That's the trouble with people. They don't know that you can always talk things out."

341

At the reunion, Ed said, one sentence from Jack "erased all our problems."

Jack, 78, died in Florida on December 19, from heart problems. He moved there after he retired from the Department of Veterans Affairs in Syracuse. His wife, Mary, died a year ago. Rosemary Fuller, Jack's sister, didn't think at first that he would come to the reunion. Jack never liked to fly. He rarely traveled without Mary.

During World War II, Jack lost his right arm and his left leg when the Japanese attacked and sank the USS *Vincennes*. Jack was in the water for 18 hours. He watched sharks kill other men. Even after Jack was rescued, the doctors warned his family there was little chance that he would survive.

He went on to raise four children and to have a fine career. "He was a fighter," Ed said. "At the House of Providence, he was always willing to take on the biggest guy around."

The brothers were put in the orphanage during the Great Depression, when Ed was nine and Jack was six. Their parents had divorced. Their father was a firefighter who worked 12-hour shifts. Their mother didn't have the money to feed her children. An aunt and uncle took Rosemary and a baby brother, Don. A judge sent the older boys to the House of Providence.

"My father dropped us off," Ed said. "Years later, he told us how hard it was for him. We stood there. We didn't know what was in store for us."

They soon learned how older thugs zeroed in on little kids. "You got slapped around by some of them," Ed said. Dinner was often peanut butter and kidney beans. Ed remembers meals that would consist of a spoonful of eggs and some puny sausages.

"I think a lot of us wound up with cholesterol problems because of those meals," Ed said. "We'd dunk our bread in the grease they used for the sausage. That was a way of getting a taste."

On Christmas, they'd each find one small toy, "a trinket," placed inside their lockers. Their relatives would come to visit them on weekends, because the younger boys rarely got to leave the orphanage. The brick walls framed their entire world. Ed recalls standing outside, watching neighborhood children running to and from their homes.

"We tried to figure out if this was the only way there was," Ed said.

In the late 1930s, Ed enlisted in the navy, "basically just to get the hell out of the House of Providence."

Jack would also enlist, three years later. Eventually they both returned to Syracuse, where their relationship slowly fell apart. After Jack moved to Florida, the brothers almost never spoke by telephone.

But Jack got on a plane, by himself, to come back for the reunion.

He and Ed talked for a long time, sitting near the cafeteria where they once dipped bread into hot grease. Ed remembered the time when an older boy was "slapping me around," and Jack came up from behind and drilled the bully with a baseball bat. The brothers laughed hard. "That was me," Jack said.

Out of nowhere, Jack said, "Remember, I'll always love you."

Ed was stunned. Jack, a lifetime tough guy, never said such things. "Same goes for me," Ed croaked in reply, as his throat got tight and tears rushed to his eyes. Neither of them knew exactly where to go from there, so they told some tales about terrifying nuns and began to laugh again. When the reunion ended, they both promised to talk soon, although Ed thinks Jack knew it wouldn't happen.

He'd already done what he came home to do.

Ed Garvey died five years later, at 85, content with the peace he'd made with his brother.

A Ripple Breaks into Billowing Wave

Monday, January 9, 2006

The six little girls stood on a bench in Section 304 of the Carrier Dome. They were high above the players, in the nosebleed seats, watching Sunday as the Syracuse University men's basketball team held on to a second-half lead against South Florida.

From Section 304, the girls could see the announced crowd of 20,686 fans spread out in a vast horseshoe around the court. Those fans were quiet. The game had settled into a kind of grinding rhythm, and the girls decided to do something about it.

Together, they shrieked and flung their arms up in the air.

Nothing happened. A couple of little boys who were with them exhorted other people to join in. The girls, disappointed, flung up their arms again. Only a few of the fans around them responded.

"You've got to keep trying," rumbled their coach, Mike Vadala, who noticed the girls seemed ready to give up.

They were all part of an excursion from St. Margaret Mary Church in Irondequoit, near Rochester. The girls play basketball for the third- and fourth-grade Catholic Youth Organization team from the church, whose CYO teams combined with a parish youth group for Sunday's trip to the Dome.

In Section 304, the girls were a long way from the court and a long way from their idol, Gerry McNamara. They decided there was still a way to make an impression: they would get the entire Carrier Dome to join in on the wave, an effort the grown-ups knew could easily end in failure.

Still, a core group of nine-year-olds—Meghan Vadala, Meghan O'Brien, Drae Kemp, Jennifer Dinolfo, and Ashton Clark, joined by

Savannah Crocetti, the only eight-year-old in the bunch—kept shrieking and flinging their arms into the air.

For a while, it was like touching a match to a wet straw. Finally, after many tries, they got a little heat. A few dozen fans joined in on the wave, which stretched to the big American flag that hung a section or two away.

That was enough to get the other girls on the CYO team—Christina Horton, Merci Young, Caitlin Maggio, and Sydney Lana—to jump up and help out. All 10 girls hurled their arms in the air. This time, the wave rippled a little farther, to the big "44" jersey hanging not far beyond the flag. For another time or two, that was as far as it went, but the girls kept going until the crowd took it all the way to the big scoreboard above the scorer's table.

The girls could feel it now. They raised their arms, and they shrieked, and people around them did the same. They touched off a response that went around the horseshoe and dropped into the bleachers and rippled through some ultra-expensive courtside seats before it came all the way back to these little girls in their SU shirts and jerseys.

One of them, Meghan Vadala, maintained she had been to the Dome "a billion times," while another, Meghan O'Brien, had never been there before Sunday. Certainly, they had never decided to get thousands upon thousands of people in the biggest on-campus arena in college basketball to join in the same cheer.

But they kept at it until the crowd around them bought in, until enough fans saw the wave coming from the far side of the Dome to send it all the way around, and then back to Section 304.

The girls, filled with joy, threw up their arms again, and an entire section filled with strangers roared in triumph at their feat. The wave kept getting bigger, rippling into both the upper and lower levels of the Dome, until even the Orange cheerleaders stepped back from the court to watch this elemental form of fan communion . . .

All started by six tiny girls in Section 304.

Mecca Matthews, an SU fan who sat near them, figured the wave came through 11 times before the crowd had enough and let it fade away. When it was over, when the girls were pounding each other and slapping hands and their parents were beaming and their older brothers wanted credit for helping to get it started, nine-year-old Jennifer Dinolfo summarized why it was such a big deal:

"For this one time," she said, "small people led big people."

Mike Vadala, the head coach, says those girls never lost that belief in what they could accomplish. Their CYO team went on to win two Monroe County middle school championships, and now—as young women—"they still inspire each other to do great things."

Francis Defies Illness to Show God's Work

Friday, January 2, 2009

Francis Geremia has trembling hands. The muscles in his throat don't always respond easily. Sometimes it is an effort for him to form words. Walking and climbing stairs can be difficult.

"They say I have Parkinson's," said Francis, 48, during an interview at Syracuse City Hall. "But can someone with Parkinson's do this?"

He held up a photograph of a leopard frog, beads of water captured atop glimmering muscles as the frog crouched in the mud.

He held up a photograph of a red-tailed hawk that stared intently at the camera, a hawk barely finished with killing a woodchuck.

He held up a photograph of a bald eagle being harassed by a crow, a drama that Francis said played out above Syracuse.

"Be ready to be amazed," Francis said, as he kept pulling out his photos. Many were taken when he balanced his camera against his foot, he said, an unorthodox method he finds to be especially effective.

"I'm not bragging on me," Francis explained. "I'm bragging on the Lord."

He is a traffic maintenance worker for the city's Department of Public Works. About 14 years ago, he began getting tremors in his hands. The doctors did some tests. He knew the truth, he said, before the specialists made it official.

Francis has Parkinson's, a progressive disease that often involves tremors, rigidity, and impaired balance. For about four years, he said, he barely noticed his symptoms. Since then, daily life has been increasingly harder.

43. Francis Geremia and his photographs. (Lauren Long/*Post-Standard*)

In the morning, it's especially tough for him to walk. There have been times when he was forced to crawl to the bathroom.

Yet he said he will not retire until the Lord gives him a signal - which will most likely happen only when he can no longer do his job.

"Francis is an inspiration," said Jeff Wright, commissioner of public works. "He could have just quit. He could have given up. He expects nothing from us, no special accommodations. For years now he's been managing things, even as they've gotten worse. Francis steps up to the plate and does a hell of a job."

He still drives a truck, and swings a sledgehammer, and takes down broken signs when they need to be replaced.

Always, at home or work, he is not far from his camera.

Francis was one of the winners of the city's "On Your Own Time" competition, which spotlights the artwork of employees. While several of his photos hang at city hall, he does not pretend to be an expert on technique. He explained that his success is more related to what books meant to him, when he was a child. If he could not travel to faraway places, the pictures in those books were a way to get him there.

Decades later, he takes delight in using photos as a way to cause people to look harder, and then look again, at "God's creation."

A wetland in East Syracuse we might drive past all the time without thinking twice? That is where Francis photographed the life-and-death struggle between a bullfrog and a blue heron. The nearby lake we often call the most polluted in the world? That is where Francis, waiting patiently, photographed a bald eagle in flight.

Those photos help him to cope with Parkinson's. If anything, he said, the disease made him a better guy.

"At first (after learning about the disease), I was very bitter," Francis said. "But the longer you stay bitter, the harder your heart gets, and I believe there is a point of no return."

Francis and his wife, Patty, build their life around their faith. To Francis, photography was God's direct means of intervention. Their teenage children often accompany Francis when he goes to take photos. The family dog, a beagle named Snoopy, also plays a major role.

The dog helped to lift Francis out of his depression. Every day, he and Snoopy went for long walks. As they wandered through the fields, Francis began noticing little dramas that had always escaped his glance.

"Nature is very competitive, and I'm a competitive person," he said. He challenged himself to capture those moments on film. He took plenty of photos that are uplifting and beautiful—flowers, tiny waterfalls, pine cones on a tree.

His most stunning work involves the drama of nature. He has countless photographs of frogs, muscles tensed, poised and ready to flee. He prides himself on being able to capture birds of prey in actual moments of attack.

It is his therapy, because Francis is blunt about his Parkinson's. "Every day you live, it gets worse," he said. So he remains active. He fights every sign of slow decline. He learns what he can of innovative treatments.

And he keeps going. His daughter is a junior in high school. He fully intends to dance at her wedding. The best way of getting there, as far as he's concerned, is to stay busy and happy. Day after day, he and Snoopy go on their regular journeys to find photos, which Francis often gives away to anyone he thinks can use them.

"He wants to give people hope like he has hope," said his wife, Patty. That's what he does. That's why she loves him.

Be ready to be amazed.

Syracuse has a new creek walk to Onondaga Lake. Regular users of the trail are accustomed to passionate conversations with a photographer who seems to know the secret patterns of every hawk and bald eagle on the lakefront. It is Francis, now retired from his job in public works, on his way to becoming a legend in his city.

At Fowler, Giving Voice to a New Syracuse

Sunday, June 26, 2011

Majay Abu Donzo vividly recalls her first moments as a middle school student in Syracuse. Majay, at 13, had just arrived from Liberia. When her teacher walked into the classroom, Majay stood up. This was typical behavior in her homeland, where educators are treated with reverence. In her new school, to Majay's surprise, other children began laughing. Even the teacher wasn't sure of how to react to this quiet girl, who stood alone.

"It's just respect," said Majay, now 18. "The kids here have so many freedoms and opportunities. They ought to take advantage. It kills me. In my country, only the rich children know they'll get an education. The rest of us would do anything to get one. It's crazy. Little kids will carry heavy things on their heads just to get a little money so they can go to school.

"My dad always thought education is the whole key to success. He values it and he taught us to value it. Here, you get everything for free, and so many kids do nothing with it. They talk back to their teachers or argue with them. It just doesn't make sense."

Saturday, in a voice shaking with emotion, Majay (pronounced MA-zhay) brought that message to a larger audience at the John H. Mulroy Civic Center. As salutatorian of the graduating class at Fowler High School, she and class valedictorian Thien Trang Ho—a native of Vietnam—offered speeches that gave voice to a new Syracuse. Of this year's 10 valedictorians and salutatorians in the city high schools, six are immigrants or refugees. Educators say that kind of high achievement is a growing phenomenon in our schools, where roughly one of every 10 students was born in another country.

351

44. Majay Donzo on Fowler High School's graduation day. (David Lassman/
Post-Standard)

The class rankings at Fowler are "not an isolated result," said Laura
Vieira-Suarez, who is in charge of English as a Second Language pro-
gramming in Syracuse. To Jackie LeRoy, an instructional specialist who
works with refugee children, Majay exemplifies an ethic common to students from abroad.

"You've got to understand the challenges they overcome," LeRoy said.
"They're asked to learn the same content as their peers while they're still
learning the (English) language. Even with those gaps, they're often able
to keep pace and go on to great success. They're welcome here, not only
because of the diversity they bring, but because their determination helps
turn them into role models."

The international influx also is transforming the neighborhoods that
shape and feed the schools. According to the 2010 federal census, Syracuse lost less than 1 percent of its population. That represented one of the
best census results for any large Upstate city in the last 50 years. Analysts

agree this new civic stability was heavily influenced by a growing refugee community.

Indeed, the Fowler commencement began with at least six students, all from different nations, offering separate greetings in their native tongues. Their relatives cheered wildly, and Majay became a spokesperson for that jubilation.

In the mid-1990s, to escape from violent rebels, her family packed up and fled the Liberian city of Monrovia. Majay left behind most of her childhood belongings, including a favorite doll. The Donzos traveled to Sierra Leone, where Majay's father obtained a house.

Yet the government ordered Liberian refugees to stay in United Nations compounds, Majay said. With thousands of others, her family was pushed into an overcrowded camp. Majay, her parents, and many of her siblings stayed there until 2006, when they were finally allowed to relocate in Syracuse.

Majay spent much of her childhood in the camp, before leaving as a teen. Throughout it all, her father drummed home one message: go to school.

"Thanks to him, I know why I'm here," Majay said. "I'm here to better myself and to show the world I can make a difference." Toward that end, while at Fowler, she ignored the noise and temptations of the street. She understood how younger children from Liberia would notice every choice she made. Her reward was a Say Yes to Education scholarship to Marist College, where she intends to study forensic science.

Her journey became the message at the center of her speech. On stage, several times, she almost gave in to tears. She spoke with appreciation of her father. She thanked her older sisters, several of whom have gone to college. She told the audience how her mother, at 3 a.m. each morning in the refugee camp, would boil water so her children could wash up before school.

Finally, Majay spoke of how each Fowler graduate should be a model for the "young ones" in the city. Half-turning toward her classmates, who were seated just behind her, Majay asked what to her is the great, unanswered question of Syracuse:

"The world is at our feet," she said. "Why are we waiting so long to pick it up?"

The crowd, deeply moved, whooped and offered its support. Majay Abu Donzo, in her new city, no longer stood alone.

As of this writing, Majay is completing her senior year at Marist.

"Internal Vision" and a Senseless Attack

Sunday, February 10, 2013

Tom Dotterer will not sit down. There is a wooden chair with a cushion just in front of him, but he insists on standing in the middle of his North Salina Street liquor store. He has a point he needs to make, and as he tries to capture it, to nail it down, well-wishers keep coming through the door—people of wildly different occupations, languages, and backgrounds—and they hug Dotterer and shake his hand and give him cards.

This is Tuesday, three days after surgeons removed his right eye. It was destroyed January 23, when a robber fired a shot into Dotterer's face. Police have arrested two men but are saying little else, and Dotterer—in deference to investigators—reveals nothing of the incident itself.

Still, there is much he wants to express, mainly his gratitude for a community's support. The problem is, every time he gets rolling on the subject—and when Dotterer gets rolling, baseball, religion, and literature soon mesh with North Side grit into wild epiphanies—someone else comes in and the thoughts go on hold, because any individual at the door, to Dotterer, becomes the most important person in the room . . .

As in Warren Bumpus, a longtime baseball umpire who stops by with a card representing all the umps in the region. Dotterer, veteran coach at Christian Brothers Academy, explains to his visitor how a bout of shingles has taken away much of the sight in his remaining eye. With a straight face, Dotterer says if his vision gets a little bit worse, then he'd "finally qualify for umpiring."

To Bumpus, the joke is a relief: Tommy is still Tommy.

"He treats the game with respect," Bumpus says. "He treats the umpires with respect. He'd never cheat or break the rules so he could win."

45. Tom Dotterer in his North Salina Street liquor store, three days after he was shot in the face during a robbery, an attack that cost him an eye. (Gary Walts/ *Post-Standard*)

There's also an appearance by a guy named Rob, a recovering alcoholic who used to buy his liquor from Dotterer. The old coach kept advising him to quit. Eight years ago, Rob did. He began living out the inspirational notes Dotterer, 77, hangs throughout the store. Now Rob and his girlfriend wrap Dotterer in hugs, and as they leave, Dotterer says:

"These people, who face their afflictions, their difficulties, their addictions every day, what they face, that (takes) courage. I'm not completely blind, even if I'm working on it, and I understand what's worse—what it means when you don't even have internal vision because you're cut off at the pipe before you have a chance, when you're still little."

At the store, the line merged long ago between his customers and friends, many of whom try to better themselves despite overwhelming circumstance. His own recovery, Dotterer says, pales next to that bravery.

"I have to attempt to feel that way," he says, "because you can get so caught up in darkness and self-pity it engulfs you."

Buddy Wleklinski, athletic director at CBA, has already said Dotterer is the school's baseball coach for as long as he wants to be. Dotterer hasn't made a decision; those who know him are familiar with his notebook, home to a mysterious system that records such details as when players swing or their incidence of contact on a particular pitch, observations spun together into a kind of mad strategy that over the years, in uncanny ways, seemed to work.

Could he keep such detailed notes after the shooting? In the middle of the store—one eye bandaged, one eye piercing above a steel gray beard—Dotterer lifts an eyebrow. Translation: he doesn't know.

He says the store was opened 79 years ago this month, by his father. Tom's hero was an older brother, Dutch, who became a major leaguer and shared the family passion for literature. Tom would spend 10 seasons in baseball's minor leagues, killing nights in cheap hotel rooms with his beloved books, until he came home for good to the liquor store, his family, and the CBA coaching job he accepted in 1980.

"Coach," he says. "It's a hell of a name. You think about all the people I've had the opportunity to meet, the players, their parents, their families, their friends, the expansiveness, the appreciation, the potentiality . . ."

He stops to mock himself for what he fears is pretension in his words. "My principal goal is to be as honest and fair-minded and supportive as I can be," he says. The kid willing to ride the bench all season may cherish the game even more than the kids who are big stars, and what childhood fate is harder, Dotterer asks, than to sit and watch someone else for whom the game seems to come so easily?

If he ever forgets the kid in the dugout, Dotterer says, then he is failing in his job.

"I love them," he says, of all his players.

The door opens again. In comes Jerry Wilcox, legendary high school basketball coach, big hand reaching out to absorb Tom's. For a moment they speak of old friends and old times, until the conversation veers into notions of forgiveness, and Dotterer comes as close to the shooting as he chooses to go:

"I'm not angry, I'm acceptant," he says. "I'm angry when I lose a sand-wich (in a round of golf) to this guy over here.

"A poor soul came in here and made a decision that impacted his life, in all likelihood, a hell of a lot more than mine will be impacted . . . For what? A dollar? Two dollars? To be a tough guy? What? He doesn't know me. It's not me . . . He acted without any degree of awareness of the impact."

Yet that can never be an excuse, Dotterer says. He offers fierce loyalty to the many customers who keep trying despite existing in a place of tattered hope, men and women who struggle but in the end would never hurt anyone except themselves. He knows the epidemic of bloodshed on our streets comes from those who lose all sight of a stranger's humanity, of the light that binds us together as human.

Tom Dotterer, in that sense, refuses to go blind.

The 2016 baseball season is underway in greater Syracuse as this book nears completion, and Tom Dotterer is again the head coach at Christian Brothers Academy. Away from the ballpark, if you need to talk to him, he's easy to find: he still holds court behind the counter of that small liquor store, his feet planted firmly in his city.

Epilogue

When you are a writer, and you walk into a new city, every street and building seems to tremble with a hidden, untold tale.

But when you have been in the same town for more than half your life, when five years shift into 15 and then—how can this be?—almost 30, the city becomes something very different.

It turns into a crucible, on almost every block, of light and ghosts and shadows.

You drive to work, or to an interview, or to get a cup of coffee, and you pass a city street of old homes where you cannot help but remember the desperate mother and children put at risk as a house burned, and the hero firefighters who risked everything to pull them out. You pass Onondaga Lake, religious epicenter of the Six Nations, where the people of the long-house believe their greatest teacher arrived in a stone canoe. You pass a street corner in Eastwood that once held a bowling alley, a place owned by an Italian immigrant whose shrewd thinking—amplified over coffee by equally inspired colleagues—would help to shape professional basketball as we know it today.

He is long dead. For an instant, you see his grin. You hear his voice.

You pass the parking lot where a beloved police officer was shot to death, and you see the house where his mother—now in her late seventies—still keeps his photo on a living room shelf. You see the tower of a landmark bank from the nineteenth century, a place designed by a young man named Silsbee, who would later move to Chicago and influence some of the greatest architects in history, including Frank Lloyd Wright. You see the come-and-go fast-food facades that eternally appear and vanish along a boulevard built atop what was once the old Erie Canal, buried now. The commerce fueled by that grand manmade channel caused a row of nineteenth-century cities to rise up across the middle of the state, cities trying even now to reassert their purpose . . .

Including Syracuse, whose old brick downtown buildings—once sweatshops, ice houses, places to store meat—have become upscale enclaves of coffee shops and restaurants and apartments. You hear and smell the noisy interstate bridges whose construction wiped out entire neighborhoods. You see the stone porch of an apartment building where F. Scott Fitzgerald played as a young child, and the downtown streets where a brooding Frederick Douglass often walked, amid his lifetime quest to set women and men free. You pass the old New York Central railroad station, now the home to a cable television company, the station where thousands of young people left for war, parents waving from the platform as each train pulled away.

The ones who came back would sometimes decide to surprise those same parents, walking in the middle of the night to houses in Eastwood or Tipp Hill or the old 15th Ward, pushing at the doorbell while the dog barked and a mother or father, sleep still in their eyes, came downstairs to open up the door, to fall into a hug . . .

With the ones who came back.

As for the ones who did not: You do not forget them, or their sacrifice. You cannot forget their children, the ones who never came to be, and what they might be dreaming, doing, changing today.

For their city.

So you keep driving. You see the homeless, standing at the corners with their signs asking for change, and you feel the raging, careening epic at their backs, the forces that so often put them on the street: The great industries that rose and fell, the jobs that came and went, the families torn by weariness, violence, and poverty, the addictions, fatigue, and mental illness that always grow from cracks where hope runs dry. Intertwined with it all, you see your own story: the city schools where your wife taught, the house where your small children turned into young adults, the green parks where you scattered the ashes of the family dogs whose passions and loyalties equate to eras, to points of time in your life.

That is with you now, all of it, on any drive through Syracuse. Almost 30 years, and all these stories and shades churn together into a riot of present, past and future, shades that call out to you about the unmarked grave, the forgotten hero, about the next untold tale that you sense is always there, in the heart of what New York calls its "Central City."

Those tales, in the end, almost always involve struggle. Yet all struggle, all effort, is built upon the innate quality that kept you here. It is the quality you still feel bursting out in every tiny child who stands up and finds the courage to take that first halting step, whether it happens on fine hardwood floors or cracked cement.

That moment, that motion, is pure faith in Syracuse.

CHRONOLOGY
OF COLUMNS

INDEX

Chronology of Columns

Index

SEAN KIRST is a longtime Upstate New York journalist, writer, and storyteller who spent nearly 25 years as a columnist for the *Syracuse Post-Standard*. Winner of the 2008 Ernie Pyle Award for human-interest writing, Kirst is also the author of *The Ashes of Lou Gehrig and Other Baseball Essays*, and coauthor of *Moonfixer: The Basketball Journey of Earl Lloyd*. He lives in Syracuse with his wife, Nora, and their three children.